Merrill's Marauders

Merrill's Marauders

The Untold Story of Unit Galahad
and the Toughest Special Forces Mission
of World War II

Gavin Mortimer

 ZENITH PRESS

First published in 2013 by Zenith Press, an imprint of MBI Publishing Company, 400 First Avenue North, Suite 400, Minneapolis, MN 55401 USA

Zenith Press titles are also available at discounts in bulk quantity for industrial or sales-promotional use. For details write to Special Sales Manager at MBI Publishing Company, 400 First Avenue North, Suite 400, Minneapolis, MN 55401 USA.

To find out more about our books, join us online at www.zenithpress.com.

Library of Congress Cataloging-in-Publication Data

Mortimer, Gavin.

  Merrill's Marauders : the untold story of Unit Galahad and the toughest special forces mission of World War II / Gavin Mortimer.

    pages cm

  Includes bibliographical references and index.

  ISBN 978-0-7603-4432-3 (hc)

  1. United States. Army. Composite Unit (Provisional), 5307th. 2. World War, 1939-1945--Regimental histories--United States. 3. World War, 1939-1945--Underground movements--Burma. 4. World War, 1939-1945--Campaigns--Burma. 5. Myitkyina (Burma)--History, Military--20th century. I. Title.

  D769.315307th .M67 2013

  940.54'850973--dc23

                    2013020172

Editorial Director: Erik Gilg
Editor: Caitlin Fultz
Design Manager: James Kegley
Layout: Brenda Canales
Cover design: Jason Gabbert

Printed in the United States of America

10 9 8 7 6 5 4 3 2 1

"When You Go Home, Tell Them Of Us And Say,
For Their Tomorrow, We Gave Our Today"
—Inscription on the Kohima 2nd Division Memorial in India,
close to the Burma border, in recognition of the Allied soldiers
who sacrificed their lives in 1944

List of Maps

Contents

TIMELINE

1943

August 19–24: Quebec Conference decision to assign a three thousand-strong Long Range Penetration force to Southeast Asia.

September 1: General George Marshall, chief of staff of the Army, issues a call for volunteers for a dangerous and hazardous mission under the classified code name "Galahad."

September 21: Casual detachments 1688A and 1688B, composed of volunteers serving in Trinidad and the Continental United States, depart San Francisco on the *Lurline*.

October 2: The *Lurline* arrives in New Caledonia to collect Casual Detachments 1688C, combat veterans of the Pacific.

October 29: The *Lurline* reaches Bombay, India.

November 1–17: The men of the 1688th Detachment train at Deolali, a British transit camp.

November 19–20: The detachments transfer to Camp Deogarh in Bengal Province and undergo further training under the command of lieutenant colonels Francis Brink and Charles Hunter.

December 31: Admiral Mountbatten, head of SEAC, agrees to transfer control of the 1688th Detachment to Lt. Gen. Joseph Stilwell's Northern Combat Area Command.

1944

January 1: The 1688th Detachment is reconstituted the 5307th Composite Regiment (Provisional) in General Order No. 1. General Order No. 2 confirms Colonel Hunter as the 5307th's commanding officer. General order No. 3 subsequently reconstitutes them as the 5307th Composite Unit (Provisional).

January 3: The 5307th is officially released from South East Asia Command and assigned to Stilwell.

January 4: Brigadier General Frank D. Merrill is appointed by Stilwell commanding officer of the 5307th, with Hunter, his second in command.

January 26–28: The 1st, 2nd, and 3rd battalions begin moving to Ledo in Assam. They will complete the movement by February 9.

February 9–21: The 5307th marches 140 miles to their jumping-off point at Ningbyen in northern Burma.

February 18: The advance elements of the 5307th arrive at Shingbiyang in Burma.

February 24–March 7: First Mission: The 2nd and 3rd battalions set up blocks along the Kamaing Road near Walawbum.

February 25: Robert Landis is the first volunteer killed in combat.

March 12–April 7: Second Mission: The 1st Battalion sets up a block near Shaduzup.

March 12–25: Second Mission: The 2nd Battalion and Khaki Combat Team, 3rd Battalion set up a block near Inkangahtawng.

March 28: The 2nd Battalion withdraws to Nhpum Ga and General Merrill suffers his first heart attack, causing his evacuation from Burma. Colonel Hunter assumes command of the Marauders.

March 31: The 2nd Battalion is cut off from the 3rd Battallion, and the siege of Nhpum Ga begins.

April 9: The 3rd Battalion breaks through to Nhpum Ga to break the siege.

April 28–May 16: Third Mission: The Marauders, supplemented by Chinese troops and Kachin guerrillas, are organized into H Force, K Force, and M Force and tasked with crossing the Kumon Mountains and seizing the airstrip at Myitkyina.

May 17: H Force under Colonel Hunter seizes the airstrip, but no attempt is made to take Myitkyina itself.

May 19: Merrill suffers a second heart attack. He eventually will be transferred to the SEAC staff in New Delhi.

May 20: A Chinese attack on Myitkyina ends in failure when they open fire on each other on the outskirts of the town.

May 21–31: K Force and M Force arrive in the Myitkyina area, and the evacuation begins of several hundred sick and exhausted Marauders.

June–July: American reinforcements, known as "New Galahad," are flown in to help defend the airstrip and to help the approximately two hundred original Marauders, known as "Old Galahad."

August 3: Myitkyina is taken by American and Chinese troops, including the last remnants of the Marauders.

August 3: Colonel Hunter is relieved of his command and ordered home.

August 10: The 5307th Composite Unit (Provisional) is dissolved. The remaining Marauders are reorganized into the 475th Infantry Regiment.

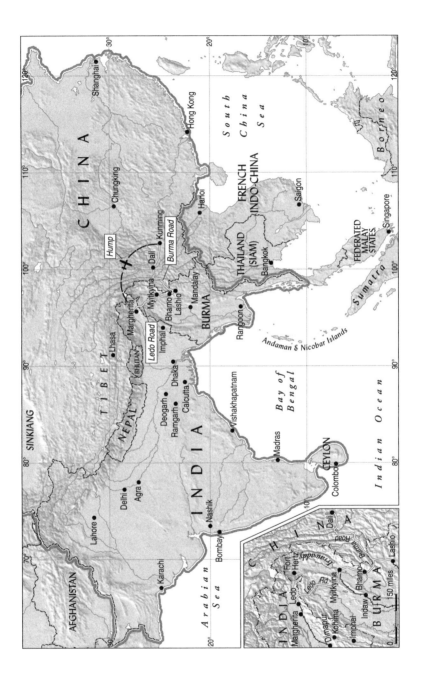

Back into Burma

April 1943. Two thousand British soldiers stagger from the steaming jungle of northern Burma. Bleeding, emaciated, worn out, these men are the remnants of the 77th Brigade. For two months, they've been fighting a primitive guerrilla campaign against the Japanese army. They are the survivors. One thousand of their comrades remain in the jungle, victims of the enemy, victims of disease, victims of hunger.

The survivors would never be the same men again. They had endured suffering the like of which few British soldiers had ever experienced: the terror of combat against a pitiless enemy, the horror of myriad diseases, the misery of searing heat, the fear of venomous snakes and bloodsucking leeches.

And for what had they suffered? How had the war in Burma been influenced by the sacrifices of so many young British men? Materially, there was little about which to brag.

An estimated two hundred Japanese soldiers had been killed, a few bridges destroyed, and a handful of railway lines severed. The Japanese war machine hadn't exactly been brought to its knees by the British guerrillas, but it had been shocked nonetheless.

In the eighteen months since it had entered the war with its spectacular attack on the U.S. Navy at Pearl Harbor, Japan's forces had swept through Southeast Asia, conquering Hong Kong, Malaya, Singapore, Indochina, and Burma.

Finally the British had struck back, jolting the Japanese out of their complacency and, with the aid of a brilliant propaganda campaign, boosting the morale of the Allies. The 77th Brigade was too prosaic a name for such a fearless band of warriors; such daring required something more exotic, more adventurous. They were rechristened "The Chindits," in honor of the Chinthe, the mythical beast—half lion, half dragon—that guarded the Burmese pagodas.

British and American newspapers heralded the operation as proof that the tide was turning in the war against Japan. In its May 21, 1943, edition, the *Washington Post* described it as a "super raid" and told its readers that the Chindits had "swept through northern Burma on a 300-mile front, wrecking railroads and bridges, and generally harassing Japanese occupation forces."

The *Ogden Standard-Examiner* called it "one of the greatest epics of the war" and devoted a full page to photographs of the Chindits and their commander, Brig. Orde Wingate. The *Waterloo Daily Courier* joined in the celebration but also offered the most perceptive analysis of the British operation. Its editorial praised the damage inflicted on the Japanese but also the fact that "the troops were supplied entirely by air." In a stroke, Wingate had disproved the theory that the jungle was inaccessible by aircraft. "Cutting an army off from its base and penetrating deep into enemy territory is an exceedingly dangerous maneuver," the paper stated. "In the past it has been possible only when the force is extremely mobile and can live off the country, or when resistance is somewhat demoralized, as was the case when General Sherman marched thru the south toward the end of our Civil war.

"But the ability to summon supplies by radio and receive them from the air makes such a maneuver more feasible. It may be that the Wingate expedition in Burma is only the forerunner of a new kind of warfare."

Following his exploits in Burma, Wingate wrote a sixty-one-page report on the mission from which he drew five conclusions:

1. Long range penetration is an offensive weapon and should be employed as a vital part of the major plan of conquest.

2. The men should be suitably equipped and trained: training is more important than physical hardiness. On this point more thought had to be given to basic jungle fighting including ambushes and close quarter combat.

3. RAF (Royal Air Force) liaison officers must work in tandem with column commanders to coordinate supply drops and air strikes.

4. There was room for improvement in wireless operations.

5. Columns need better training in river crossing, otherwise the operation easily becomes a shemozzle.

The candor that suffused the report was in places openly critical of the British campaign in Burma. Many of the senior officers blanched at its findings, regarding Wingate as a dangerous renegade whose methods were unethical and not worthy of the British Army. But eventually the report landed on the desk of Prime Minister Winston Churchill. How he rejoiced!

Here was a kindred spirit, a man of independent mind not afraid to risk opprobrium in pursuit of the unorthodox. "A man of genius and audacity," was how Churchill summarized Wingate. "There is no doubt that in the welter of inefficiency and lassitude which has characterized our operations, this man, his force, and his achievements stand out." Summoned to London by Churchill, Wingate arrived on the morning of August 4, 1943, and that evening dined with the prime minister. By the time the dessert was served, Churchill knew he needed to take Wingate to the impending Quebec Conference so that he could "explain his theories to President Roosevelt."

Churchill was anticipating a tense encounter with the Americans at the conference. President Franklin Roosevelt and his chief of staff were pressing for an invasion of France, but they also wanted some belligerent action in the Far East.

Since its conquest by the Japanese in the spring of 1942, Burma had posed a threat to American interests in the Pacific because of its proximity to China. Even before the capital, Rangoon, had fallen, Roosevelt sent a small force of 440 military personnel to China to help train its army to fight the Japanese. Their commander was Maj. Gen. Joseph Stilwell. He reported to Chiang Kai-shek, the Chinese leader, on March 6, 1942, the day before the Japanese entered Rangoon.

Stilwell was confident that the British, together with the 3 million Chinese soldiers (organized in three hundred divisions), had the capacity to launch a counterattack from their strongholds in central Burma. Neither the British nor the Chinese shared Stilwell's belief, and as the Japanese advanced north crushing all before them, the American mission was forced into a desperate retreat toward India.

After a brutal 140-mile trek, Stilwell emerged from the jungle in May looking, in the words of one war correspondent, "like the wrath of God and cursing like a fallen angel." Stilwell had never felt so humiliated, and he told the world so, in words that made him a worldwide sensation as the straight-shooting general. "I claim we got a hell of a beating," Stilwell told reporters. "We got run out of Burma and it is humiliating as hell. I think we ought to find out what caused it, go back, and retake it."

The causes were obvious. The Allies were novices in jungle warfare compared to their enemy. By the end of 1942, the Japanese had pushed right up into the north of Burma, seizing the vital airstrip at Myitkyina.

Here was Roosevelt's problem. The speed with which the Japanese had swept through the Far East astounded the Chinese. The so-called invincible British Army had turned out to be anything but, and even the respected General Stilwell had been chased out of Burma.

Roosevelt was determined not just to restore the prestige of the Allies, but to keep China an active partner in the alliance. It was envisaged that further down the line, China would provide American bomber aircraft with the bases from which to attack the Japanese mainland.

British opinion diverged on the subject. Their preoccupation was India, and Winston Churchill was wary of having anything to do with the Chinese, fearful that if they ever entered Burma—a British colony—they would never leave.

Roosevelt's opinion won out over Churchill's, and the British placed Burma under their Southeast Asia Command and not their India Command. One British general called the idea "wild and half-baked." In response, Churchill told his general that the United States viewed the supply of munitions to China as "indispensable to world victory."

With Burma in Japanese control, to resupply China from India meant the Americans flying twelve thousand tons of supplies into the country each month on one hundred DC-3 transport planes. It was a perilous route even before the Japanese seized the airstrip at Myitkyina, as the turbulence over the Himalayas was a force of nature that challenged the most skilled pilot. With Japanese fighter aircraft now able to attack the United States Army Air Force from Myitkyina, the supply line to China was jeopardized. Another route had to be found—an overland route.

In November 1942, construction began on a three-hundred-mile road starting in Ledo, in the very far northeast of India close to the border with Burma. The road would cut through the unoccupied northwestern corner of Burma, tapping the Burma Road at the Chinese frontier, an existing route that ran from Rangoon in the south through mountains, jungles, and valleys, all now occupied by the Japanese. Simultaneously, a pipeline would be laid to run parallel to the road in order to increase the flow of motor fuels to China.

In February 1943, engineers crossed into India. They celebrated their three months of toil with a sign: "Welcome to Burma! This way to Tokyo!" Their jubilation at the rate of their progress was premature. Constructing a road in India was the easy part; continuing it through Burma's nightmarish terrain was altogether more daunting. In May the monsoon arrived, and for three months Burma was saturated with tireless rain. There were no more triumphant signs hammered into the soil, and Stilwell became more irascible with every tropical downpour.

Stilwell wasn't alone in voicing his frustration at the lack of progress being made in Burma. Winston Churchill was beginning to doubt if any of his senior officers had the aggression and initiative to take the fight to the Japanese. Then Wingate's report fell into his lap.

★

Wingate was a hit with the Americans at the Quebec Conference. "You took one look at that face, like the face of a pale Indian chieftain, topping the uniform still smelling of jungle and sweat and war and you thought, 'Hell, this man is serious,'" recalled General H. H. Arnold, commander of the USAAF. "When he began to talk, you found out just how serious."

Wingate first talked to the Americans on August 17, explaining in a presentation that long-range "penetration affords greater opportunity of mystifying and misleading the enemy than any other form of warfare. . . . To sum up, long-range groups should be used as an essential part of the plan of conquest to create a situation leading to the advance of our main forces."

The following day, Wingate repeated his presentation in front of Churchill and Roosevelt. The prime minister was impressed, praising the Chindit leader for having "expounded a large and very complex subject with exemplary lucidity." Roosevelt also approved, and agreed to deploy for the first time, American ground troops in Burma.

The telegram authorizing the deployment was sent to General Stilwell on August 31 from Washington's Operations Division (OPD) of the War Department General Staff. It was headed "Information Pertaining to Three American Long Range-Penetration (LRP) Groups," and it informed Stilwell that a "total of 2,830 officers and men organized into casual detachments will arrive in India in early November. They will all be volunteers. 950 will be battle-tested troops in jungle fighting from the South and Southwest Pacific. 1900 will be from jungle-trained troops from the Caribbean Defense Command and the Continental United States. All will be of a high state of physical ruggedness. Above volunteers have been called for with requisite qualifications and commensurate grades and ratings to form three Independent Battalions after their arrival in the theater. They must be intensively trained in jungle warfare, animal transportation and air supply in a suitable jungle area in preparation for combat in February [1944]."

This final sentence was a stipulation of Gen. George Marshall, U.S. Army chief of staff, who, though impressed with Wingate's concept of long-range penetration, nonetheless recoiled at the British general's callous attitude for his wounded during the first Chindit expedition. No wounded American soldier would be abandoned to the mercy of the Japanese; rather, the proposed LRP unit would be reliant on air support for supply and evacuation.

Stilwell was delighted with the news, writing in his diary on September 2: "Only 3,000, but the entering wedge. Can we use them! And how!" His good humor was brief, lasting until he learned that the American force—code named "Galahad"—would not be under his command. That honor fell to Orde Wingate, now promoted to major general, who had been given permission to raise eight new LRP groups for operations in Burma at the same time as the American troops. Additionally, the USAAF accepted Wingate's request for close air support in Burma and put its special air unit, No. 1 Air Commando, at his disposal for the forthcoming operation.

Stilwell was mad as hell, and for once he had some justification. Hadn't he been the man calling for American troops for months? Wasn't he, commander of Americans in the China Burma India (CBI) Theater, the man who should lead them? Yet instead, as Stilwell raged in his diary, "We get a handful of U.S troops and by God they tell us they are going to operate under WINGATE! We don't know how to handle them but that exhibitionist does! He has done nothing but make an abortive jaunt to Katha, cutting some railroad that our people had already cut, get caught east of the Irrawaddy and come out with a loss of 40 percent. Now he's the expert. That is enough to *discourage Christ*."

CHAPTER 1

Wanted: Men for a Dangerous and Hazardous Mission

Charles Newton Hunter was born in Oneida, New York, in January 1906. From an early age, he knew that soldiering was the life for him. He graduated from West Point Military Academy in 1929, in the same class as a young officer from Massachusetts named Frank Dow Merrill.

Hunter was a popular cadet, a lively young man whose traits, and his Scottish ancestry, were described in his entry in *Howitzer*, the West Point yearbook:

> Newt has worn the gray of the Corps with distinction, yet, we hope sometime to see him in wee kilts, and to hear him dreamily squeeze the bagpipe for our benefit. His ruddy countenance, slightly tilted nose, sandy hair, and twinkling blue eyes carry an appeal that can pass unnoticed by no mortal lass. Fortunately for us, Newt's forefathers failed to transmit to him their most famous trait. His helpful generosity would do credit to even the Good Samaritan. Newt is a precious bundle of wit and humor, with more than his share of common sense and good fellowship. He is the type that one enjoys to have around and whom you daily learn to appreciate more and more. These characteristics are certain to gain him the best in life wherever he goes.

From West Point, Hunter joined an infantry regiment. He served three years in the Philippines and two and a half in the Canal Zone, the ribbon of U.S. territory in Panama that included the Panama Canal. Neither posting was challenging. His time was spent instructing soldiers from the 14th

Infantry in the art of jungle warfare. After the Japanese attack on Pearl Harbor, Hunter was recalled to the States and sent to the infantry school at Fort Benning, Georgia. Now a lieutenant colonel in his thirty-seventh year, Hunter was appointed chief of the Rifles and Weapons Platoon Group of the Weapons Sections—a long-winded title for a tedious position. The war seemed to be passing Hunter by, even if all the training kept him in shape. "Five feet seven and very muscular with no excess fat" was how one contemporary described Hunter. "His athletic appearance and firm facial features created an aura of authority."

In late August 1943, Hunter was one of several officers who responded to a call from the War Department for a "hazardous mission." It was a chance to escape the boredom of Fort Benning. When Hunter was summoned to Washington, he had no idea what he gotten himself into. "My only clue," he wrote later, "was that I had been selected from all other volunteer lieutenant colonels because of my extensive tropical jungle experience."

Hunter spent a week in Washington, learning all about the hazardous mission code named "Galahad"* and the force of three thousand troops that had to be raised in a month. Hunter was also briefed on the complex situation in the China Burma India Theater—the intrigues, the personalities, the egos. Finally, Hunter was informed that the War Department expected the force—which, for the sake of expediency, was designated for the time being the 1688th Casual Detachment—"would suffer approximately 85% casualties" during its three-month mission.

At the end of the week, Hunter left Washington clutching a set of secret orders and made for Fort Mason, California, where he was to report to the commanding general, San Francisco Port of Embarkation, no later than September 20. Hunter was told that secrecy was paramount and, therefore, they would be sailing "under the not very convincing cover of medical replacements" for the South Pacific Theater.

As Hunter headed west, a memo was on its way to General Thomas Troy Handy, assistant chief of staff in charge of Operations Division, updating him on the progress of the 1688th Casual Detachment's recruitment. Dated September 18, it ran:

1. The following personnel for the American Long-Range Penetration Units for employment in Burma are being satisfactorily assembled at the San Francisco Port of Embarkation:

"Galahad" remained a classified code name for many months and was not known among its volunteers.

960 jungle-trained officers and men from the Caribbean Defense Command

970 jungle-trained officers and men from the Army Ground Forces.

2. A total of 674 battle-tested jungle troops from the South Pacific are being assembled at Noumea (the capital city of New Caledonia) and will be ready for embarkation on the Lurline 1st October.

3. General MacArthur was directed to furnish 274 battle-tested troops. He was able to secure only 55 volunteers meeting our specifications. He was accordingly authorized to secure volunteers from trained combat troops that have not been battle-tested. These troops will be picked up by the Lurline at Brisbane.

Among the volunteers heading to San Francisco were two handpicked by Hunter: Sam Wilson and William Lloyd Osborne. Wilson, a nineteen-year-old first lieutenant, had been raised on a 150-acre tobacco and corn farm in Southside, Virginia. His mother was a public schoolteacher from whom he inherited an abiding love of literature as well as "discipline, self-control, and how to think logically." From his father, Wilson and his four siblings were imbued with a love of nature and the psychological tools required to survive in the great outdoors.

Wilson, who had lied about his age to enlist in the National Guard in 1940, first came to the attention of Hunter at Fort Benning. Upon graduating from Officer Candidate School in August 1942, Wilson was selected to remain behind as an instructor, imparting his expertise in raiding by infiltration, patrolling, and ambushes. "We taught them out on the sides of the hill or in the swamps and marshes along the Upatoi Creek on the Chattahoochee River," remembered Wilson. "There was very, very little actual class time and now a whale of a lot of bleacher time."

Wilson was assigned to the Office of Strategic Services (OSS) in the summer of 1943, just as the 1688th Casual Detachment was initiated. Hunter, recalled Wilson, "invited me to go with him on an unnamed escapade that sounded pretty mysterious." Wilson had no idea what or where the "escapade" involved, but he trusted Hunter. "He was a lieutenant colonel and, obviously, an extraordinarily capable officer," remembered Wilson. "He gave me all the responsibility as a young lieutenant that I could handle. So when he asked me if I would like to join him on a rather dangerous mission, there was only one answer."

The other officer to receive an invitation from Hunter was in marked contrast to the young and inexperienced Wilson. Major William Osborne was the recipient of a Distinguished Service Cross for a feat of extraordinary daring that turned him and another officer into national celebrities in the fall of 1942.

In 1941, Osborne had commanded a battalion of the Philippine infantry. But following the fall of the Islands in April that year, he fled into the jungles around Bataan, evading the Japanese forces for several months. Eventually, a group of Philippine partisans put Osborne in touch with an escaped Air Force lieutenant, Damon Guase. Together, the pair set sail for Australia in a twenty-two-foot, native-built motorboat with only a *National Geographic* map and an army field compass to navigate the 3,200 miles of ocean. "We arrived here not by any expert navigation but by the grace of God," declared Osborne when he stepped ashore in Australia.

The twenty-nine-year-old Osborne, a married man who had been born in Prescott, Arizona, was nothing special to look at. On arriving in San Francisco from Fort Benning—where he had been lecturing students in jungle warfare—a fellow volunteer for the 1688th Casual Detachment was surprised at his appearance. "He reminded me more of a young assistant professor of mathematics than anything else," wrote Charlton Ogburn, who later was to discover that Osborne possessed a characteristic "rare among those who have actually been through war: he liked battle."

Lieutenant Ogburn had learned of the call for volunteers while idling away his time at Camp Van Dorn in Mississippi. Serving in the 99th Signal Company, 99th Infantry Division, the thirty-year-old Ogburn was an unlikely recruit to what the War Department had in mind for the 1688th Casual Detachment. He was an intellectual with little military lineage of which to boast; his father was a corporation lawyer and his mother a writer of mystery novels. Ogburn had graduated from Harvard in 1932 and moved to New York City, where he made a respectable living as a writer, including reviewing books for the Book of the Month Club. On the outbreak of war, Ogburn enlisted in the Signal Corps with the ambition of becoming a photographer. Eighteen months down the line, he had yet to lay eyes on a camera.

Ogburn was alerted to the 1688th Casual Detachment by a fellow officer at Camp Van Dorn. Standing in the chow line, swatting away mosquitoes, Ogburn was told by his buddy that the War Department was seeking "volunteers with jungle training." That ruled Ogburn out unless, as his messmate joked, Mississippi counted as the jungle.

What the hell, thought Ogburn, nothing to lose. He put his name forward, more in hope than expectation, but a few days later he received Special Orders 218, instructing him to report to Camp Stoneman, forty-five miles northeast of San Francisco, on September 17.

Ogburn arrived a day ahead of schedule, and when he checked in to a modest hotel he found himself sharing a room with Sam Wilson. Eleven years Ogburn's junior, Wilson was "ardent and idealistic, yet unfailingly self-possessed, self-disciplined and coolly analytical," Ogburn wrote. The youngster told Ogburn all he knew about the force being assembled, that it was for a "dangerous and hazardous mission" under the command of the redoubtable Lt. Col. Charles Hunter. The first thing that struck Ogburn was how the hell could a mission be dangerous and *not* hazardous?

The next day, Ogburn reported to Camp Stoneman. Already wondering if he hadn't made an awful miscalculation, his heart sank still further when he discovered he was now an infantryman. Then he heard a rumor that a casualty rate of 85 percent was anticipated for whatever the War Department had in mind. The "final and worst blow of the day" came when Ogburn was appointed commander of the communications platoon of Casual Detachment 1688-A, which came to be called 1st Battalion.*

As a Signal Corps officer, Ogburn had trained in field wire and telephone, but his experience of radio was negligible. A crash course awaited him, but in the meantime Ogburn had the opportunity to run an eye over some of the men who would be serving under him in the 1688th Casual Detachment. "I remember the word 'pirates' crossed my mind," he wrote later. "An assemblage of less-tractable soldiers I had never seen." One of his fellow officers, Capt. Tom Senff, a former law student from Kentucky who took life in stride, grinned as he eyed up the men. "We've got the misfits of half the divisions in the country," he said.

One of the men who stood in front of Ogburn was Robert Passanisi. A nineteen-year-old from Brooklyn, Passanisi was the son of Sicilian immigrants, his father a stonemason who had worked on many of the brownstone houses of Brooklyn. Passanisi was the youngest of twelve children and, as a result, grew up tough, ambitious, and with a strong fighting spirit. He was clever, too, and self-confident, excelling at school in science and track and field. When he wasn't watching the Brooklyn Dodgers, Passanisi helped repair neighborhood radios.

Passanisi enlisted in April 1942 after watching newsreel footage of the fall of Bataan. He was underage, but his height (he was over six feet), plus a little tampering with his birth certificate, fooled the Army. Having qualified as an aircraft radio equipment repairman, technician fifth grade (T5), Passanisi was posted to the 76th Signal Company at Camp A.P. Hill.

For months, Passanisi chafed at the torpor of life in Virginia. He had brothers fighting in Europe, and here was he, wasting away in the States. Then one Friday afternoon in September 1943, the 245 men of his signal company were addressed by the first sergeant. "He proceeded to read a request for

*Some Marauders never got out of the habit of referring to the battalions by "A," "B," and "C," but for the sake of clarity, this author will use the official 1st, 2nd, and 3rd appellation.

volunteers," remembered Passanisi. "He explained that the mission would be for six months—three months training and a three-month mission. I don't remember hearing the words *dangerous* or *hazardous*, but he did say casualties were expected to be very high." The sergeant asked for volunteers. Passanisi needed no second invitation. "As I stepped forward, I looked around and was amazed to see that of the 245 men, I was the only volunteer."

Over the weekend, Passanisi was restricted to company area. Then early Monday morning, he was put on a train to San Francisco, a journey that gave him plenty of time to reflect on his decision to swap an easy life for an unknown one. "There are many reasons that swirl around in a soldier's mind that lead to a decision to volunteer for some life-threatening mission," he said. "The great majority did so because they were young and adventuresome, restless and desirous of getting involved more actively in the war."

CHAPTER 2

Destination Unknown

The 1688th Detachment sailed from San Francisco on the morning of September 21, 1943, on board the SS *Lurline*. Two destroyers provided the escort. A purple dawn and the sight of the Golden Gate sliding from view provided a wistful backdrop.

The *Lurline* was eleven years old, a cruise liner that before the war had transported wealthy passengers between the west coast of the United States and the tropical paradise of Australasia. Then it had been a glamorous ship, spotless white on the outside with lavish furnishings inside. Now its hull was naval gray, and the interior giltwork had been removed. There were armaments instead of ornaments, with the *Lurline* boasting four .50-caliber machine guns and one 5-inch gun on the stern. The marines who manned the weapons were confident that they would never be called into action; with its maximum speed of 22 knots, the *Lurline* could outrun any predator.

When it was launched in 1932, the *Lurline* could accommodate 715 passengers on seven decks. The exigencies of war increased that figure threefold. The smaller cabins were modified to sleep six soldiers, while the larger cabins slept as many as sixteen. Conditions were cramped with no privacy, and men squeezed into pipe-frame bunks with a laced-on canvas sheet for bedding.

The officers had it better. Charlton Ogburn of the 1st Battalion was billeted in one of the ship's staterooms, and Thomas Bogardus of the 2nd Battalion was in a well-furnished cabin along with five other officers.

Bogardus, a twenty-six-year-old from Illinois, was an enterprising and steady young man who had received a Reserve Officers' Training Corps (ROTC) commission at the University of Montana in 1940 before graduating from the Officers School in Infantry Communications at Fort Benning. From there, he was posted to Trinidad and the Headquarters

Company of the 33rd Infantry Regiment. Life in the Caribbean was fun but unsatisfying; a lot of tennis, volleyball, and climbing coconut trees, but not much excitement.

The chance to volunteer for the secretive mission had been too tempting to turn down for Bogardus, and he was soon in San Francisco. While waiting to board the *Lurline*, he was approached by two high-ranking officers from the Inspector General's Department of the Army, almost certainly at the quayside to try and trip up some of the detachment's officers into disclosing classified information.

"Captain," the officers inquired of Bogardus, "what unit are you from?"

"I am not at liberty to say."

"Well, Captain, what are you doing?"

"I have no idea, sir," replied Bogardus.

After a few more questions, the officers departed, satisfied that Bogardus had revealed nothing that could compromise their presence in San Francisco.

On board the *Lurline*, Bogardus found the atmosphere far less intimidating. In fact, he could have been going on vacation, such were the facilities on offer. His six-man cabin on A Deck came "with a shower and complete basin and toilet facilities. It had an opening onto an outside promenade deck." The presence of the regular cruise ship crew, the waiters resplendent in their dress whites, also lent a touch of allure to the voyage. Best of all, several pretty young nurses were among the couple hundred other military personnel on their way to the Pacific.

For T5 Robert Passanisi and the other men in the Communications Platoon of the 1st Battalion, there were no waiters attending to their needs and no comfortable billet. Instead, they were exposed to the elements on a semi-open deck. When they weren't there, Passanisi and his comrades spent much of their time in the mess hall on deck D. "Chow consisted of two meals a day, and the chow line was about ten hours long," recalled Passanisi. "One pretty much would leave the mess hall and get back on the chow line."

On the fourth day at sea, the *Lurline*'s public address system developed a fault and Passanisi was told to report to the bridge with his tool bag. He had little in the way of tools, just "bullnose pliers, wire cutters, a screwdriver, and a pocket volt-ohm meter," but he fixed the system and earned the praise of the captain. There was a reward, too: an extra meal, new quarters in the radio room, and a job presenting the evening's music request show on the public address system.

Tommy Dorsey's jazz instrumental "Song of India" was the show's theme tune, chosen by Passanisi, who had learned of the *Lurline*'s ultimate destination through his privileged position. The clue was lost on most of his buddies, who remained ignorant of where they were headed.

The men had been given vaccine shots in San Francisco without knowing what for, and the clothing issued them shed no light on the subject. "We thought we had learned something when we got wool clothing," recalled Capt. Fred Lyons of the 2nd Battalion. "But the next day we were issued another outfit of cotton uniforms. The rumor factories were put in production, but we still had no inkling of our real destination."

★

As the *Lurline* steamed west, the officers became better acquainted with their men. Charlton Ogburn had led a sheltered life up to that point, going straight from school to Harvard to a white-collar profession. Now for the first time, he was in the presence of "adventurers, musicians, drunkards, journalists, delivery boys, wealthy ne'er-do-wells, old Army Hands, investment brokers, small-town Midwesterners, farm boys from the South, offspring of Eastern slums . . . idealists and murderers."

Ogburn soon identified Passanisi among his Communications Platoon as exceptional, more for his "precocious skills in radio repair" than for the fact that at nineteen he was the youngest man in the section. Passanisi for his part was initially impressed by the erudite and efficient Ogburn.

Senior among the "Old Army Hands" was forty-five-year-old Master Sgt. Joseph Doyer from New Jersey. Doyer had fought in the First World War, a veteran of the trenches in France who served in the Canadian Army after the American military rejected him on account of poor eyesight.

Doyer was accepted by the U.S. military after the war, and throughout the 1930s he drilled National Guard units in Wisconsin. In 1943, he was serving in an administrative capacity at the Port of Embarkation in San Francisco when the 1688th Casual Detachment assembled. Still with a thirst for adventure, Doyer volunteered for the mission and was accepted by Col. Charles Hunter. He knew a good master sergeant when he saw one.

Hunter established his headquarters in one of the *Lurline*'s saloons and called each of the detachment's officers for a brief interview. Ogburn stood before Hunter, a little in awe of his commanding officer. He noted the "mouth that was a straight line across a firm jaw [and] the gaze of command in a countenance that sometimes surprised you with its boyish look." As he had the officer in charge of 1st Battalion's Communications Platoon in front of him, Hunter asked Ogburn if he was fully conversant with radio. Ogburn confessed that he wasn't. "Then, lieutenant," said Hunter impassively, "you had better learn something about it."

★

Not long into the voyage, Lieutenant Colonel Hunter introduced the detachment's officers en masse to Lieutenant William A. Laffin and his fourteen Nisei interpreters. *Nisei*, Hunter informed the uninitiated, was a Japanese word meaning second generation. It was a Japanese word, but the fourteen men standing in the state room were loyal Americans who had volunteered for the 1688th Casual Detachment.

Roy Matsumoto was among the eldest Nisei. Born in Los Angeles in 1913, Matsumoto had spent his adolescence in the city of Hiroshima living with his grandparents and learning the culture. In 1931, he returned home to California, enrolled in Long Beach Polytechnic High School, and combined his English studies with a part-job job in a wholesale produce market. His industry paid off when he graduated. "Jobs were hard to come by because it was the height of the Depression," said Matsumoto. "But there was a Japanese grocery store and because I knew about fruit from the wholesaler, and because I could speak good English, they gave me a job as a delivery driver."

The job provided Matsumoto with a living during the Depression and enabled him to master the Japanese language. "Most of the grocer's customers were Japanese who spoke a variety of dialects," explained Matsumoto. "At school in Japan I'd just learned standard Japanese, but through the delivery work I got to learn these strange dialects."

The Japanese attack on Pearl Harbor had devastating consequences for Matsumoto. He had been born, raised, and schooled in the States, but in the paranoid minds of the authorities he was "an enemy alien." In January 1942, he was arrested and sent first to California's Santa Anita Assembly Center and then to the Jerome Relocation Center in Arkansas.

"Relocation center" was a craven euphemism for internment camp. "It was very hard when I lost my freedom," said Matsumoto. "I lost just about everything—almost all my personal property and financial assets, including my bank deposits. The government's excuse: It was enemy alien property. They were never returned to me. I was so mad."

Being classified 4-C (an enemy alien) insulted the pride as well as the patriotism of Matsumoto. He might only have been five foot two, but Matsumoto had run and swum for his high school, and the many hours spent lifting heavy sacks of produce at the wholesalers had honed his physique. He was 1-A, not 4-C, another reason to be "mad" with the American government.

After six months of internment in the Jerome Relocation Center, Matsumoto was informed by the commandant that the Military Intelligence Service (MIS) was looking for personnel fluent in Japanese. Matsumoto volunteered and was sent to the MIS Language School at Camp Savage in Minnesota, one of several hundred Nisei who volunteered to serve America despite their shabby treatment.

Matsumoto cruised through most of the classes held at Camp Savage. The level was aimed at the weakest student, the Americans of Chinese ancestry and the Caucasian officers learning the language, not the likes of Matsumoto, who was already fluent.

In early September 1943, a notice was posted on the bulletin board of Camp Savage seeking Nisei with a "high rate of physical ruggedness and stamina" and a good command of the Japanese language. The volunteers were asked about their "marital status, health, language proficiency." When it came to Matsumoto, he was given no choice. "I did well at the language school, so without an interview I was ordered to join," he recalled. A few days later, Matsumoto and the other thirteen Nisei were on a train with shades down headed for San Francisco.

l

CHAPTER 3

India

Captain Thomas Bogardus recalled that as the *Lurline* sailed west across the Pacific, "some troop training of sorts" was carried out on deck. "The main swimming pool was drained and turned into a training area, as were several different corners of the ship and state rooms," said Bogardus. "We did some training in first aid, map reading, and the like. . . . One of the unique training sessions consisted of learning how to give blood transfusions."

The transfusions were demonstrated by the detachment's 104-strong medical personnel, one of whom was Technician 4th Grade Richard Murch, a twenty-two-year-old who before the war had worked for the Continental Bank and Trust in New York City. Murch had initially been rejected by the Army on the grounds of poor physique, a rebuff that caused him to wander the streets of Manhattan in "shame." Six months later, the Army relaxed the recruitment criteria and Murch was in, assigned to Fort Dix in New Jersey and then to Billings General Hospital, where he qualified as a medical surgical assistant and anesthetist in early 1943. Murch remembered that on board the *Lurline*, the medical personnel "would meet every morning for three or four hours, trying to find the strengths and weaknesses of each person, assigning duties to fit each person's capabilities."

As the voyage wore on, the initial excitement dissipated and the 1,800 soldiers began chafing at their humdrum existence. At night, all portholes and doors had to be closed for security purposes. The heat inside the ship was unbearable, remembered Bogardus, "and we were soaking wet with perspiration a good part of the time."

To break the monotony, a boxing ring was installed on one of the decks and men fought each other over two rounds. Richard Murch was beaten by a fellow medic, Thomas Finnegan, but in the poker school that he ran from a cabin, he met with greater success. When the green hills of New Caledonia were spotted after twelve days at sea, Murch was $600 richer than he'd been in San Francisco.

Within a few hours of arriving in the broad harbor of Noumea, capital of New Caledonia, the men were pressed against the deck railings watching 670 combat veterans of the South Pacific climb up ladders from the iron barges below. Their uniforms were dirty, their boots scuffed, and their unshaven faces a strange shade of yellow from their anti-malaria pills. To Lt. Phil Weld, a Harvard graduate and former journalist with the *Chicago Daily News*, the men coming aboard appeared to be ascending "from another world."

The veterans were similarly intrigued by what they discovered once on board the *Lurline*. Edward C. Kohler, a twenty-two-year-old sergeant who had spent weeks fighting the Japanese in the jungle of Guadalcanal and then in the swamps of New Georgia, expected more. "The ship could stand a good cleaning and the food needed a lot of improvement," he remembered.

Like their spick-and-span comrades who had sailed from San Francisco, the South Pacific veterans reflected their country's rich diversity. Kohler was from St Mary's, Ohio, a National Guardsman mobilized into the 148th Infantry, 37th Division and shipped to the Pacific in 1942.

Werner Katz was a twenty-one-year-old German Jew who had fled his homeland in the late 1930s and arrived in New York.* Katz had enlisted in the U.S. Army in early 1941 while he was still waiting to receive his citizen papers, and in January 1942 he volunteered to go with the 182nd Infantry Regiment to Australia. From Melbourne, the 182nd shipped out to Guadalcanal in November, and Katz distinguished himself during the fighting on the Pacific island.

Bernard Martin also landed on Guadalcanal, but during his stint on the island with the 43rd Signal Company, he had seen little in the way of action. The twenty-one-year-old from Rhode Island was one of the best radio operators in his unit, capable of sending twenty words a minute when the average was half that figure. "I spent about two weeks on Guadalcanal before being transferred to another island," recalled Martin, a man who lived on the sunny side of life. "I was furnishing messages to base when all of a sudden a message came in stating 'looking for volunteers for a dangerous mission.' I thought it over for two days and volunteered. I was bored with what I was doing. I wanted to be involved; I wanted to fight."

Two officers newly arrived on the *Lurline* had both volunteered despite weeks of heavy fighting in the South Pacific. First Lieutenant Ted McLogan, twenty-three, was reading political science at the University of Michigan on

Later Katz Anglicized his name to Warner, but for the purpose of clarity, he shall be referred to as Werner throughout.

December 7, 1941, when the news broke in his fraternity house of the attack on Pearl Harbor. McLogan recalled that he and his friends "picked up a long-handled broom and we marched around the room, almost as if it were a big joke, not realizing the seriousness of it at that moment."

Having served in the ROTC at Michigan, McLogan was commissioned into the 35th Infantry Regiment, 25th Division, and then shipped to the South Pacific, where he was blooded in combat on the island of Vella Lavella. Not long after the island had been secured, McLogan received an order to assemble his men for an important announcement. "So I got my guys out of their foxholes and this major came along," remembered McLogan. "He opened up a file and said: 'The War Department is looking for volunteers for a dangerous and hazardous mission in another theater of operations. You may have one minute to think about it, and if you're going to volunteer take one step forward. We need you here; there's no pressure for you to volunteer. It's entirely voluntary and the option is yours.'"

For a few moments, no one moved. McLogan then heard a stage whisper from behind. "Here's your chance, Mac." It was McLogan's sergeant, a laconic West Virginian by the name of Paul Michael. "So I said, 'I will, if you will,'" remembered McLogan. "I knew he wasn't going to [volunteer] because he was one of these regular Army guys. He had challenged me, and I had to respond in front of the men." But McLogan had underestimated his sergeant. Michael volunteered, and so did he.

The pair was among the thirty-two men from the five hundred-strong 35th Infantry Regiment who volunteered for the unknown assignment. Included in that sparse number was Pvt. Gabriel Kinney, a twenty-two-year-old from Cullman County, Alabama. On the day of Pearl Harbor, Kinney was working the day shift in the iron ore mines of Birmingham. The death of his father the following month delayed Kinney's enlistment into the Army, but by the end of 1942 he was a member of Company F of the 35th Infantry Regiment, McLogan's company. Kinney recalled being enticed into volunteering with the promise that "when the mission was complete we would be returned to the States . . . that sounded good to me."

Another officer who joined the *Lurline* in New Caledonia was Lt. Logan Weston, a twenty-nine-year-old Pennsylvanian drafted into the heavy weapons unit of the 145th Regiment of the 37th Infantry Division in early 1941, while studying to become a preacher at the Transylvania Bible School. Two years later Weston, now an officer, took his first life fighting on Guadalcanal. "My self-condemnation weighed heavily on my mind," he wrote later. "But then I began to understand. The way I saw it, I was not only preserving my own life but doing what was necessary to see that our democratic freedoms remained intact." Weston turned to God for guidance and "felt peace in my heart that I was doing the right thing."

On board the *Lurline*, Weston lectured those of his fellow officers untested in combat on what to expect when the day arrived. Some of what he imparted was practical information: that grenades were the most effective weapon in thick jungle, and moving through the dense undergrowth was similar to feeling your way across a dark room.

But Weston was also at pains to dispel the popular image back home, spread in the newspapers and on the newsreels, that the Japanese soldier was weak and cowardly. Not at all; he was tenacious, cunning, and bewilderingly brave.

There were other lectures, too, from the newly arrived combat veterans, including talks from medical officers on the importance of halazone tablets to sterilize water* and of taking atabrine to combat malaria, regardless of the fact that it turned the skin yellow.

The *Lurline* stopped briefly at Brisbane on the east coast of Australia to collect the final detachment of volunteers—270 officers and men from the Southwest Pacific Command, of whom the majority had no combat experience. The ship, accompanied by a Dutch destroyer, then continued around the southern tip of Australia, sailing up a channel into the port of Fremantle on the west coast of the country. "The houses as you enter this channel are on the right side on steep cliffs," remembered Capt. Thomas Bogardus. "As we came in through this channel, the people of almost every house came out with bed sheets, pillow cases, and towels and waved them in the air. This was probably the first troop ship that they had ever seen, and they were welcoming the Americans."

Once the *Lurline* was at anchor, the men of the 1688th Casual Detachment were allowed ashore for the first time in six weeks. The 1st Battalion disembarked first, followed by the 2nd, and then the 3rd. They marched through the streets of the quaint town, whose design owed much to the English emigrants who had first settled Fremantle, and were cheered all the way by the Australians. "Barmaids from the local pubs came out with their hands filled with mugs of beer, passing them to the troops," said Bogardus.

The *Lurline* took on supplies in Fremantle and then headed northwest into the Indian Ocean. But to where exactly? "To our knowledge there weren't any American troops in combat in this area of the world," recalled Bogardus. "It left us up in the air as to where we might be going, although India seemed our next area where we might stop."

Not long out of Fremantle, Colonel Hunter opened "the ship's safe, and sealed material from Washington was delivered to the various battalions indicating what kind of equipment we were to have and what kind of

---

*It was subsequently discovered by the unit's medical officers that halazone did not kill the amoebic ova responsible for intestinal infections.

organization we would finally become." The orders also revealed their destination—India.

The *Lurline* docked in Bombay, halfway up the west coast of India, on October 29. The 1st Battalion was first off the ship, followed a day later by the 2nd Battalion. Captain Thomas Bogardus was appalled by what he saw of Bombay as they marched through the city to the railway station. "The native Indians were living in cardboard boxes for shelter," he recalled. "You could see people on the verge of dying right along the railroad tracks. I shall never forget the soulful look of these starving masses of humanity as we passed."

The 3rd Battalion remained on board the *Lurline* for a further twenty-four hours, much to the annoyance of one of its medical officers, Capt. James Hopkins. "The only entertainment was provided by watching the Indian dockworkers [and], the attitude of the men was further disturbed by the heat, not only on the outside but also on the inside of the poorly ventilated ship," he recalled. Hopkins's great-great uncle was Johns Hopkins, founder of the famous hospital, university, and medical school in Baltimore, from where he himself had graduated in 1941. Pearl Harbor compelled Hopkins to interrupt his first year of surgical training to enlist, and he was soon serving as a surgeon with the 18th General Hospital in Fiji before volunteering to join the 148th Infantry Regiment on Guadalcanal as their assistant surgeon.

Imprisoned on board the *Lurline* in Bombay, Bernard Martin struck up a friendship with a fellow member of the 3rd Battalion. Wilbur Smawley—he preferred "Bill"—came from Pullman, Washington, and was the same age as Martin. "Bill and I became instant friends," recalled Martin, who was delighted to find someone who shared his interest in radios. "He was bashful and shy, a really nice kid."

The 3rd Battalion eventually disembarked on October 31 and marched through the city to the station, where they boarded a train. It took several hours for the antiquated train to cover the 125 miles to a village called Nasik. The men sat on wooden benches facing inwards, and trips to the bathroom were fraught with danger as the train jolted northeast. There was nothing but a hole in the floor that opened to the tracks below, and a good sense of balance was required if a soldier wished to return to his bench with his boots still respectable.

When the Americans arrived in Nasik, they encountered a town that conformed to the western stereotype of India. The bazaar sold exotic spices, sparkling jewels, and ornamental rugs. Natives organized cobra and mongoose fights in the alleyways, and British officers strode down the street trailed by their Indian servants.

Not that men of the 1688th Detachment were given much time to take it all in. They marched through Nasik and onward two miles to a transient camp at Deolali, where the men were billeted in tents. The officers, recounted

Capt. Thomas Bogardus, were quartered in "row after row of small cubicles about twelve feet square, with two bunks in each cubicle and a door to an outhouse that was perhaps three or four feet square." To each cubicle was assigned a local boy whose job it was to "bring us hot tea and shake us, which in essence was our alarm clock," Bogardus said. In return, the boy received thirty-three cents a week, with a shave costing an additional three cents for officers and men alike.

Captain James Hopkins wasn't alone in finding the food at their camp substandard. "The quality and quantity were poor," he recalled, and meals were eaten in "disappointment and revulsion." On one occasion, a soldier bit into his bread and into a mouse. "The mouse must have fallen into the dough and then been baked with the bread," said Richard Murch, who witnessed the incident. Already, the relative luxury of the *Lurline* was a distant memory.

CHAPTER 4

Teaching, Training, Teamwork

Asurprise awaited Lt. Col. Charles Hunter at Deolali in the formidable shape of Col. Francis G. Brink, General Staff Corps. A former light-heavyweight boxing champion at Cornell University, Brink had worked for the American Embassy in Tokyo before the outbreak of war. Hunter admired Brink's "can-do" attitude but found him a little too "secretive" on certain subjects. He was also "puzzled" to discover that Brink had been appointed the 1688th Detachment's training officer, a role Hunter had more than adequately fulfilled during their voyage to India.

Hunter remained responsible for discipline and administration, but he was troubled by the division of leadership. He suspected that were it not for the fact that Brink was a member of the General Staff Corps—and thereby ineligible by military law to exercise command of troops—he would have replaced him as the detachment's commander.

Hunter's common sense and good fellowship made for a generally happy camp in Deolali. Hunter respected that the men had all volunteered, and while his standards were high he treated them as adults. As a commander, he was hard but fair, authoritarian but approachable. There was just one line that could never be crossed. "I don't want to see anyone taking sunbaths," he informed the men. "I don't know why it should be, but I've found that people who take sunbaths are difficult to get along with."

Thanks in no small part to Hunter's approach in Deolali, the sinews of the volunteers were strengthened by an *esprit de corps*. "This period of relative inactivity and freedom did a lot for the physical and mental outlook of the men," said Capt. James Hopkins. "I do not recall any criminal activity, significant complaining, or fights among the men or with the natives. The minimal classroom-like training and organized marches were completed with good humor."

One of the first visitors to the detachment's camp was Maj. Gen. Orde Wingate, an event that aroused much curiosity among the men. Here at last was the fabled guerrilla fighter, the scourge of the Japanese, the man labeled a "genius" by none other than Winston Churchill.

Even by the eccentric standards of the British officer class, Wingate was a maverick. In Burma, the pious forty-year-old rarely went anywhere without a fly gun, and it was his custom to tie an alarm clock to his person so he wouldn't be late for appointments.

Wingate's reputation as a guerrilla fighter had been forged in the British Mandate of Palestine in the late 1930s; there he had raised a unit of counter-insurgency troops, Night Squads, to protect oil pipelines from sabotage by Arab fighters. He was eventually posted back to Britain when his commanders grew concerned that Wingate was fighting more for the Jewish cause than to protect British interests in Palestine.

At the outbreak of the Second World War in September 1939, Wingate was sent to Ethiopia, where he deployed similar guerrilla tactics to those used in Palestine in helping the army of Emperor Haile Selassie defeat Italy.

A period of depression followed for Wingate, culminating in an attempt to kill himself in a Cairo hotel in July 1941. But he returned to England, recuperated, and then set off for Burma in 1942 with orders to organize a guerrilla campaign against the Japanese.

Ted McLogan was struck by Wingate's size—"he only stood about five foot five inches with a great beard"—while Bernard Martin found him "nice and easy to talk to" after he was required by Wingate to send a couple of radio messages back to his headquarters in Jhansi.

At Brink's behest, Wingate addressed the officers of the 1688th Detachment in the mess hall, a lecture that was well received by some and less so by others.

Captain Fred Lyons of the 2nd Battalion listened wide-eyed with amazement as Wingate "told us every detail of his famous Raider campaign in Burma the year before so we could profit by his experience and come out of the jungle alive." Lyons, who had yet to see combat, gobbled up every morsel of information thrown his way by Wingate. "I see him now," he recalled, "his hawk-like face animated as he warned us never to speak above a whisper in the jungle, never to try to pull away a blood-sucking leech, never to drink jungle water without sterilizing it."

Lieutenant Sam Wilson was "aware of his innovativeness" but was somewhat surprised by his size and the high pitch of his voice. "He was rather Messianic," said Wilson. "He reminded me a little bit of a fundamentalist preacher at a revival. He would get kind of worked up. He was obviously a brilliant man, but also a very strange man."

Captain James Hopkins was less impressed with what he heard from Wingate. A veteran of Guadalcanal and a skilled surgeon, Hopkins stared in disbelief when the British general declared emphatically that "dysentery can be controlled by the wearing of a tight band about the waist."

Not all of Wingate's advice was nonsensical. He recommended the use of heavy machine guns in the jungle as an effective means of inflicting casualties on an enemy close at hand but concealed by the dense undergrowth. He also reassured his American allies that in all his time in the jungle, he had yet to come face to face with a man-eating tiger. Elephants, yes, but not tigers. As for the jungle itself, Wingate said there was no need to fear it. It was large and deep, like a placid ocean, but with a map and compass it was just as navigable. In fact, from a junior leader's standpoint, the jungle offered far more opportunity to display individual initiative and responsibility than any other theater of war. The crucial point, stressed Wingate, was that the "best defence in the jungle is to seek out the enemy and attack him, and thus impose your will on him . . . therefore what are needed are self-reliant, alert-minded officers and men who will act with vigor according to the situation confronting them."

★

Unbeknown to Wingate, as he expounded his theories on jungle warfare to the 1688th Detachment, a storm was brewing with Gen. Joseph Stilwell at its epicenter. As well as being the deputy commander of South East Asia Command, Stilwell was also commander of Americans in the China Burma India Theater and chief of staff to Chiang Kai-shek. It still rankled Stilwell that the first American force of ground troops earmarked for operations in Burma had been placed under British control. He vowed to wrest their command from Wingate.

Stilwell was especially cantankerous in the second week of November 1943, so much so that in his diary he took out his anger on President Roosevelt by referring to him as "Rubberlegs," a grievous mockery of his leader's polio. Stilwell believed that the president was being weak in his dealings with Chiang Kai-shek over Chinese military assistance.

Stilwell already had in mind a large-scale operation for Burma, a plan he conceived "as a jerk to the sleeves of his allies that could not be ignored." What the general envisaged was a three-phase advance into northern Burma, the main attack coming from two Chinese divisions and the 1688th Detachment—but only if they were under his direct command.

Stilwell planned that this force would march south from India into Burma along the Ledo Road and then push into the jungle, advancing through the Hukawng and Mogaung valleys to capture the airstrip at Myitkyina, the strategic jewel in northern Burma.

Stilwell took his plan to the Cairo Conference, which was billed as the largest gathering of its kind with "all the British and American officers of whom one had ever heard." Winston Churchill was present, as was Roosevelt, and when Stilwell arrived in the Egyptian capital on November 20, he had among his entourage Col. Frank Merrill.

★

On the same day that Stilwell arrived in Cairo to discuss plans for an offensive in Burma, the 1688th Detachment completed its move from Deolali to a new base. The seven-hundred-mile journey northeast to the Jahklann station in Bengal Province took three days. Once the force (each battalion traveled separately twenty-four hours apart) alighted from the train, they were obliged to march ten miles "across dry, rugged land, irregularly covered with spine-producing bushes about six feet high," recalled Capt. Thomas Bogardus.

Their new home was Camp Deogarh, a former British military establishment approximately eighty miles to the south of Wingate's Chindits at Jhansi. The camp was not electrified, and there was no running water or telephone system. Everyone, officers and men, was billeted in tents. "A tent city consisting of British cotton tents," was how Bogardus described Deogarh. "They were double-layered to keep the heat down in the midday sun of India—extremely cold at night but very hot in the daytime."

Each battalion was allocated its own section of the camp where its men slept, ate, and trained, independent of the other two battalions. It was an arrangement that concerned Colonel Brink, who believed that the 1688th Detachment would prosper if the combat-experienced soldiers of the 3rd Battalion were divided up among the other two battalions.

Hunter opposed the idea, advising Brink not to tamper with the camaraderie that was taking root in the unit. But Brink went ahead and transferred 6 officers and 160 men from the 3rd Battalion into the 1st and 2nd battalions.

Private First Class Gabriel Kinney, the iron ore miner from Alabama, was torn from the bosom of the buddies he had fought alongside in Guadalcanal. "My reaction to being transferred was total disappointment," he reflected. "There were five of us volunteers from F Company, 35th Regiment, 25th Division. When we left Vella Lavella, we thought we would stay together."

If the transfer was difficult for 3rd Battalion personnel, it also raised issues among the 2nd Battalion. Kinney was now the sole combat veteran in the 1st Platoon of E Company, 2nd Battalion, under the command of Lt. Larry Lindgren. "Other than being totally yellow because of the [atabrine] pills, I was the one the other members of the platoon asked questions about combat," said Kinney. "That didn't stand me in good stead with Lindgren."

Kinney now had to answer the same questions that he himself had asked combat veterans on Guadalcanal when he had arrived on the island in December 1942 to relieve the 1st Marine Division. "The answer I gave was the one I'd been told: 'If you're still alive in the morning, you know what you're doing is right.'"

One of the six officers uprooted was Lt. Ted McLogan, moved to the Green Combat Team of the 2nd Battalion, a comeuppance he said he deserved for "lording it over the other two [battalions] because they hadn't had combat." Transferred into McLogan's platoon from the 3rd Battalion was Sgt. Ed Kohler. "After a few days with these men, I knew we had our work cut out for us," he recalled.

McLogan accepted his fate with equanimity and became acquainted with his new commanding officer, the taciturn Lt. Col. George Alexander McGee. McGee was from Denver, a West Pointer from the Class of 1937 whose yearbook photograph depicted a neat, dark-haired young man, handsome yet intense. "Plebe year was safely passed before we saw him smile," ran his yearbook biography. "But now his own ready wit makes life more enjoyable for all."

"Maggie," as McGee was known to his fellow West Pointers, wore chevrons in an exemplary manner; enjoyed poetry, music, and lacrosse; and longed to own a horse and a dog. "A hard worker, he enjoys working for experience's sake," continued the yearbook. "Graduation will embark him on a career for which his preparation is complete, a career in which his fine qualities will ensure him continued success away from these walls."

On the outbreak of war, McGee was commanding officer of the 2nd Battalion, 33rd Infantry Regiment, recently returned from Fort Clayton in the Panama Canal Zone. Within days of Pearl Harbor, the regiment was ordered to Trinidad to protect the newly acquired Lend-Lease bases on the Caribbean island. For more than eighteen months, they remained on the island until the day, to McGee's unbridled relief, he was ordered to find volunteers for a unit code named "Galahad."

One of the first officers summoned to McGee's office was Capt. Fred Lyons. "'Do you want to volunteer for a dangerous and hazardous secret mission in an active theater?' he asked me," remembered Lyons. "A dangerous and hazardous secret mission! My heart gave a jump. But wasn't this what I'd been waiting for? 'Sure as hell,' I replied, 'When do we start?' Colonel McGee asked the same question of all the officers and men in the regiment, and everyone gave the same answer."

Lyons was accepted by McGee, as were captains Henry Stelling, one of the 33rd's medical officers, and Thomas Bogardus, who recalled that more than one thousand soldiers volunteered so that McGee had the luxury of deciding which men to select and which to omit.

The soldiers selected by McGee were soon on their way to the States. "Our Trinidad unit boarded every available plane that landed there and was flown to Miami as quickly as possible," recalled T5 George Rose, who hailed from Emporia, Virginia. Rose had quit his job in a furniture store to enlist underage in the 33rd Infantry. Now he was in Florida, with the sense of excitement mounting. "Men who had volunteered for the mission were pouring into the hotels; cavalry men from Jamaica, engineers from Puerto Rico, riflemen from Panama, radio experts from Washington. They were all confined to their hotels and were not allowed even to walk around the streets or telephone home. Nobody knew anything about where we were going or what we were to do."

★

With the experience of the 3rd Battalion now running like a seam through the unit, Colonel Brink divided each battalion into two jungle columns, as advised by General Wingate, a man Brink admired greatly. Nevertheless, Brink decided not to ape the British in calling them "columns" but instead designating them "combat teams."

Each of the six combat teams was color-coded and each trained to operate as a self-contained unit, comprising a heavy weapons platoon, a rifle company, an intelligence and reconnaissance (I&R) platoon, a communications platoon, and a pioneer and demolitions detachment (see table on page 37).

Lieutenant Colonel William Osborne was assigned command of the 1st Battalion, with its Red and White combat teams under the command of Major Edward Ghiz and Major Caifson Johnson, respectively. The 2nd Battalion, led by McGee, comprised the Blue Combat Team under Major Richard Healy and the Green Combat Team under Captain Thomas Bogardus.

Lieutenant Colonel Charles Beach, a thirty-five-year-old from Cincinnati nicknamed "Old Ranger," commanded the 3rd Battalion. Major Lawrence Lew led the Orange Combat Team, and Major Edwin Briggs was in command of the Khaki Combat Team.

"Colonel Beach was a nice guy," recalled Bernard Martin, who was in the communications platoon attached to the Orange Combat Team. "A courageous and straightforward man, he wasn't afraid of anything. He would never hide behind his rank."

By now, the 3rd Battalion had been renamed the "Chow Raiders" because of their constant assaults on the camp's kitchens, a moniker that the men recognized with their own battalion insignia pinned to their lapels—the small can openers that came with 10-in-1 ration packs.

While Hunter busied himself with administrative tasks at Deogarh, Brink oversaw the detachment's training. He was careful not to step on the toes of the three battalion commanders, and his tact was appreciated by Lieutenant Colonel McGee, who praised the "wide latitude" afforded by his approach and the way he "rarely if ever convened the battalion commanders, instead he visited them individually and observed training frequently, and in a soft-spoken but firm manner made suggestions and otherwise provided guidance."

The training was punishing, conducted in countryside that reminded Thomas Bogardus of the photographs he'd seen of central Africa. "Brush and scrub and fair to middling high grasses," he recounted. Aside from the hours spent on the firing range, the men practiced ambushes, casualty evacuation, trailing, and trail concealment. They launched attacks against enemy pillboxes, learned how to receive an airdrop, and mastered the art of crossing a river in the shortest time possible.

The M1919 Browning machine gunners were encouraged to fire as much ammunition as they wanted. There was too much ammunition of all caliber in Deogarh to be taken to Burma, so it was expended in the scrubland around the camp. In addition, soldiers were taught how to fire every type of weapon, from a Browning Automatic Rifle to a semi-automatic M1 Garand rifle to a Thompson submachine gun and carbine. The idea, wrote Hunter, was "that when the chips were down they could employ them collectively to create a sledge hammer effect to crush the heretofore 'Banzai' charge of the hysterical, hopped-up Asians."

Different men preferred different weapons. As a sergeant, Roy Matsumoto had been given a Garand, but he found its 4.3 kilograms too heavy so he traded it for a carbine, which was two kilograms lighter. Bernard Martin and Robert Passanisi, though both radio operators, would be infantrymen just like everyone else on the march through the jungle. The pair preferred the Garand, Martin because it was easy to clean and Passanisi because of its accuracy.

Other skills were honed in the scrubland around Deogarh, such as how to handle a hand grenade. The green troops were told to forget what they'd learned in training about using two hands to remove a pin from a grenade. That could be fatal in combat. Never take your eyes off the enemy, not even for a couple of seconds to locate and squeeze the pin that would release the spoon (or handle). Instead, as T5 Robert Passanisi recalled, they were taught to "squeeze the pin most of the way, then place the ring over one of your fatigue buttons and then button the button. When the situation called for a grenade, all you had to do was reach over with one hand, without looking. Grab the grenade and spoon, like you would a baseball, then with a sharp tug pull the grenade free, leaving the ring and cotter pin still on the button, and never taking your eyes off the action."

The communication platoons held classes in which the men familiarized themselves with their radio equipment (which arrived in December). This consisted of AN/PRC-1s and SCR (Signal Corps Radio) 284s, as well as SCR 300s, portable radio transceivers worn on a mounted backpack and better known as walkie-talkies. "The SR300 was a tremendous asset," remembered Passanisi. "It weighed about sixty-five pounds with a thirty-pound battery and with eighteen tubes. It was state-of-the-art." The SCR 284, a combination transmitter and receiver with a hand crank generator, was far more cumbersome. Passanisi considered it "very inefficient compared to the others and very hard to generate power."

Each battalion also had its own medical detachment, composed of five doctors and approximately thirty medics of varying abilities. Their role would be of paramount importance, for in Burma disease was an enemy far more prevalent and inestimably more merciless than the Japanese. In 1943, the British and Indian troops were a hundred times more likely to be struck down by illness than they were an enemy bullet.

Technician Fourth Grade Richard Murch was a medical surgical assistant and anesthetist in Red Combat Team, 1st Battalion. "Physical disability, incompetence, etc., during our training in Deogarh thinned the ranks of the NCOs," he recalled. Murch gained an extra stripe as a result of this depletion of the battalion's medical staff, rising in rank to Tech 3.

While at Deogarh, the 1688th Detachment carried out several training exercises with Wingate's Chindits, themselves preparing for a second mission to Burma. "The Chindits were really tough guys; they put us through our paces," recalled Bernard Martin. "We went on these long marches with fifty pounds on our back, and sometimes in the middle of the night they would start firing their weapons, shouting, 'We're the enemy, we're the enemy.' Other times, they would just burst into our tents and throw a bucket of cold water over our faces, and we had to react. They taught us well and trained us well."

Lieutenant Sam Wilson also found the time spent with the Chindits instructive. "They were much leaner, more conservative, in what they carried and in what kinds of external support they expected," he reflected. "We were sort of, by nature, a little spoiled . . . you can do more with less, and you really don't need most of the things you think you do." Wingate called the tendency of soldiers to carry a surfeit of nonessential items into combat "Christmas treeing"; it was an aversion he bequeathed to the officers of the 1688th Detachment.

Wilson was selected by Lieutenant Colonel Osborne to lead the 1st Battalion's intelligence and reconnaissance platoon, a singular honor given his age. Chosen to command the 2nd Battalion's I&R platoon was 1st Lt.

William Grissom, a man described by one of his soldiers as a "a fine officer and well respected by his men."

Logan Weston held a similar standing among the 3rd Battalion's I&R platoon, one of whom, Sgt. Alfred Freer, described their officer as "a tall, lanky, soft-spoken man [who] did not act like the typical officer. He wasted few words."

Nearly two hundred soldiers applied to join Weston's outfit (which was soon affectionately rechristened the "Ignorant & Rugged" platoon). Knowing he could only select fifty-four men, Weston meticulously screened all candidates, looking for those who had distinguished themselves in the South Pacific and further whittling down the list by recruiting soldiers who "had trusted the Lord to deliver them under combat situations."

The men selected for the I&R platoons had to be tough, alert, and supremely fit. Their task once operations started would be to "snoop" several miles ahead of their battalion, reconnoitering the dense jungle not only for the enemy but for routes of march, bivouac camps, and suitable areas for airdrops.

Conscious of what General Wingate had said about the need for self-reliant, alert-minded officers and men able to take the initiative, Lt. Sam Wilson instigated a set of standard operating procedures (SOPs) for hand signals with little verbal communication. "I was a little nutty on things like that," he recalled. "If you come under fire, or something is going wrong, you flash a signal and at least you execute something quickly and in a well-organized fashion. If you can explode in the face of an enemy in that way when he thinks he's got you in an ambush, you can come at him so hard that he doesn't know what has hit him."

Wilson saw parallels between his I&R platoon and a football team, in that certain plays are developed and practiced over and over until everyone "can do them in their sleep," even when wounded or frightened.

★

By the middle of December, Hunter was concerned by the lack of official recognition accorded the 1688th Detachment by South East Asia Command. Neither its supreme commander, British vice-admiral Lord Louis Mountbatten (a cousin of King George VI), nor his deputy, General Stilwell, had acknowledged their presence in the region, and save for the visit from Wingate, they might not have existed. Worse, the force hadn't even been given a name or an insignia that could be invested with pride.

Hunter "began to put pressure on the Rear Echelon Headquarters of CBI to do something about the situation," he recalled, but with little success. He wasn't alone in feeling a sense of mounting frustration at the pace of events in the CBI Theater. The Cairo Conference hadn't gone well for Stilwell, and Chiang Kai-shek—whom the American referred to in private as "Peanut"—was being more capricious than ever, one moment agreeing to commit large numbers of Chinese troops to an offensive in Burma, the next day withdrawing his consent.

Matters reached a head on November 25, 1943, when President Roosevelt informed Stilwell that Chiang had accepted SEAC's plan for a Burmese campaign. In the evening, he was summoned back to the president's residence to be told that the generalissimo had had second thoughts. "Louis [Mountbatten] is fed up on Peanut," wrote Stilwell in his diary. "As who is not?"

Stilwell could at least derive a measure of satisfaction from the knowledge that Churchill and Roosevelt had seen firsthand in Cairo what Chiang was like, what he had had to endure for more than a year. "They have been driven absolutely mad," was how Mountbatten described the reactions of the two great Western leaders.

Nonetheless, a declaration was signed at Cairo, made public on December 1, in which Britain and the United States recognized China as a great power and promised the return "of all the territories Japan has stolen from the Chinese." In addition, the Allies agreed to an amphibious assault on the Andaman Islands off the southern Burmese coast, an operation Chiang believed would divert Japanese troops from the mainland and make the land invasion easier.

Four days after the promulgation of the declaration, the amphibious assault was abandoned when the Americans and British agreed that logistically it wouldn't be possible to spare so many landing craft so close to the invasion of France.

Roosevelt telegrammed the decision to Chiang, also inquiring whether he was prepared to still support a land offensive in northern Burma or wait a year when the Allies would be better able to launch a major amphibious landing in Southeast Asia.

Chiang was furious with what he saw as another Western betrayal, but he played the abandonment of the operation to his advantage. Yes, he would still support a land offensive, but only in return for more financial support from the United States. While the Chinese and American governments argued over the exact nature of the monetary aid, Stilwell began preparing to invade northern Burma.

On December 18, Chiang agreed that Stilwell would command the 22nd and 28th Chinese divisions assembling on the border between Assam and Burma, making it the first time an American would lead Chinese soldiers into battle. "It took a long time, but apparently confidence has been established," Stilwell wrote in his diary. "If the bastards will only fight, we can make a dent in the Japs."

Stilwell's plan, code named "Capital," called for a three-pronged attack; the Chinese Y (Yoke) Force would cross from China into northeast Burma, fording the Salween River and attacking the Japanese around Lungling, and the British IVth Corps would strike in the west across the Chindwin. Meanwhile, his two divisions would drive down the middle of northern Burma and seize Myitkyina while supported by Colonel Hunter's 1688th Detachment. They would be confronted by the Japanese 18th Division, regarded as one of the outstanding divisions in the Japanese army under the command of General Shinichi Tanaka, conqueror of Singapore.

On December 24 the offensive began, watched by Stilwell from his Burmese headquarters at Shingbwiyang. Wearing a steel helmet instead of his usual battered felt infantry campaign hat, Stilwell braved sniper fire to encourage the 38th Division as they advanced into the Yubang Ga. In the first week of fighting, the Chinese lost 750 men killed or wounded, but they forced the Japanese to fall back, a direction they had seldom gone since their occupation of Burma.

Emboldened by the initial gains of the Chinese, Stilwell now turned his attention to finally gaining control of the only American infantry unit then on the Asian continent—the 1688th Detachment.

★

General Stilwell, nicknamed "Vinegar Joe" early in his military career, found much of humanity objectionable, but he hated the British more than most. As a chief intelligence officer for the IV Corps in France during the First World War, Stilwell was attached to the British 58th Division in France. It was a chastening experience for a young officer trying to make his way in the world. The British were "so damn snotty," with their condescending attitude gnawing at Stilwell's innate insecurity.

Now in the CBI Theater, where he was commanding general of the United States Army Forces, Stilwell believed the British were guilty of docility. "Yellow Limeys," he called his Allies in his diary, an opinion only marginally tempered by Orde Wingate's Chindit expedition into Burma in February 1943.

Since the Cairo Conference, Stilwell had agitated for the transfer of the 1688th Detachment to his command, and finally at a conference in Delhi on December 31 he got his way, as an exasperated Mountbatten declared: "For God's sake, take them off my hands."

Undoubtedly, Stilwell's relationship with General Marshall had contributed to the latter's decision. The more Marshall observed Wingate's methods, the greater his concern that American lives would be squandered by the ruthless British general.

It fell to Lieutenant Colonel Hunter and Col. Francis Brink, both of whom were present at the Delhi Conference, to inform Wingate that he was no longer in charge of the 1688th Detachment. It was a task neither relished.

Hunter and Brink located the Chindits' leader at the airport as he prepared to board a flight to Jhansi. "Wingate greeted us affably," recalled Hunter, and then Brink informed him that the 1688th Detachment was now under the command of Stilwell. "With this Wingate's piercing black eyes clouded with anger and he blurted out, 'Brink, you tell General Stilwell he can take his Americans and stick 'em up his ass.'"

Wingate's pique was understandable; in losing the 1688th Detachment he had also lost face, but the ethos that he believed underpinned long-range penetration had also been compromised by the decision to transfer command of the American force. "Ignorance is our main weakness," Wingate had written in his report of the first Chindits mission. "Long Range Penetration will prove a dismal failure unless it is conducted from one centre, with one plan, one doctrine, one training and one control in the field."

Wingate's anger was fueled by a fear that in decentralizing command of the LRP, South East Asia Command had made a grave mistake that would have serious repercussions in Burma.

Brink soon had his own reason to curse Stilwell. Within days, he was unceremoniously relieved of his position as the detachment's training officer. "Vinegar Joe" was living up to his nickname.

CHAPTER 5

Merrill and His Marauders

Hunter returned to Deogarh from Delhi "apprehensive" of the future now that Stilwell was in command of the 1688th Detachment. He recalled what Wingate had said a few weeks earlier, that should the unit "be employed under Stilwell's command, they would not be withdrawn after three months," as he had been led to believe by Washington, but instead would be used to spearhead Chinese advances deeper into Burma.

Hunter's fears were well-founded. On January 1, he was instructed to issue General Order No. 1, which at last gave a name to the 1688th Detachment. From now on, they were to be known as the 5307th Composite

	Battalion HQ	Combat teams		
		No. 1	No. 2	Total
Officers	3	16	16	35
Enlisted men	3	456	459	928
Aggregate	16	472	475	963
Animals (horses and mules) . .	3	68	68	139
Carbines	6	86	89	181
Machine guns, Heavy		3	4	7
Machine guns, Light		2	4	6
Machine guns, Sub	2	52	48	102
Mortars, 60mm		4	6	10
Mortars, 81mm		4	3	7
Pistols		2	2	4
Rifles, Browning Automatic . .		27	27	54
Rifles, M1	8	306	310	624
Rockets (Bazookas)		3	3	6

..giment (Provisional). The men were astonished. "Where'd they ever get such a number?" wondered one officer in the 1st Battalion. "It sounds like a street address in Los Angeles."

General Order No. 2, also issued on the first day of 1944, proclaimed Colonel Hunter the unit's commanding officer. General Order No. 3 changed the 5307th from a regiment to a unit "since it would not be fitting for a mere regiment to have a general officer commanding it." General Order No. 4, published on January 4, appointed Brig. Gen. Frank Merrill as the new commanding officer.

The men were surprised and a little dismayed by Hunter's treatment. "It had been our hope all along that Hunter would be the man who would be anointed to command us and carry us into combat," reflected Sam Wilson. "He put the unit together, trained the unit, got us into fighting fettle, and then we became a political football between the British . . . and Stilwell's CBI command."

Stilwell appointed Merrill because he could rely on him to carry out his instructions to the letter, but it was a crass and potentially dangerous appointment. Stilwell knew that Merrill was not a physically robust man; on the retreat from Burma in 1942, Merrill had suffered heart trouble and was carried part of the way on an air mattress. Now Stilwell wanted him to lead an infantry unit into the hostile Burmese jungle.

But Stilwell knew that Merrill possessed something that Hunter didn't—obeisance. Merrill was a "yes man," a man who preferred consensus to confrontation. In short, Merrill wasn't one to rock the boat.

Merrill was born with an astigmatism that threatened to wreck his adolescent ambition of becoming an Army officer. Six times he took the exams for West Point before the Academy eventually agreed to overlook his poor eyesight, which he hid behind a pair of gold-rimmed spectacles. Once at West Point, his physical deficiencies amused his peers, who nicknamed him "Pee-Wee" and used his yearbook entry to poke fun at his character: "Tasks have not always been easy—he holds a special order of commendation from his Division Commander for displaying unusual initiative and energy in performing engineering work under adverse conditions. We refuse to make predictions as to Pee-Wee's future, for it is ever changing. First of all, his goal was to be a lawyer, then a politician, and last a soldier. Even this is slightly uncertain."

Merrill graduated from West Point in 1929, in the same class as Hunter, aware that he was better suited for a role behind a desk than a rifle, even if he did like to imagine himself a warrior. In 1932, he gained a bachelor of science degree in military engineering from the Massachusetts Institute of Technology, and in 1938 he was dispatched to Tokyo as the military attaché, an appointment that furnished him with a solid grounding in Japanese military culture. Subsequently, Merrill joined Gen. Douglas MacArthur's staff in the Philippines and was in Rangoon when the Japanese attacked Pearl Harbor. He remained in Burma—now promoted to major—and was appointed to Stilwell's staff when he arrived in March 1942.

Despite his physical collapse on the retreat through Burma, Merrill caught the eye of Stilwell and was promoted to his assistant chief of staff for Plans and Operations, G3, in the CBI Theater. At the start of 1944, he wore the rank of brigadier general over a heart that had not gotten any stronger.

Merrill must have felt a degree of discomfort replacing Hunter as the commanding officer of the 5307th. Since graduating from West Point fifteen years earlier, Merrill had risen higher in rank than his old classmate but not through any great feats of leadership. Hunter was the better infantryman, but it was Merrill who was tasked with leading an elite force of guerrilla fighters into what Winston Churchill described as the "most forbidding fighting country imaginable."

Merrill had his strengths. He was eager, charming, intelligent, and outgoing, far more so than Hunter, who wasn't one of life's extroverts. "Merrill was a neat guy, very softly spoken and easy to get along with," reflected Bernard Martin, who worked as his radio operator for a brief spell in Deogarh. "With Merrill it was possible to negotiate with him, and he would listen to what people said."

Sam Wilson found Merrill "brilliant, innovative, and probably a better strategic thinker than Hunter," even if he did also regard Merrill with a little wry amusement. "Merrill reminded one very much of Franklin Delano Roosevelt," reflected Wilson. "He looked like him, had some of the same mannerisms, including this cigarette holder with the cigarette on tilt. Probably a bit affected because he realized that he looked like and sounded like Roosevelt, so he played it."

★

Merrill's first challenge on assuming command was what to do with the scores of soldiers who had gone AWOL over Christmas. A thick report detailing the myriad incidents sat on his deck—most concerning the 3rd Battalion. Incensed that they had not been given a furlough since volunteering three months earlier, the South Pacific veterans simply walked out of camp and made their way by train to Bombay. Sergeant Ed Kohler of the 2nd Battalion had gone, too, taking a couple of buddies along for the ride. "We decided if we are going to get killed in combat, we might as well have one last fling," he recalled. "After a couple of days of drinking we ran out of money, so we turned ourselves into the British MPs. They said they could let us sleep in jail until the Red Cross could make arrangements to get us back to camp."

Back at Deogarh, Kohler was busted in rank from sergeant to private. "It didn't matter since I didn't think we would make it out of Burma in one piece," said Kohler.

Merrill didn't have time, or the inclination, to court-martial more than one hundred men, so he dropped all charges. It was a deft piece of man management from Merrill; in a stroke, he had won over the unit.

Merrill now turned his attention to the question of transporting 800 tons of supplies 1,200 miles to Dinjan in Assam, just west of Ledo, where a series of bamboo warehouses had been procured by the superbly efficient Maj. Edward T. Hancock, the 5307th's supply officer.

There was an additional headache regarding the mules, which were needed to transport radio equipment, medical supplies, crew-served weapons, and packaged ammunition through the jungle. Three hundred mules had arrived in late December, along with eighty muleskinners from the 31st Quartermaster (QM) Pack Troop, but a second consignment of three hundred sunk to the bottom of the Arabian Gulf when the troop ship was torpedoed. Faced with a serious shortage of animals, the 5307th had to make up the shortfall with inferior mules and a consignment of horses from Australia of dubious quality.

"I was assigned a mule to carry part of my medical equipment," said Tech 3 Richard Murch, the New York bank worker turned medic. "I was given a serial number branded on the mule and then told to go down to the corral, pick him out, and bring him back. I knew what a mule was, as I had seen pictures of them, but a real mule. . . ."

There were dozens of mules in the corral, around seventy-five in Murch's estimation. Twice he tried to find his mule only to be kicked hard in the shins for his trouble. Eventually, he waited until the corral had been emptied of mules and then went back in to lay claim to his animal. Murch christened him "Bozo."

As the Chindits had discovered the previous year, mules made superb transport animals in Burma. They were strong—capable of carrying two hundred pounds of equipment—were reliable, and could live off the bamboo leaves. Horses ate only grain, twelve ounces a day per animal, which was three more ounces than a mule required.

But mules did have to be handled with care. "A mule's every bit as intelligent as a human," cautioned Col. Ralph W. Mohri, CBI Theater veterinarian. "To get along with him you need to have as much sense as the mule."

Muleskinners from the 31st QM Pack Troop put selected infantrymen through a crash course in maintenance, giving practical demonstrations outside the warehouse tents at Deogarh before heading down to the Betwa to practice river crossings. Regrettably, the mules had not had their vocal chords removed as requested before being shipped out to India, something

Wingate advocated. It was discussed as to whether it should have been done at Deogarh, but the decision was made not to debray the animals.

Next came lessons in saddling, loading, and leading. As one of the muleskinners explained, it was necessary for a soldier to lead each mule because normally they moved at around five to six miles per hour, a steady pace that allowed the 1,500-pound animal to pick his own gait. That was practical in a platoon of men, but in a column at that speed the mule would constantly overrun the foot soldier.

★

On January 11, Lord Louis Mountbatten, the supreme commander of SEAC, arrived at Deogarh to inspect the 5307th, looking at each battalion in turn before watching a series of demonstration exercises. "We found him to be friendly, unostentatious, soldierly in appearance, sensible, kind, and considerate of our problems," said Charles Hunter. Before departing, Mountbatten addressed the American troops and expressed his hope that they would be used as originally envisaged—as a complement to Stilwell's Chinese drive into Burma, and not as its spearhead.

On January 20, there was another visit to Camp Deogarh, this one from the press corps greedy for more details about the first American infantry unit on the Asian continent. Among the correspondents was Dave Richardson, a twenty-eight-year-old redhead from New Jersey whose application to join the infantry had been rejected on health grounds.

Richardson had vowed to see combat in some form, and eventually he was sent to the Pacific as war correspondent for *Yank* magazine, the weekly read by the GIs stationed abroad. Richardson earned a reputation for fearless reporting, and in January 1944 he arrived in India in search of a good story to go with Stilwell's drive into Burma. "Little did I expect what I would luck into on my very first day in India," he later recalled. Richardson was summoned by the Army's public relations department in New Delhi and told "about a whale of a story that was coming up very soon, one he thought was right down my alley as a combat correspondent."

Richardson hightailed it to Deogarh and arrived on January 20 in the company of Charles Grumich of the Associated Press, Frank Hewlett of United Press, and James Shepley of *Life* magazine.

General Merrill was there to greet the reporters, welcoming them to India and promising them that his boys were the best in the CBI Theater. The reporters lapped it up. In Hewlett's eyes, the 5307th was "the roughest, toughest bunch of infantrymen the U.S. Army has ever put together," while its leader "is one of the youngest and most brilliant line officers in the American Army." Hewlett described how Merrill "had learned how to fight the Japanese the hard way" during the bitter retreat from Burma with Stilwell two years earlier.

Merrill also gave the correspondents a lift down to the Betwa River in his jeep so they could see how his men got their mules across water. On their way, the men talked about this and that and about the name of the outfit. The 5307th didn't exactly trip off the tongue. Some of the correspondents began to bounce around alternatives, something that might capture the imagination of the public back home. It needed to be gung-ho and glamorous. Then it came to James Shepley: Why not call the unit "Merrill's Marauders"?

The name stayed in the jeep, however, and soon the correspondents left Deogarh for other assignments—except Dave Richardson, who felt such a kinship with the 5307th that he obtained permission from Merrill to accompany them into Burma. "It was a greater mix than I'd ever run into in an outfit," he recalled. "It had among its volunteers not only West Pointers but tough kids from the east side of New York, country boys from the plains, Sioux Indians from Idaho, who were expert shots, several Harvard eggheads as platoon commanders . . . in other words everybody had different reasons for wanting to volunteer."

To Richardson, the men of the 5307th weren't "Merrill's Marauders," they were "Dead End Kids," and that's how he started to refer to the unit in his dispatches. "He was right—we knew we were the castoffs," said Bernard Martin. "But we were proving to the Army that castoffs could be damned good soldiers."

The 3,000 volunteers—now reduced through illness and accidents to 2,600—were unrecognizable from the ragtag collection of volunteers who had stepped ashore at Bombay three months earlier. The 5307th lacked a name of which to be proud, and an insignia, but what they did have was a belief in themselves.

Captain Fred Lyons recalled that months of training had left them as "hard as our green helmets, tough as our green GI brogans. I weighed 146 pounds, and there wasn't an ounce of fat on me. I could run for twenty miles and still enjoy a brisk walk in the cool night air of an Indian village."

On January 27, the 1st Battalion was the first of the three battalions to entrain for Margherita, 1,200 miles east in Assam. It was a ten-day voyage in total, including a trip on a paddle wheeler that made the southern boys pine for the Mississippi. For officers such as Charlton Ogburn, it was a perfect opportunity to unwind after the rigors of Deogarh. "It was bliss," he reminisced, "to be able to lie about all day even on wooden benches, eight to a compartment, with nothing to do but talk, eat, buy tea from the vendors at the stations."

CHAPTER 6

Down the Ledo Road to Burma

The English painter and writer Robert Talbot Kelly was instrumental in opening up Burma to the West. For many years he lived in Egypt, traveling into the interior of the desert and painting the Bedouin tribesmen with whom he lived. At the turn of the twentieth century, Kelly visited Burma. At once he was entranced by the mysterious eastern country, describing it as "one of the most interesting and beautiful in the world." The south, in and around Rangoon, he found exotic and bustling. The north was a different country, where "ranges of hills form a barrier between Burma and the frontier provinces of India, and when I tell you that all these mountains are densely covered with forest and jungle, and that the rivers are wide, and in many cases unnavigable, you will understand how it is that Burma is not better known."

Kelly found northern Burma stunning, a paradise, albeit one where the traveler had to be wary. In luxuriant prose, he threw open this land to his reader. "Sparkling rivulets spring from the mountain-side, and, overhung by ferns and mosses, flow gurgling over their pebbly beds to the deep valley below, there to join the swiftly-flowing river, which, by many waterfalls and rapids, eventually reaches the level of the plains."

But the prose, like the terrain he was describing, grew less attractive the deeper one delved. "The forest is dense, and in places almost impenetrable, and as you ride or cut your way through the thick undergrowth, monkeys of large size follow you through the tree-tops, scolding and chattering at your intrusion," wrote Kelly. "On the lower levels, where paths are more frequent, little bridges of picturesque design cross the streams, from which rise warm miasmic mists. In the early morning dense fogs fill the valleys, often accompanied by frost; but as the sun gains power and the mists are sucked up, the heat is intense; and these extremes of heat and cold, combined with the smell of rotting vegetation and exhalations from the ground, render this region a perfect fever-den, in which no white man can safely live."

Disease wasn't the only danger lying in wait for the uninitiated. There were tigers, leopards, elephants, pythons, and the terrifying king cobra. Burma, warned Kelly, was not for the fainthearted.

★

When the 1st Battalion stepped off the train on February 6, they were in a new India compared to the one they had left in the arid scrublands of Deogarh. Assam was lush, wet, and hot—so hot that it was like walking into a steam room. By the time the men had marched to the staging area at Margherita, they were squelching with sweat.

Margherita was a village of *bashas*, small houses constructed from bamboo with palm-thatched roofs and elevated four feet from the ground on stilts. A harassed supply section worked furiously to ensure that the unit was properly equipped before it set off along the Ledo Road into Burma.

During the afternoon of the 6th, the 1st Battalion was addressed by Harold Young, an American Baptist missionary (whose son William would become a legendary CIA agent during the "secret war" in Laos in the 1960s). It was a lecture Young would repeat to the other two battalions. "He demonstrated how to get water from bamboo and banana trees, how to build an insect-proof bed, and gave many other practical suggestions on what to do and not to do in the area we were to operate in," recalled James Hopkins. You got water from banana trees by simply squeezing, but bamboo required more effort. Hack into the joints of the bamboo, Young explained to the soldiers, where one cylinder joined another. That's where the water is found.

★

On the morning of February 7, the 1st Battalion made its final preparations for the march into Burma. All equipment not required for the operation was placed into large individual barrack bags on which was painted the soldier's name. The men also put their personal effects into the bags: battlefield souvenirs, knick-knacks bartered for in Indian bazaars, journals, photos of family back home, letters from wives and sweethearts.

The cotton uniform that the 5307th had been issued in Deogarh met with general approval. It was not, recalled Capt. Fred Lyon, "the splotched camouflage uniforms of the New Guinea boys, but solid dark green outfits that offered even more complete concealment in the bush. Our fatigue blouses and our pants, our undershirts and drawers, even our handkerchiefs and matches were green." On their feet, the men wore either calf-high, rubber-soled canvas boots or standard combat shoes, except Bernard Martin, who sported a pair of handmade boots. "During training we occasionally got the chance to sneak into town, and one time I had a cobbler make me a pair of boots," he remembered. "They cost me about ten American dollars, and they were beautiful."

Each soldier had been given a choice of three backpacks in which to carry his essential equipment, such as mess gear, blanket, poncho, and a change of socks and underwear. (Once in Burma, the men would also carry three to five days of combat rations). Ammunition, radio equipment, and medical supplies would be carried on the mules and horses.

The 1st Battalion was scheduled to march out from the staging area at 2000 hours on February 7, but a short while before H-Hour the scene was one of utter confusion. "Rear-base supply officers were running about with clipboards," Charlton Ogburn recalled. "Platoons were being disentangled one from another, missing soldiers were being discovered (blinking in the beam of a flashlight) behind bushes fortifying themselves with a last, unauthorized meal, loads were being wrestled with by the light of campfires, freedom-loving pack animals were being rounded up in the woods."

It was nearly midnight when the column finally formed on the Ledo Road, with the men spaced ten feet apart. For a few moments, an awesome silence descended on the 1st Battalion, as if the mules and the horses sensed the enormity of the occasion as well as the men. Then, from the front of the column, a command was passed back through the warm, damp blackness: "Put 'em on. The column's moving."

Absent from this auspicious moment was Sam Wilson and his I&R platoon, which had moved out ahead of the rest of the 1st Battalion to scout the road and select bivouac areas. Wilson had a recent addition to his I&R platoon, a twenty-five-year-old sergeant from California named Clarence Branscomb.

Branscomb was a veteran of Guadalcanal, a member of the 161st Infantry Regiment that had helped drive the Japanese from the Matanikau River Pocket in January 1943. Over the course of eleven bloody days in January 1943, the six-foot Branscomb proved himself an adept jungle fighter. "I enjoyed fighting," he reflected. A loner by nature, Branscomb was shrewd, outspoken, and daring. But he wasn't reckless, and his reputation as an outstanding soldier, in his opinion, owed more to "common sense" than courage.

Branscomb had volunteered for the 5307th because it was either that or a spell as an instructor, and he knew he wasn't cut out for training recruits. With the rest of the South Pacific veterans, Branscomb boarded the *Lurline* at New Caledonia and spent the entire voyage to Bombay in the sick bay. "I had dengue fever. I was really sick," he said. "When we got to India I was transferred to another hospital, and I didn't join the unit for several weeks."

When Branscomb finally reported to the 5307th in Deogarh, he discovered he'd been transferred from the 3rd to the 1st Battalion under the command of Lt. Col. William Osborne. Osborne assigned him to the Red Combat Team's I&R platoon. "When we went down the Ledo Road, I didn't really know any of the names of the men in my platoon," recalled Branscomb. "I just didn't have time. That's a bad situation; you should get to know your neighbor."

Branscomb was unsure what to make at this stage of Wilson, whose youthful idealism was a counterweight to his own intrinsic skepticism. "Sam had never been out of the USA before Burma, and he had never been in combat," said Branscomb. "He could be a little clumsy, and I wasn't sure he was ready for the job."

Branscomb's opinion was reinforced by an incident along the Ledo Road. "The column had fallen out for a rest break, and as usual I was taking advantage of the chance to unlimber the horses a bit," recalled Wilson. Unable to resist the temptation, Wilson took "Big Red" for a gallop along the road, past the column of foot-weary soldiers, with the horse picking up speed with every yard. "We came careening around a bend in the road, and right in front of me was the command group with General Merrill, standing there with his clipboard," remembered Wilson. Merrill waved his helmet in the air as Wilson thundered past with a fixed grin on his face as he tried desperately to rein in Big Red.

★

The 2nd Battalion struck out for Shingbwiyang twenty-four hours after the 1st. "Lining both sides of the road as far as I could see ahead were the bobbing heads of men in green helmets, with green packs riding high on their backs," remembered Capt. Fred Lyons, who, like most of the other officers, had removed all evidence of rank from his uniform so as not to invite the attention of enemy snipers. "Mules ambled along, their packs lurching from side to side in rhythmic movement with the marching feet. Behind me stretched an endless line of faces chalky white in the iridescent light from a Burma moon." The men talked in snatches, passing comments rather than conversations. "I hope this thing's over with in a hurry," Lyons heard Sgt. Stan Sokoloski mutter. "I have a feeling this is going to be no jaunt."

★

Merrill had instructed the battalions to march by night and rest during the day in a bid to conceal their presence from the Japanese. It did no good. Hours into their march, the 2nd Battalion tuned into the radio to listen to Tokyo Rose, the generic name given to the female broadcasters used to spread Japanese propaganda over the airwaves. "To our astonishment, we heard her say there was a regiment of American infantry on the Ledo Road moving toward Burma," recalled Lt. Ted McLogan. "And that his Royal Majesty's 18th Japanese Division knew all about us and were ready and waiting for us."

The 3rd Battalion left the staging area at 1830 hours on February 9, just around the time the 1st Battalion was experiencing its first tragedy. "We had one misfit in our group on the Ledo Road," remembered Robert Passanisi. The soldier had trained under Passanisi's tutelage as a radioman, but he failed to make the grade. Charlton Ogburn reassigned him as an infantryman, but as they closed on Burma the man became more agitated. "We tried to get the medics to move him out and take the Tommy gun from him," said Passanisi. Nothing was done, however, and on the evening of February 9, as the battalion bivouacked for the night at a spot chosen by Sam Wilson's I&R platoon, the soldier disappeared into the undergrowth with his Tommy gun and killed himself.

Another unfortunate incident occurred when one of the mobile kitchen trucks loaned to the 5307th for the march along the Ledo Road suffered a brake failure. Twenty soldiers from the 2nd Battalion were injured and one killed as the vehicle careened out of control down a steep incline.

The mess trucks provided the soldiers with hot and plentiful meals at daybreak and dusk. There was also the opportunity to barter for additional food with the British and Chinese troops they encountered, with the unit's men getting whatever they wanted in exchange for the much sought-after American cigarettes. Occasionally, the battalions passed a field hospital or an engineer camp, and a further chance was had to barter goods. As the 1st Battalion marched by one engineer unit, staffed entirely by black American soldiers, a band struck up "God Bless America" followed by "Dixie."

On February 10, the 3rd Battalion also encountered some homespun hospitality, which was good enough for Sgt. James McGuire, a twenty-six-year-old from Arizona, to describe in the diary he carried in his pack: "14 mi. tonite, saw some nurses and Red cross women last nite, they passed out cookies along road."

★

On leaving Assam, the Ledo Road wound up through the Naga Hills and into the country occupied by the Kachins, a tribe that had been helping the Allies in the fight with Japan for two years. For much of that time, the Kachins had been engaged in a guerrilla campaign organized by Lt. Col. William "Ray" Peers, commander of Office of Strategic Services Detachment 101, formed in April 1942 to fight the Japanese in Burma. Peers described the average Kachin as "a hardworking, industrious, and trustworthy individual." The jungle to the Kachins is as Main Street is to Americans, continued Peer, and "their sense of direction and junglecraft is uncanny." Some Kachin warriors carried homemade blunderbusses, but most favored a long, razor-sharp knife called a *dah*. It killed the Japanese with less noise. "All in all," concluded Peers, "in his jungle the Kachin is a good man to have as a friend and a poor choice as an enemy."

Once in Kachin country, the 5307th marched on average ten to twelve miles a day, singing as they went, until they began climbing the eight-mile gradient that led to the Pangsau Pass. "Hell's Gate" was the troops' name for the five thousand-foot pass. On the summit was a sign that read, "Welcome to Borderville. God be with you."

The 3rd Battalion rested on the summit for ten minutes, a chance to massage sore feet and drag deeply on a cigarette. It was also an opportunity to take in the awesome view. To the north were the snow-capped peaks of the Himalayas; to the south lay Burma—and the enemy. "Entered Burma tonite," wrote Sgt. James McGuire in his diary, who also noted that the weather was muddy and rainy. The men had no way of knowing, but they had walked into a freak spell of weather in Burma in which the supposedly "dry" months of January and February produced thirty days of heavy rain. On top of the pass, McGuire discarded fifteen pounds of equipment to reduce the weight of his pack to "about 40 pounds." His diary remained.

There was no respite in the terrain as the 5307th pushed into Burma. In fact, the road turned into something that was akin to a mountain track, narrow and precipitous and hell to negotiate. Colonel Hunter discovered what every other soldier of the 5307th was learning—that being burdened with a heavy pack going down was just as bad as going up. The thighs screamed in agony when ascending the slope, but on the descent "the pack was urging you on and bowing the back as each foot was extended below the other, stretching muscles not designed for this kind of work."

It was the "shakedown" the unit needed. When the 1st Battalion reached Shingbiyang on February 18, every soldier glowed with satisfaction at the completion of the 140-mile march. "It was quite evident that we were becoming a cohesive force and great pride was beginning to show," said Richard Murch, one of the medics, who was pleased with how he personally had fared on the march. "I was doing well. The many miles I had walked each day to save a nickel on the subways of New York programmed me."

The shakedown had allowed the 1st Battalion's medical team to develop a daily routine that would continue for the rest of the mission. "The life of a medical corps man is a hard one," said Murch. "You are up early, wash, eat breakfast, feed the mule, and then hustle over to the aid station to hold 'sick call.' Dismantle the aid station and pack it on the back of the mule. During the day's march, the column halts every hour for a ten-minute break. During the break, the aid man is working, patching blisters, cuts, and treating whatever. When the column halts for the evening, unload the mule, set up the aid station, feed and brush the mule, and then 'sick call' . . . anything the company aid man could not handle he would send to us."

Life was just as thankless for the muleskinners during the brief rest periods. War correspondent Frank Hewlett marched some of the route with the 3rd Battalion, his typewriter and that of colleague Dave Richardson carried on a mule supplied by General Merrill. "An Infantryman, after hours of brisk marching, could flop and relax fully during a ten-minute break," wrote Hewlett. "Not so with a muleskinner. He must adjust the load and let the animal pull him along while grazing, or cut a handful of bamboo leaves to satisfy the restless animal. But the muleskinners' worst grief results when the column is stopped and orders are issued to disperse the animals off the trail, because the mules hate being alone and become a problem when out of sight of other mules—especially a bell mare."

★

By the time the 5307th Unit entered Burma, General Stilwell had relocated his HQ to Ningam Sakan, fifteen miles southeast of Shingbiyang. Ten miles farther on was the village of Ningbyen, selected by Merrill as the unit's assembly area. It was too dark to proceed through the wild terrain of the Hukawng Valley that night, so the 1st Battalion bivouacked at Shingbiyang, feasting on what would be their last proper hot meal for months. A novel order was then issued, one that reinforced the fact that they were closing in on enemy territory: "All fires out by dark and no lights thereafter."

The next morning, February 19, Merrill ordered the 1st Battalion to shave and wear their helmets. In a couple of hours, they would march past General Stilwell's HQ en route to Ningbyen, and Merrill wanted the 5307th to make a good impression on their commanding officer. But Stilwell wasn't there—he couldn't be bothered to make what Charlton Ogburn described as an "inexpensive gesture." Slighted, the battalion marched to the assembly area wondering if they'd ever encounter their commander.

On the same day, the 3rd Battalion still had some distance to go after two days of tough marching. Sergeant James McGuire complained to his diary on February 17 that they had climbed eight miles that evening before bivouacking on top of a mountain nine thousand feet above sea level. The mess truck had been unable to reach their camp, so they ate cold rations.

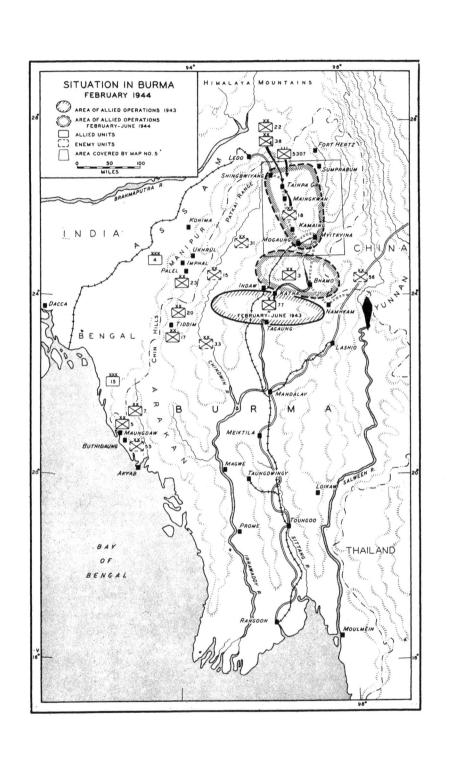

SITUATION IN BURMA
FEBRUARY 1944

AREA OF ALLIED OPERATIONS 1943

AREA OF ALLIED OPERATIONS
FEBRUARY-JUNE 1944

ALLIED UNITS

ENEMY UNITS

AREA COVERED BY MAP NO. 5

0   50   100
MILES

The morning of February 19 brought better news. "Breakfast at colored kitchen, pancakes 1st in over mo[nth]," wrote McGuire. "Wearing same clothes now for mo[nth]."

The 2nd Battalion followed on the heels of the 1st, passing through Shingbiyang late on February 20. Lieutenant Colonel George McGee was pleased with how his men had come through the long march down the Ledo Road in good shape, a fact he attributed not to luck but to their "awareness and understanding" of their new environment.

McGee misjudged the environment on the evening of February 20. That night, he ordered the battalion to continue marching in an attempt to reach the assembly area at Ningbyen. But the Burmese jungle at night was not a place for the uninitiated. "Even though the moon was bright, the light that seeped through the tangled mass of vines, banyan trees, and verdure was hardly enough to make a tree visible two feet away," recalled Capt. Fred Lyons. "Each man passed back to the one behind him the information on what to expect for his next step." Lyons was behind one of the battalion's medical officers, Capt. Henry Stelling, a thirty-seven-year-old doctor from Augusta, Georgia, who carried more than one hundred pounds of medical equipment on his back.

Captain Thomas Bogardus had first encountered Stelling in Trinidad and soon learned that while the "short and stubby, red-faced, red-haired" officer was a first-rate physician, he wasn't so skilled in the ways of the world. "Old Doc Stelling seemed to be a gullible sort," recalled Bogardus. "He was a boy scout and very proper in his demeanor. He never swore, never drank, everything was done to perfection . . . everybody enjoyed him but he was the butt of a number of jokes and he seemed to fall for anything."

Stelling's opinion of how the battalion had stood the march down the Ledo Road differed from his battalion commander. On the second day of the march, twenty men had to ride on trucks because of bad backs or sore feet, and a few were sent for treatment at the 20th General Hospital in Margherita. Stelling was at a loss to understand why "anyone in command ordered such a long first-day march with full packs," yet he spoke as a medical officer. For McGee, the brutal pace was necessary to harden men and animals for the rigors that lay ahead as infantrymen, a fact understood by Lt. Ted McLogan, who unlike most of the 2nd Battalion knew from first-hand experience that combat was no place for the weak. "McGee was tireless," he recalled. "Following each day's hard march, and while the rest of us were getting ready to flop down, he would show up to see exactly how each platoon was positioned in case of trouble. He never ordered any unnecessary action, and valued every man's life as precious as his own."

Nonetheless, McGee was as ignorant as the rest of his battalion of the Burmese jungle, underestimating its unpitying vastness in leading his men through the darkness toward Ningbyen. Stelling was furious with what he viewed as a dangerously foolhardy decision. "In the pitch black dark only those who have attempted to do so can possibly appreciate the utter impossibility of keeping a column of loaded pack animals and men moving along such a trail with thick vines and bamboo and underbrush growing up to the very edge of a narrow winding trail and with fallen logs and roots every few feet," he wrote later. "The disgust generated by our battalion commander on the first night march by stubbornly ordering the battalion on for three or four hours after dark during which we moved nearly one-half of a mile, of course without any light whatsoever, caused him to reach a new low in the estimation of all the men and most of the officers."

Stelling's opinion of McGee was the exception among the 2nd Battalion. Like all the best commanders, McGee didn't court popularity. His job was to lead, not to be liked, and if his men thought him a son-of-a-bitch for his tough, uncompromising approach to leadership, he cared not a hoot.

When the 2nd Battalion finally reached Ningbyen on the morning of February 21, they were drenched from the heavy rain that had fallen throughout the night. As the men dried their clothes and cleaned their weapons, they began nudging each other and pointing to the man at the side of General Merrill—Stilwell had finally put in an appearance. Not everyone recognized the old man in the dirty field jacket, baggy pants, and Chinese army-issue peaked cap. "One of my men came up when I was talking to him and took one look at him," recalled Lt. Phil Piazza, a twenty-four-year-old from Stratford, Connecticut. "He said, 'Jesus Christ, dad, things must be pretty rough back in the States when they sent an old SOB like you over here to fight.'" Piazza said Stilwell just laughed, and later in the day, when the general encountered the 3rd Battalion coming up from Shingbiyang, he was insulted again, this time labeled a "duck hunter" by George Kotch, a rifleman in the Orange Combat Team who was oblivious to Stilwell's real identity.

To his credit, Stilwell reprimanded neither man, though the jibes must have struck a nerve. In his youth, Stilwell had been a fine specimen, five foot nine and 145 pounds, fit, wiry, and tireless. He was a brilliant athlete during his time at West Point, the captain of the cross-country team in 1904 and the cadet credited with introducing basketball into the Academy. But he was now in his sixties, and that retreat from Burma to India two years earlier had taken its toll on his aging physique. He had been left practically blind in the left eye by an accident in World War I, and the sight in his right eye was also now poor.

Nevertheless, the presence of Stilwell at Ningbyen was a morale boost for the unit. McGee said the men of the 2nd Battalion "appreciated his interest" and were also impressed by the "easy and comfortable relationship that clearly existed between General Stilwell and General Merrill. It was one that could only exist between two individuals who knew and understood one another."

Lieutenant Sam Wilson was given a glimpse of the strength of this relationship when his I&R platoon received a visit from the two generals. To reach the platoon, Stilwell had to wade the Tanai Hka*, a shallow river in which was an island used as Wilson's bivouac area. Stilwell called Wilson and his men together and issued a little pep talk. Then he dismissed them, and while the I&R platoon brewed some coffee, Stilwell and Merrill sat on a log talking. Wilson gradually became aware that he was the subject of their conversation. "I had already done some things during exercises for Merrill that he kind of liked," explained Wilson. "I noticed Merrill sort of gesturing in my direction, nodding his head, and Stilwell turned and looked directly at me." For the twenty-year-old Wilson (he had celebrated his twentieth birthday on the *Lurline*), it was a moment he would never forget.

Merrill might also have mentioned to Stilwell that Wilson's I&R platoon had selected the area for the unit's first drop of supplies by air. The area, on the south side of the Tanai Hka, was free of jungle foliage and adequate for the momentous event. Colonel Hunter organized the drop in a slick procedure that the men would grow wearily accustomed to in the weeks that followed.

First, a set of fluorescent panels were laid on the ground "to indicate the center of the drop zone (DZ), the surface wind directions, the direction of approach of the aircraft to the drop zone, and the direction of turn on leaving the drop zone." When laying out the panels, the soldiers on the ground took care to direct the aircraft away from the drop zone in the direction considered the safest from both enemy bandits and dangerous terrain features.

Before the drop, the radio operator set up the SCR 284 radios on the edge of the DZ and tuned them to the 4 MHz frequency used by the C-47 transport aircraft of the First and Second Carrier units. There was a small speaker with the 284, so Hunter could listen for the flight leader's report as he neared the drop zone and began searching for the fluorescent panels, a task subsequently undertaken by air liaison officers attached to each combat team.

Over time, the 5307th Unit developed a deep respect for the C-47 pilots and their skill in approaching the DZ at a height of 400 feet or less. The pilots risked a stall as they lowered the front of the aircraft and raised the tail to make it easier for the "kickers" to perform their task. The kickers were responsible for heaving out the supplies, a job that married physical strength with perfect timing. Failing to heave a container out the door at the right moment could result in vital supplies drifting out of reach of their comrades on the ground.

*Hka *is the Kachin word for* water.

Clothing and grain for the animals were free drops from 150 feet, but all other supplies came down in bundles that weighed approximately 120 pounds from 200 feet on the end of a parachute, each one a different color and texture. A blue 'chute was nylon and denoted ammunition, white was cotton and used for rations, and green signified medical supplies.

The drop on February 21 passed without hitch, the bundles all landing on the DZ. Speed was of the essence in harvesting the supplies, for though on this occasion there was no threat from Japanese attack, future airdrops would be deep inside enemy territory with the very real threat of molestation.

Men ran forward with mules, loaded the bundles onto the animals, and headed to a distribution point where the supplies were opened and shared among the unit. Among the supplies dropped on February 21 was a great quantity of 10-in-1 rations, the favorite ration pack among American soldiers. The 10-in-1 provided three meals—breakfast, a midday snack, and supper—for ten soldiers, but they were considered a rare treat by the men. Normally they had to survive on the K-ration, which provided the soldier with a daily intake of barely three thousand calories and was designed to be carried in his pack and consumed when no alternative food source was available.

The breakfast K-ration consisted of chopped ham and egg, the K-1 biscuit, the K-2 biscuit, a compressed fruit bar, five grams of soluble coffee, sugar tablets, and a packet of chewing gum. Lunch was even worse: more biscuits along with a can of processed American cheese, maltrose, dextrose tablets, and a tasteless concoction rumored to be lemon juice powder. Supper was possibly the most challenging meal of the day with its dubious delicacies that included a corned pork loaf, bouillon powder, and a two-ounce D-bar that was alleged to contain chocolate.

K-rations, packaged in a wax-covered paper box approximately ten by four by one and a half inches, came to be detested by every member of the 5307th. For Colonel Hunter, it was the cheese that he found "particularly obnoxious." Robert Passanisi referred to the ham and egg yolk for breakfast as "the greasiest garbage." And Charlton Ogburn recalled that the "flat and musty" biscuits left him feeling queasy.

Each K-ration meal also held a pack of four cigarettes, which contained unheard-of brands such as Fleetwood, Chelsea's, or Wings. They tasted bad and burned lips, but they were better than smoking nothing.

CHAPTER 7

"I Fear No Son-of-a-Bitch"

February 22 was a day of comparative rest for the 5307th. The 3rd Battalion soldiers had joined their comrades at Ningbyen, and Sgt. James McGuire wrote in his dairy: "Took it easy got plenty of sleep." When he woke, he washed his clothes in the river, listening to the distant rumble of Japanese artillery fire and from time to time catching on the wind the "smell of dead Japs."

There was a further series of airdrops, and at 0800 hours on February 23 Merrill held a staff conference at which all battalion commanders, combat team commanders, and I&R reconnaissance platoon leaders were present. Merrill began the conference by pointing on a map to the disposition of Japanese forces in the Hukawng Valley. It was the fabled 18th Division they were facing, with the 55th Regiment dug in east of the Kamaing Road and the 56th Regiment to the west of the road, which was the main line of communication for the Japanese. Intelligence also pointed to the presence of artillery with twelve 70mm mountain guns and four 105mm guns.

The seven thousand Japanese troops were well dug-in and exploiting the local terrain to their advantage. William Peers, the OSS commander, explained how they utilized a variety of Burmese bamboo known as *bullaca*:

It is from four to eight inches in diameter and is capable of withstanding light artillery fire. The Japanese had perfected this bamboo into a concrete-strong barricade. Clumps of the bamboo grew ten to fifteen feet in diameter; the enemy had burrowed underground, as if building a tunnel, until they reached the center of the clump. Then, coming up to the center, they had chopped away enough so that they were absolutely surrounded by the natural obstacle, protected against light and heavy fire.

For two months, the Chinese 22nd and 38th divisions had been trying to dislodge the Japanese from the Hukawng Valley, but it was proving slow and bloody work. Progress was being made, however, and the 38th, along with the Chinese 1st Provisional Tank Group commanded by Col. Rothwell H. Brown, were driving south along the Kamaing Road toward Maingkwan, the principal Japanese base in the valley, while the 22nd covered their left flank.

Stilwell had issued Merrill his orders during their meeting of February 22. It was his favorite jungle tactic of launching a frontal assault on the enemy while the most powerful attack came from the flank with a block behind. Surrounded by his staff, Stilwell brought his briefing to an abrupt halt. "Aw, to hell with this," he said to Merrill. "Come on outside, Frank, and let's get this thing settled." The pair walked to a tree, where they studied a map laid out on the ground. Stilwell traced a finger to Walawbum, fifteen miles south of Maingkwan on the Kamaing Road. No written orders were issued by Stilwell; that wasn't his way. He gave his commanders the objective and allowed them some leeway in fixing their schedule. "I want you to hit there on March 3" was all he told Merrill.

"There" was Walawbum, the village that the Chinese would attack head-on while the 5307th swung around the east (or right) of the Japanese flank, cutting their way through the jungle and establishing blocks on the Kamaing Road to the south of Walawbum—in effect, preventing the enemy from withdrawing south.

Having briefed the 5307th officers of their mission, Merrill then issued orders for their inaugural operation. He instructed Sam Wilson's 1st Battalion I&R platoon to head south at 1130 hours (3 1/2 hours hence) on a reconnaissance of a series of villages to the east. The 2nd and 3rd battalions' I&R platoons, under the command of lieutenants William Grissom and Logan Weston, respectively, were ordered to depart a few hours after Wilson on the same trail for approximately eighteen miles before turning south and seeking out the enemy's flank. Merrill reminded the three I&R platoon leaders that they were to operate under regimental control, communicating through their own battalions until they reached the village of Nzang Ga. He also reiterated that they were "not to fight unless necessary—your mission is purely reconnaissance."

The I&R platoons had a vital task to perform for the 5307th. Aerial reconnaissance of the area was, in the estimation of Colonel Hunter "unsatisfactory," a situation that was not to improve over the course of the campaign. It didn't take Hunter long to understand that "we were working from an artist's sketch of the campaign rather than from architectural drawings by one who knew the details of construction."

The rest of the 5307th would follow the I&R platoons along the trail, marching east to the abandoned village of Ngukun Ga, then turning south toward Tanja Ga, fording the Tawang and Tanai rivers before heading west to establish the roadblocks as Stilwell's Chinese infantry launched its frontal attack.

Early in the morning of February 24, the men of the 1st Battalion emerged from under their ponchos and prepared to hit the trail. Many were still acclimating to the jungle: its blackness, its sounds, its smell. It was never a constant odor, fluctuating from day to day, hour to hour. It was sometimes earthy, almost fresh, other times putrid and sour.

Men took the opportunity of tasting hot coffee for one final time, aware that from the moment they started down the trail, campfires were forbidden. A detail was instructed to remain at Ningbyen for forty-eight hours and keep the campfires burning in order to deceive the Japanese spotter planes.

The 1st Battalion started down the trail at 0600 hours on February 24, followed half an hour later by the command group. The 2nd Battalion broke camp at 0900 hours, and two hours later the 3rd Battalion soldiers were the last to bid farewell to Ningbyen. After the conference with Merrill the previous day, Lieutenant Colonel Beach, commanding officer of the 3rd Battalion, had returned to his men and briefed them on the mission. Bernard Martin remembered that Beach told them they were facing the same Japanese troops who had taken Singapore. "The boys all whooped and yelled, 'That's the bastards we want,'" recalled Bernard Martin. "What Beach told us was like pouring gas on a fire. 'Kill the yellow bastards'— that's all we could think about."

In between discovering their mission from their commanding officer and heading down the trail, the 3rd Battalion had time to attend to last-minute matters. Sergeant James McGuire's entry in his diary for the 23rd ran: "Told what mission is. Expect air-raid tonite. We sent out decoys to build fires away from our area. Issued 3 day rations. Issued all equipment will need behind Jap lines. Firing in distance."

One soldier wrote his family back home, reassuring them he was well and ending by telling them: "My pack is on my back, my gun is oiled and loaded. As I walk into the shadow of death, I fear no son-of-a-bitch."

CHAPTER 8

Death on the Trail

There were three types of trail in northern Burma. There was the elephant trail, which meandered through the jungle with no concern for the shortest route from A to B. Then there was the main trail that Kachin natives used to get from their village to the next, constructed by rolling a large teak log behind an elephant. The third and final trail was the hidden trail, the route that once had linked villages but long since had been abandoned for a more fertile area of jungle. These trails were overgrown but still passable.

In time, the 5307th would learn of the trails from their Kachin guides, but on February 24 the three I&R platoons were advancing down the main trail. Logan Weston had divided his 3rd Battalion platoon into three squads and a headquarters group, a strategy he'd learned in the South Pacific. "A soldier even under the best of conditions often feels quite isolated because of the lack of visibility among the group," he explained. "Our unit was therefore organized into buddy teams. Each man was supporting a buddy, and he could rest assured that his buddy was supporting him. That gave us a psychological feeling of security."

Even on the trail, the foliage was so dense that Weston's platoon had to walk single file, six yards between each man. The undergrowth on either side of the trail joined overhead to create a tunnel effect, blocking out the sun's rays and further reducing the scouts' visibility.

They were arrayed in a wedge formation, the first squad out in front—with two scouts at point followed by Weston himself—and the second and third squad slightly behind and to the left and right. The platoon headquarters, including five mules and a horse, brought up the rear. "If we ran into the enemy, I would be in a position to make a quick estimate of the situation," said Weston. "If the enemy located our trail and tried to attack from the rear, the men in the platoon were to make an about-face. The platoon sergeant would then make his estimate of the situation, and the men moved into position: even men to the right, odd to the left. As the first squad in line established a base of fire, the platoon guide would stop the headquarters and direct the second squad into its wedge position beside the first squad. The third squad would then come up and form its wedge position on the other side of the first squad, forming a perimeter that looked like three points of a star."

Dave Richardson, the flame-haired war correspondent for *Yank* magazine, had attached himself to the 3rd Battalion, intrigued by some of its characters. Along with Weston—"The Fighter Preacher," as Richardson called him—there was Cpl. Werner Katz, "a burly first scout," and Sgt. William L. Grimes, "who won the Silver Star for knocking off 25 Japs at Guadalcanal." Richardson had a particular soft spot for Norman Janis, an Ogala Sioux and former rodeo rider from Deadwood, South Dakota. "We called him 'Chief' although he really wasn't one," recalled Richardson. "He was a loner who indulged in little of the usual chit-chat among his fellow soldiers, but he did love his gun and [was] known as a sharp-shooter."

The first day, February 24, passed without incident, and Weston located a suitable bivouac area for the 3rd Battalion that evening. "Walked 14 mi. Bivouacked in bamboo overnight. Crossed 2 rivers not bad going," wrote Sgt. James McGuire in his diary before settling down to sleep. At some point during the night, Capt. James Hopkins, one of the battalion's medical officers, was awakened by some men's reaction to a green flare bursting in the sky night. "Some said this was a signal from a Japanese patrol that the Americans were on the march," said Hopkins.

★

Weston's I&R platoon was on the trail early the next morning. Corporal Werner Katz was the lead scout as they neared the village of Nzang Ga. Despite his reputation for fearlessness, Katz was well acquainted with the emotion. "You're always scared like hell but you still keep alert and do your duty," he reflected. His combat experience in the Pacific, seeing men either side of him getting killed, had left Katz a fatalist. By the law of averages, he believed, it was only a matter of time before his time came.

A little after 1100 hours, Weston's platoon turned right off the trail and took a spur that led southeast in the direction of Nzang Ga. They were now twenty miles southeast of Ningbyen and approximately five miles in front of the rest of the unit.

The jungle became denser. The elephant (*kunai*) grass was as high as twelve feet in some places, and the trail, such as it was, was crisscrossed by elephant trails. "I was dreaming of New York going through high elephant grass," recalled Katz. Suddenly, he stopped and threw up a hand. The scout behind him stopped. So did Logan Weston five yards further back. None of the men moved. Weston saw Katz scrutinize the trail ahead, his head slightly cocked to the jungle. Weston padded noiselessly down the trail. "What is it?," he asked softly. Katz whispered that he "had heard sounds ahead." Yet the latest intelligence reports indicated the Japanese were twenty miles south. Most likely a Chinese patrol. Katz indicated he would press on. "Be careful," Weston warned him. "Don't shoot unless you're positive they're Japs." Katz moved down the trail as far as a bend. Up ahead was a figure. He was about fifteen yards ahead, standing in the middle of the trail as if he were expecting the Americans. The man smiled and waved. Katz relaxed. Weston remembered that Katz "looked back at me and said, 'Come on, it's okay.'" Katz took a step down the trail toward the Chinese soldier still holding a hand in the air. Suddenly, the arm dropped and the smile vanished. "Son of a gun," murmured Katz. "This is a Japanese."

A soldier untested in combat might not have reacted the way Katz did; he might have hesitated for a second or two. Not Katz. He fired and dived in the same movement, hitting the Japanese soldier "right between the eyes." In the next instant, the Japanese machine gunner concealed in the elephant grass fired a burst toward Katz. "The machine gun opened up on me and I was fortunate enough to fall on the ground and find a little indentation in the ground," he recalled. A Japanese bullet hit Katz's watch and ricocheted up into his face, causing a deep cut to his left cheek.

Weston and the second scout silenced the machine gunner with two short, accurate bursts. Katz leapt up from the indentation, and the men withdrew down the trail toward the rest of the I&R platoon. They soon encountered Dave Richardson, who was clutching his camera and hoping for a good story. The moment he saw Katz pumped with adrenaline, Richardson knew he'd struck gold. "They had just grazed his cheek so I said to Werner, 'I would like to take your picture,'" recalled Richardson. "I don't know why but when I took the picture his helmet was askew and I thought this was very odd, but I was in a hurry, bullets were still flying in that area, and we both had work to do. So I snapped it quickly . . . but it does capture his wonderful personality. He was a remarkable guy."

Joe Gomez, the I&R platoon's medic from New Mexico, stitched Katz's wound. Katz felt "embarrassed" at so much fuss over so small a wound, but his spirits soared when Gomez informed him that he had the "honor of being the first Marauder wounded in combat and also the first to kill one of the enemy."

★

Sam Wilson's I&R platoon heard the unit's first contact with the enemy and froze in a "moment of paralysis." The jungle's other inhabitants were less mute at the sound of machine gun fire. Scores of birds flew from the trees, and monkeys shrieked as they swung from the branches. And then the silence descended once more. Wilson waited a few seconds. One of his men said, "It's behind us." There was nothing they could do. "All right, let's go," said Wilson, and his platoon pushed on down the trail.

A few miles south of Wilson, a patrol from the 2nd Battalion's I&R platoon approached the village of Lanem Ga. They were hot and tired, sick of the sun that beat down on their heads.

The patrol leader was Sgt. Joe Freer, a New Yorker. With him were Sgt. Stanley Cobb and privates Eddie Eiskant, Vincent Melillo, and Robert Landis. Melillo carried an M1 with eight rounds of ammunition in its magazine. Eighty more rounds were stored in his belt, and another eighty were in a bandoleer worn crossways over his shoulders.

Melillo's surname was too much of a mouthful for his buddies, so they called him "Maxie." He was one of McGee's boys, a professional soldier who had joined the 33rd Infantry Regiment in 1940 and served in Panama and Trinidad. Melillo liked the Army. It was his substitute family. A baby when his mother died of influenza in New Jersey during the pandemic of 1918, Melillo had been raised in a series of Catholic orphanages for the first eleven years of his life.

Melillo, Freer, and Eiskant had been together in the 2nd Battalion since the beginning, but Cobb and Landis were veterans of the South Pacific, members of the 3rd Battalion who had been transferred to share their combat experience among greenhorns. Captain James Hopkins knew both men from his time in the 3rd Battalion, and Landis, in particular, struck him as an "intelligent, cooperative, patriotic young man." A native of Mahoning, Ohio, Landis was a handsome and muscular man who had proved himself as a soldier serving with the 37th Infantry Division in the Solomon Islands.

Joe Freer was the lead scout as Lanem Ga came into view. Like most Kachin villages in the jungle, it was nothing more than a few bamboo huts, in this case built on a slight rise in the ground. There were three trails into the village: one from the south, one from the north, and one from the east. The Americans approached from the east. The village had been abandoned several weeks earlier, and nothing appeared untoward. The patrol paused on the track, and Melillo listened to Freer's instructions as the sergeant "sent Cobb and Landis around to the left flank and told me to cover the rear."

Cobb and Landis stepped off the trail, and in the blink of an eye they were swallowed by the jungle. Freer and Eiskant continued up the trail with Melillo covering their rear. The village was now no more than a hundred yards away. Everything was quiet, the air heavy with the sultry heat of the jungle. Suddenly, the world exploded with noise. "When the firing started it seemed like my whole life went passing through my mind," recalled Melillo.

As they fell, the men's training kicked in. They were heads up as they hit the ground so that their backpack didn't push their helmet up over their eyes, leaving them blind. Freer and Eiskant returned fire, and Melillo scanned the jungle to make sure they weren't being encircled. He saw nothing—no Japanese and no sign of Cobb or Landis. "That was the first time I'd been under enemy fire," said Melillo, "and I sure was scared."

The firefight was brief. Freer estimated that there was an enemy squad concealed in the village, and he ordered Melillo and Eiskant to fall back into the jungle. The three withdrew without incident, and they moved back down the trail toward the platoon area where Lieutenant Grissom and the rest of the men were encamped. "Cobb was already back there," remembered Melillo. "He had lost his helmet and rifle. He was crying and he was saying, 'They got Landis, they got Landis.'" Landis had been killed instantly when the machine gun opened fire.

A messenger was dispatched down the trail with a situation report for Lieutenant Colonel McGee, but Grissom knew that the rest of the 2nd Battalion was still several miles to their rear. For the next few hours, they were on their own. Grissom set up an ambush and waited for the Japanese to appear on the trail. But none came. At first light the next morning, February 26, the rest of the battalion appeared and scouts were sent forward. They returned with the news that this time the village really was deserted.

Landis's body was found in the center of the village. "The Japs had stripped everything off him except his pants," recalled Melillo. McGee ordered the young Ohioan to be buried, and after the simple ceremony he examined the recently vacated Japanese positions. The machine gun nest that killed Landis had been well concealed in the jungle close to the southern trail. On either side were foxholes carpeted with spent cartridge. McGee pushed further into the jungle along narrow paths and discovered that a "bamboo lean-to had been constructed for unit sleeping-quarters and in front of it was a single communal fireplace." Approximately three feet above the paths, the Japanese had strung lengths of bamboo so that if surprised during the night they could feel their way from their sleeping quarters to their gun emplacements.

McGee was impressed at the "thoroughly professional manner" with which the Japanese had gone about their tasks. Prior to the war, the pervading view in the West was that a conflict with Japan would be bloody but brief. Their officers lacked imagination and their soldiers initiative— two flaws that combined to produce a "a third-rate army." That at least was the opinion of Capt. Evans Carlson, an observer at the Battle of Shanghai in 1937. Four years later, this supposedly fragile military machine had brought the might of the British Army to its knees in a matter of weeks. Soldiers apparently low on initiative had surprised the British at Moulmein in Burma by advancing not on the roads in columns but in small bands through the jungle. They wore clothes adapted for the terrain, carried all their ammunition and rations on their backs, and relied on animals for transport. Their fitness became the stuff of propaganda legend, so much so that *Reader's Digest* even carried an account of the Japanese battalion that set a world record for endurance marching in 1942 with a hundred-mile dash down the Malayan Peninsula. It took them just seventy-two hours.

★

News of the first Marauder to fall in combat filtered back to the rest of the 5307th. In the 3rd Battalion, there was much sadness for a soldier who up until recently had belonged to them. Captain James Hopkins said the mood of the men "changed noticeably when they learned of his death." After the grief came a thirst for revenge, an eye for an eye, but then later Hopkins noticed that many of the men appeared to be contemplating the fact that "it might have been me."

Vincent Melillo wasn't the brooding sort, despite being close to Landis. "I never thought about dying; it just didn't cross my mind," he reminisced. "I had a job to do and that's what I had been trained to do, so I did it." Werner Katz also put duty before thoughts of his own mortality. "When you see a guy get killed, when you kill somebody or you see somebody lose a limb, you become so scared or you become later on so fatalistic," he said. "You don't stay in there because you want to be a hero. You only stay in there because you do your duty."

★

On the same day that Robert Landis was laid to rest, Sam Wilson led his I&R platoon into the Tanja Ga. Like all villages in this region of Burma, it amounted to little more than another collection of bamboo huts in a clearing surrounded by jungle. There were fresh prints on the trail, the distinctive hobnailed imprints of Japanese boots, and Wilson found similar defensive positions to the ones McGee had discovered at Lanem Ga. While some of the platoon moved into the gun emplacements, Wilson took a patrol as far south as the mile-wide Tawang River in search of the enemy. None was encountered, and Wilson returned to the village confident that they had gotten beyond the right flank of the Japanese. The information had to be relayed to General Merrill as a matter of urgency.

I&R platoons carried on their mules the heavy SCR 284 radios because they probed so far in front of the rest of their battalions that they were generally out of range of the portable SCR 300s. Once the SCR 284 was unloaded from the mule and set up, Wilson waited eagerly for the regimental net to open so he could pass on the news. Contact was made, but the atmospheric conditions deep in the jungle prevented the communication of the message.

The message had to be relayed, so he and Clarence Branscomb saddled up the platoon's two horses and galloped off down the trail. Between Tanja Ga and General Merrill were twenty-two miles of trail. The precise whereabouts of the enemy was unknown.

Other dangers lurked in the jungle at night. As Wilson spurred his mount across a stream, something up ahead spooked the animal. The horse bolted up the bank with such force that Wilson was unseated, slipping from the saddle with one foot caught in the stirrup. He looked around for Branscomb, but his sergeant was still several hundred yards back down the trail.

Suddenly, Wilson heard what the horse had heard a few moments earlier, the sound of two wild animals "spitting and snarling as if they were fighting." They were about thirty yards down the trail. To Wilson's ears, they were cats, big cats, either tigers or leopards. "You don't want to tackle me, you crazy cats!" he yelled, while still frantically trying to untangle himself. "I'm too damned tough for you! Stringy and full of bones!"

Wilson freed his foot and grabbed his carbine from the saddle, firing a shot in the direction of the snarls. The animals fled into the jungle, and Wilson spurred the horse down the trail.

Just after dawn on February 27, Wilson and Branscomb encountered the 2nd Battalion's I&R platoon. Lieutenant Grissom briefly described events of the previous day, and then the two riders galloped west to deliver their message to General Merrill. Elated at the news, Merrill consulted his map and directed the three battalions to converge on Tanja Ga. Wilson and Branscomb rode back to their platoon in Tanja Ga, and within twenty-four hours the village was hosting all three battalions.

The village was a hive of activity on February 28. Colonel Hunter, as he recalled, organized a resupply "using as a drop zone a large sand bar around which the river curved to the west," while General Stilwell gave Merrill fresh orders. The Chinese were advancing toward Maingkwan on schedule, and Stilwell instructed the 5307th to close on Walawbum "as quickly as possible."

Between Tanja Ga and Walawbum lay forty miles of thick jungle, so time was of the essence. Merrill ordered Lieutenant Colonel Beach to lead his 3rd Battalion south at dusk. The 2nd Battalion would follow soon after, with Osborne's 1st Battalion moving out at first light on February 29.

The march toward Walawbum was uneventful, though the further south the Americans advanced the more they understood the Kachins' hatred of the Japanese. "Saw a lot of Burmese women and men dead in village, Japs killed them," wrote Sgt. James McGuire in his diary on March 1. "Dogs eating on their bodies. It stinks."

The 3rd Battalion covered fourteen miles during the night of March 1–2. To guide them through the darkness, some men tied their luminous wrist compasses onto the tails of their donkeys. Others discovered that the rotting vegetation that carpeted the jungle glowed in the dark and could be used as a beacon if attached to the backpack of the soldier in front. The humidity was unbearable. "We were soaking wet most of the time from sweat," recalled radioman Bernard Martin. "Always the worst for me was at the back of the knees, but on the long marches our boots would be squelching with sweat and after a while our socks just rotted away." The handmade boots that Martin had bought in India for ten bucks proved a waste of money. Within days of arriving in Burma, they were falling apart and Martin was left cursing the cobbler as their cardboard soles disintegrated.

A mule carried Martin's communications equipment, the radio secured on top of the saddle and the rest of the kit stored in panniers on either side, with everything covered by canvas to protect against the frequent rain. Sergeant James Ballard was the communications platoon sergeant, and he left Martin in no doubt as to who would be held responsible if the radio were damaged. Ballard was from Washington State, a huge man who stood well over six feet and weighed somewhere in the region of 250 pounds. "There wasn't an ounce of fat on him, and he wasn't scared of anything," recalled Martin. In fact, Martin was growing increasingly confident that the 5307th would be more than a match for the Japanese, despite some earlier misgivings. "I had doubts before we went into combat about some of the volunteers; they really didn't give a crap," he reflected. "Most of the soldiers were bums and castoffs, but they straightened out when we went into the jungle."

Beach drove the 3rd Battalion even harder in the early morning of March 2, leading them eighteen miles in eleven hours. "Today hard day, it's really hot," McGuire told his diary. "Crossed River 4 times. Saw a lot of natives that have come back to this Village." The local men wore small loincloths and the women were bare-breasted, a fact that, according to Capt. James Hopkins, made them "quite a hit" with the men.

The fourth river crossed by McGuire's 3rd Battalion was the Tanai, the last major obstacle before Walawbum, which now lay just a few miles to the southwest. By early afternoon on March 2, the whole force was across the river and preparing to receive an airdrop. Merrill gathered his commanders and issued combat orders for the forthcoming operation. The 3rd Battalion would move out at 1600 hours, "pass through Sabaw Ga and Lagang Ga, [and] secure control of the Kamaing Road at Walawbum by seizing the high ground along the Numpyek River east of the road."

Merrill turned to Lt. Col. George McGee. The 2nd Battalion was instructed to "proceed via Wesu Ga, cut a trail through the jungle westerly to strike the Kamaing Road just east of the Numpyek River at a point 2 1/2 miles west of Walawbum, and there construct and hold road block."

Merrill split the 1st Battalion. Some platoons were tasked with establishing blocks on the trails at Sana Ga and Nchet Ga to prevent Japanese movement southward, and to perform a similar function on the trail leading north out of Walawbum. The rest of the 1st Battalion was kept in reserve at Wesu Ga to be deployed as and when required.

Finally, Merrill stressed that the 5307th must maintain the blocks on the Kamaing Road until the Chinese drove the enemy out of Walawbum and relieved them.

At 1600 hours, the 3rd Battalion moved out as instructed, heading toward Lagang Ga approximately eight miles to the southwest. After six hours on the trail, Lieutenant Colonel Beach called a halt to the march, and the exhausted men fell asleep were they lay, heads resting on packs. Further down the trail, Lt. Logan Weston and his I&R platoon bivouacked. They rose early on March 3. It was unseasonably cold, and a thick fog filtered through the trees. Suddenly, the mules began to bray. In the next instant, Weston saw through the fog "the huge form of an elephant approaching." The beasts saw each other at the same time. Pandemonium ensued. As petrified mules fled north, taking with them the Americans' supplies and radio, the startled elephant turned tail and thundered back down the trail. It took Weston and his men several hours to round up the animals from the jungle, a laborious task that left them well behind schedule.

Anxious to make up time, Weston led his I&R platoon toward Lagang Ga at a relentless pace. Luck was with them. No Japanese were encountered until half a mile from the village, when the thump of a machine gun shattered the stillness. Instantly, Weston's platoon moved into wedge formation, the squads to the left and right advancing through the jungle to support the lead squad, which had established a base of fire. As veterans of the South Pacific, they were all familiar with the enemy's method of ambush. The S-shaped ambush began with the Japanese pinning down the lead squad with machine gun fire and then firing mortar rounds over their heads to prevent reinforcements coming up quickly. The Japanese would disengage once the firefight intensified, then fall back one hundred yards or so and repeat the tactics, in effect funneling the enemy down a trail—or so they hoped. It had worked against the British and the Chinese, but Weston's I&R platoon knew what to expect, and their wedge formation took the Japanese by surprise. They withdrew to beyond Lagang Ga, enabling Lieutenant Colonel Beach to stride into the village just after noon at the head of his men.

Among the 3rd Battalion was Capt. James Hopkins. "The [Numpyek] river ran directly north and south on the opposing side of the village," he recalled.

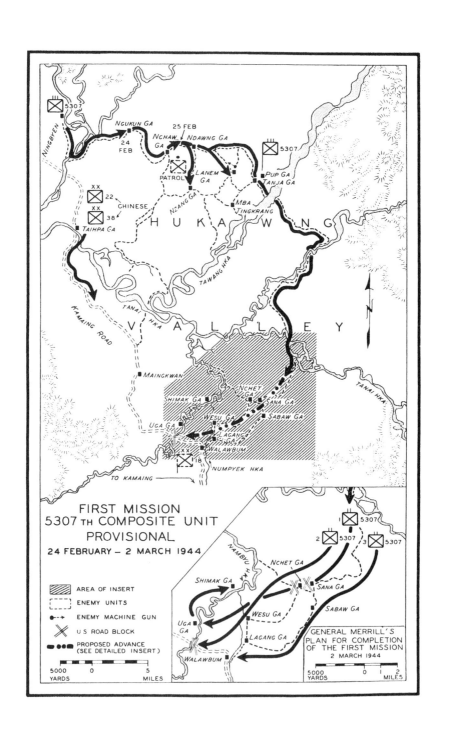

**FIRST MISSION
5307 TH COMPOSITE UNIT
PROVISIONAL**

24 FEBRUARY – 2 MARCH 1944

AREA OF INSERT
ENEMY UNITS
ENEMY MACHINE GUN
U.S. ROAD BLOCK
PROPOSED ADVANCE
(SEE DETAILED INSERT)

5000 YARDS   0   5 MILES

GENERAL MERRILL'S
PLAN FOR COMPLETION
OF THE FIRST MISSION
2 MARCH 1944

5000 YARDS   0   1   2 MILES

"Straight ahead and to the south, our trail entered the jungle just to the left of the river, where it continued two miles to reach Walawbum." Suddenly, seven Japanese appeared on the trail, trotting south with a litter resting on their shoulders. They saw the Americans a few seconds later. One soldier reached for the rifle over his shoulder, but he was too slow. "All hell broke loose," recalled Hopkins. "Many men fired and five of the enemy were instantly killed." The two survivors ran toward the river, but they too were shot.

★

Later in the day, Weston led his I&R platoon across the Numpyek River with orders from Lieutenant Colonel Beach to protect the battalion's north flank as they advanced toward Walawbum. War correspondent Dave Richardson remained on the bank watching as the men "crossed it Indian file, wading forty feet to the other side through crotch-deep water. Then, rifles cradled in their arms, they climbed the bank."

Weston and his men were now effectively isolated from the rest of the 3rd Battalion and deep inside territory held by the Japanese 18th Division under the command of Gen. Shinichi Tanaka. He was aware of the American presence. Confident that his troops could contain the Chinese 38th Division at Maingkwan, fifteen miles north of Walawbum, Tanaka ordered the bulk of the 55th and 56th infantry regiments to move south and "destroy" the Americans who were threatening their flank.

By the time Weston and his men crossed the Numpyek, the advance elements of the Japanese reinforcements were already headed their way. Twice in the late afternoon, Weston's I&R platoon spotted enemy scouts up ahead—spectral apparitions in the gloom of the jungle. As dusk approached, so did the fog. Weston ordered his men to bivouac in a swamp, instructing them to make no noise and use their helmets as latrines. "That night it was real foggy and we bedded down in the swamp, and the next morning at daylight we observed a high rise in the terrain and a bend in the river," recalled Weston. The platoon moved to the high ground, and Weston established his command post (CP) between the two trees while a perimeter was formed that afforded them good protection and a field of fire up and down the lazy river. The men began digging foxholes, three feet wide and six feet long and to a depth of about a foot. It took them until around 0700 hours to finish the job.

Pete Lettner from Lake Okeechobee, Florida, was the first to finish the foxhole. He went off to gather some branches for camouflage and was shot in the stomach by a Japanese sniper. Weston and Sgt. Paul Mathis dashed out to the wounded man and carried him back to the CP. As platoon medic Joe Gomez dressed Lettner's wounds, the rest of the unit scrambled into their slit trenches and readied themselves for the main attack. "We didn't have to wait very long," recalled Weston.

The sun had burned away the dawn fog, and the tan uniforms of the Japanese were clearly visible as they advanced through the brush. Weston let the Japanese come close enough so that he could make out the twigs sticking out of their helmet netting. Then he gave the order to fire. "The enemy soldiers hit the ground and fanned out, crawling closer and shooting ferociously," he said. "They chattered among themselves. Some seemed to be giving orders." Weston then heard a sound he knew all too well—a hollow snap. "Mortars!" he yelled. The first rounds exploded in the trees, raining down shards of red-hot shrapnel on the foxholes. There was a second salvo, and Sgt. Lionel Paquette collapsed due to a wound to his head. Gomez finished pouring sulfur powder into Lettner's bleeding stomach and crabbed over to where Paquette lay.

The enemy pushed toward the perimeter. Some crawled, some ran, some crouched. Others laid down a suppressing fire. Spotting several Japanese trying to outflank them on the right, Harold Hudson eradicated the threat with a burst from his Tommy gun that took out the rear man first and the lead man last. Sergeant William Grimes picked off any Japanese who exposed his head above the brush, and Pvt. Raymond Harris raked the undergrowth with his Browning Automatic Rifle. But for every enemy soldier hit, another one took his place. Soon they were moving around both flanks. Weston could still see them talking to each other, as could the I&R's Nisei interpreter, Henry Gosho, a twenty-three-year-old from Seattle who had been sent to Japan by his father in the late 1930s to learn the language. He returned to the States in September 1941 after being required in Japan to attend their equivalent of Reserve Officers' Training Corp (ROTC).

Now, in between the mortar shells and small arms fire, Gosho could hear quite clearly the orders been shouted by the Japanese officer. "I was amazed to find that this firing order was exactly the same order that I had learned in ROTC while going to college," recalled Gosho. "So I said to Weston, 'I'm not sure this is right, but he's giving firing orders.' So Logan turned round and said, 'What are they?' I told him, and he rearranged our firepower so we were able to respond to theirs."

The precious inside information checked the Japanese encirclement, allowing Weston a small window of opportunity to withdraw his men to safety before they were overrun. Weston's radioman, Benny Silverman, called up Bernard Martin on his SCR 300 walkie-talkie. Martin was with the rest of the 3rd Battalion on the other side of the Numpyek. We need assistance, and fast, Silverman told Martin. Support arrived in a matter of minutes. An 81mm mortar round looped over the river and exploded just behind the Japanese rear. Weston yelled new coordinates to Silverman.

The second shell was still too short. "Anybody got a compass with mills on it instead of degrees?" Weston asked his men. Joe Gomez fished into his medical bag and produced just what Weston required. "We medics have everything," said Gomez, grinning at his commander.

Silverman relayed precise coordinates to Martin, and mortar rounds started to land slap-bang among the Japanese soldiers closest to the Marauders' positions. Weston seized the moment. Back across the river, he barked.

As the I&R platoon began to fall back, carrying their wounded on litters constructed from combat jackets and bamboo poles, Lt. Victor Weingartner led his central platoon to the eastern bank of the river. Weingartner was wearing the same dirty mechanic's cap that he had in New Georgia, where his sartorial inelegance was matched only by his daring. He ordered his men to form a skirmish line and cover their comrades who were scrambling down the western bank and wading their way with all the haste they could muster. Dozens of Japanese were also visible, screaming, whooping, the scent of blood in their nostrils.

"As we started to withdraw, Weston made a temporary litter and gave me and another fella the order to take this fellow [Lionel] Paquette across the river," recalled Werner Katz. Katz and the other man, John Clark, slid into the river with their cargo and struck out for the opposite bank. Katz glanced around and "saw a Japanese with a Nambu machine gun. I was praying, thinking 'this is it, I'm going to die.'"

Katz, ever the fatalist, turned his face from the enemy and braced himself for the inevitable bullet. But on the eastern bank of the river, another soldier had seen the Japanese machine gunner. "He squatted down behind the gun so I shot for his head," recalled Norman Janis, the Ogala Sioux known as "The Chief." The Japanese was dead before he had a chance to draw a bead on Katz. "Another one got in his place," continued Janis. "I hit him, got him out of the road. There was seven of them, dragging them away, and then another one. That last one he kinda crawled back. I said, 'By gosh, I'm going to get you and keep you there.' So I shot him twice.'" Janis had a name for his M1 Garand: "Betsy." Betsy fired eight bullets across the river, and seven brave Japanese died as a consequence.

Weston waded into the middle of the river and stood there exhorting his men to hurry, disdaining the enemy fire that threw up spurts of water on either side of him. Only when the last member of the I&R platoon was being pulled up the bank by their comrades did Weston follow "as calmly as he were out for a walk in the sun."

The Japanese, furious that their prey had eluded them, charged across the river, but they were easy targets for Weingartner and his men. "They just kept coming across and we kept shooting at them," he remembered.

★

Colonel Charles Hunter was with the 1st Battalion at Lagang Ga, the village the 3rd Battalion had passed through the previous day. A noon airdrop was scheduled on a strip that had been fashioned five hundred yards to the east of the village, the shells and ammunition much needed in light of the 3rd Battalion's activities. With everything set up for the drop, Hunter decided to take advantage of the lull to read the airmail edition of *Time* magazine that had arrived an hour earlier in an L-4 liaison plane of the 71st Squadron.

These light aircraft were agile enough—in the hands of a skilled pilot— to land on sandbars or rice paddies and evacuate a badly wounded soldier to rear airstrips, where the casualty would be loaded into a C-47 ambulance aircraft. He then would be flown to the 20th General Hospital in Margherita or the 14th Evacuation Hospital situated nineteen miles along the Ledo Road.

One L-4 had arrived late in the morning to evacuate Pete Lettner, the I&R man who had been shot in the stomach just after dawn. His comrade, Lionel Paquette, had died shortly after being carried back across the Numpyek, and Lettner also succumbed to his wounds. Nevertheless, the fact that the pair, along with other less severely wounded soldiers, had been evacuated so quickly had a noticeable effect on their comrades. "The knowledge that our sick and wounded could be taken out by plane from improvised airstrips was a big boost to the morale of the men," said Capt. James Hopkins.

With the first of the wounded evacuated, Hunter browsed *Time*, but his eyes soon began to droop in the midday heat. Suddenly, he was "jarred back to reality by the screaming jeemie sound of an artillery shell bouncing off the terrain." Hunter leapt from his chair as the shell exploded in the middle of the airstrip, mud and dirt erupting from the smoking crater. He looked about and realized that most of the 1st Battalion had never before experienced an artillery barrage. Men looked stupefied, unsure of what to do, waiting for instructions. Another shell screamed onto the airstrip, and another. Hunter began yelling instructions, ordering the men to the flanks while telling his radioman to contact the transport planes and cancel the resupply.

Charlton Ogburn and his communications platoon were among the men caught in the open. One moment, Ogburn was comparing the tranquility of the afternoon to "an English painting of the eighteenth century," and the next he was scrambling for his weapon and helmet and looking for cover. Mules and horses broke free and bolted for the woods as another salvo of shells dropped on the airstrip, making a shu-shuing noise that to Lt. Phil Weld sounded "like evil buzzards flying overhead."

Men began to tear at the soil with whatever came to hand. Many used their entrenching tools, but others were cursing their decision to jettison the small shovel along the Ledo Road. They dug with their helmets, shoveling the soil for all their worth as more shells landed close by. Those minutes were long and harrowing for the 1st Battalion, a baptism of fire that none would ever forget. "I found myself on the ground, shaking, and thinking this was the end and I would never see another day," reflected Richard Murch, the medic. "The only way I can explain it is [you think] your time has come, this is the end, why am I here, please God, help me."

Robert Passanisi, the nineteen-year-old from Brooklyn, had marched into Burma cloaked in the armor of youthful invincibility. Death was what happened to others, not him. Not once had Passanisi given his survival a conscious thought, but now, under shellfire, he understood fear. "When you are in imminent danger, your pulse rate may be 150 and you are truly scared," he reflected. "It is not easy to describe; you're afraid of dying, but you're not consciously thinking about it."

Nonetheless, Passanisi and the rest of the 1st Battalion came through their initiation in what Col. Hunter regarded as a "gallant manner." When the shelling stopped, the animals were rounded up and Hunter instructed a contingent of men to prepare a new airstrip two miles to the north at Wesu Ga, where Merrill had situated his HQ.

Later that afternoon, Ogburn led a small group of men and mules to Wesu Ga to collect some of the supplies that had just been dropped. On their return toward Lagang Ga, they passed a steady stream of men coming from the opposite direction. A voice in Ogburn's head screamed that he, too, should head to Wesu Ga, but he knew he needed to first report to Lieutenant Colonel Osborne at the battalion CP and gather the rest of his communications platoon. Osborne was "singularly unruffled" despite the barrage breaking around his CP, but elsewhere at Lagang Ga panic was spreading. Ogburn didn't dawdle once he'd located his platoon. "We mustered what additional mules we could, loaded whatever equipment they could carry and, leaving much behind, joined the exodus," he said. Robert Passanisi seethed at the manner of their hasty departure, particularly the abandonment of the radio equipment and a bag containing $250 in silver rupees that was part of the Marauders' intelligence funds.*

Passanisi had initially held Ogburn in high regard, in thrall to his seniority, his Harvard education, and his intellect, but in recent weeks he had glimpsed another side of his personality. "Ogburn was well educated and smart . . . a great officer in training," said Passanisi. "In the jungle, however,

*For many years after the war, Ogburn believed this money had been lost until informed by Charles Hunter that he had buried the money at Wesu Ga "in order to lighten loads on our depleted complement of mules."

he "was entirely too much by the book," an inflexible and unimaginative officer who lacked what Passanisi called the "free-thinking aspect" of other Marauder officers.

For weeks Passanisi had been simmering with discontent, and on the morning after their withdrawal from Lagang Ga a confrontation erupted. "My mule was left behind with all the 1st Battalion radio equipment and it was Ogburn's fault," recalled Passanisi. "I approached him with my M1 in hand and told him that he and I were going back to get the radio equipment. There was dead silence. Everyone stopped what they were doing. No one moved or made a sound. From my expression and manner, they knew I was dead serious."

The thirty-year-old officer and the nineteen-year-old radio operator glared at each other. Ogburn knew what Passanisi was insinuating. He could see it in his expression, what he described as "his head back, his lips set in a pained half-smile, his eyes narrowed, feeling on my account a shame that I was apparently beyond feeling myself."

Ogburn had a healthy respect for Passanisi, a brilliant operator whom he called "one of the most valuable members of the platoon," yet this was insubordination borne of the "lofty, inaccessible disapproval of youth."

Ogburn countered the rebellion with sarcasm, asking Passanisi if he thought he could "conjure mules up out of nowhere to load the stuff on?" Passanisi's reply was brief and to the point: "If we hadn't been in such a hurry, we could have put more on the mules we had."

Ogburn wrote in his memoirs that it was his suggestion they go in search of the missing radio equipment. Passanisi has a different recollection of events. "In my eyes the welfare of the whole 1st Battalion was in jeopardy, and it was essential that I get that equipment," he recounted. "Going back bordered on suicide, but shouldn't the man responsible also extend himself?"

The two men untethered a mule and were about to start down the trail when orders came through instructing the platoon to move out. The search mission was abandoned, but the relationship between Ogburn and Passanisi never recovered. Ogburn would have been within his rights to report Passanisi to Lieutenant Colonel Osborne, but that never happened. He needed Passanisi in his platoon. "I didn't give any thought to the consequences of my actions; the radio equipment had to be recovered at all cost," stated Passanisi. "This candidness wasn't really very common, but there is always the thought: What are you going to do to me, save my life by sending me back to rear echelon for a court martial?"

CHAPTER 9

"Like Shooting Fish in a Barrel"

Following the airdrop at Wesu Ga on the afternoon of March 4, Col. Charles Hunter asked General Merrill if he could borrow his horse. He considered it prudent to ride the four miles south to check on Lieutenant Colonel Beach and the 3rd Battalion. Hunter was pleased with what he saw when he arrived on the east bank of the Numpyek. The Khaki Combat Team was at Lagang Ga while the Orange Combat Team was well dug in on the high ground overlooking the river with machine guns covering their front and flanks. Perched high up in a tree was Sgt. Andrew Pung, the mortar section's observer. Since midmorning, he had been spotting targets in Walawbum and relaying the information into his walkie-talkie. Over a hundred rounds had been fired into the village and onto the Kamaing Road. It appeared the Japanese were in the act of withdrawing.

Hunter returned to Wesu Ga and reported to Merrill, who in turn radioed the news to General Stilwell. "FRANK MERRILL IS IN WALAWBUM," he bragged to his diary. Stilwell retired for the night in high spirits; not only could the Chinese 38th Division now attack Maingkwan, but they could do so under the gaze of Admiral Lord Louis Mountbatten, scheduled to arrive at Stilwell's HQ the next morning to monitor the progress of the offensive.

That same evening, radio operators Bernard Martin and Bill Smawley were hunkering down for the night in a field behind the hill occupied by the Orange Combat Team. They had arrived from Lagang Ga a few hours earlier, led by Kachin guides who effortlessly chopped their way through the jungle before leading them into the open field. Martin reported to Lieutenant

Colonel Beach on arriving, and "he told me to get my [radio] gear running as close to the hill as I could." Martin and his team began digging a hole for the radio; it needed to be six feet by four feet and four feet in depth. The soil was soft, but it still took Martin, Smawley, and their muleskinners nearly three hours to carve out a hole with their small entrenching tools. With that done, they set up the radio while the muleskinners led the animals back into the safety of the jungle.

Martin and Smawley took turns transmitting messages. The one whose turn it wasn't had to crank the generator, a wearisome chore in the steaming jungle. Battalions rarely communicated with each other; rather, communications went straight to Merrill's radio operator, whose job was to route the messages to their destination. In that way, HQ was kept informed of every new development—not always easy in Burma, where the nature of the terrain mitigated against commanders issuing orders to their subordinates face-to-face.

With the radio working, Martin was given a guided tour of the Orange Team's position on the west bank of the river by Sergeant Ballard. Then, at about 1900 hours, he was instructed by Lieutenant Colonel Beach to encode a message and send it to Merrill. A short while later, Martin received the response in clear text and handed the message to his runner, Tony Colombo, who disappeared into the gloom to deliver it to Beach.

Martin and Smawley dined on their cold K-rations, a can each of corned pork loaf. As they were doing so, another message was received in clear text. This one said simply, "You're real close, Joe." "I knew it was from a Jap operator," said Martin, who was in the mood for some banter. "My answer was 'no, we just installed a new transmitter. Much more power.' He came back with 'listen to Tokyo Rose tonight, all Glen Miller music.' I answered with 'will do.'"

★

March 5 was a Sunday, a day that began with a dawn mist lingering along the Numpyek River and in the slit trenches of the Americans dug in on its eastern bank. Among their number was war correspondent Dave Richardson, who was up and about chatting to some of the red-eyed soldiers eating their breakfast. To Richardson, they were still the "Dead End Kids." One explained how much he'd enjoyed the firefight of the previous day. "Combat seems to seduce a guy," the soldier said. "He's scared as hell while he's in it but get him back in garrison and he'll start longing for those foxholes and shellings and bombings."

As the 3rd Battalion's Orange Combat Team prepared for another day on the banks of the Numpyek, the 2nd Battalion continued its move southwest toward the Kamaing Road. The previous day, March 4, Lieutenant

Grissom's I&R platoon had scouted the route, and now the rest of the unit was following in its wake. "We left the tangled jungle behind and walked through waving seas of elephant grass, like sugar cane, towering above our heads," remembered Capt. Fred Lyons. "The men ahead had pushed stalks aside and cut them with Gurkha knives, but we had to be careful not to brush against the stalks and cause ripples along the way."

Private First Class Gabriel Kinney recalled that the 2nd Battalion developed a technique for forcing a way through the elephant grass more discrete than the noisy chop-chop of a blade. Two men held opposite ends of a rifle and then jumped on the grass stalks to knock it down, allowing the following pair of Marauders to walk across the flattened foliage before repeating the process, and so on.

Captain Lyons was feeling apprehensive as the battalion advanced toward the enemy. "I was going into my first battle action, and I was scared," he said. "As I picked my way along the wavering patch of grass, I thought of all the things I had to do. I thought how I would set up the mortars on the edge of the road ready to pour shells into the Jap emplacements; how I would group the machine guns to hit from all sides at once. As twilight grayed into night, we moved to within a mile of the road and grouped in the familiar wagon wheel for the night."

Lieutenant Colonel McGee ordered his men to go into bivouac just short of the Kamaing Road. The Japanese were now so close that they could be heard through the jungle. "It gave me little chills down my back," said Lyons.

At dawn on March 5, the I&R platoon reported to McGee that the Japanese had withdrawn from their defensive positions on the road and had moved toward Walawbum. McGee at once led his men onto the twenty-foot wide road and instructed the two Combat Teams—Blue and Green—to establish a perimeter roadblock facing north and south. "The Japs had moved down the road during the night . . . leaving their foxholes wide-open and inviting," recalled Lyons, who was in charge of a heavy weapons platoon. "We set to work digging the foxholes deeper, so two men could occupy one at the same time. Meanwhile, the gunners were setting up their pieces and the mortar men were putting their three-piece stovepipes together. I was moving around, checking to see the crossfire covered all the approaches."

The I&R platoons pushed further along the road in both directions to set up ambush points. McGee then radioed his position to General Merrill. The 2nd Battalion was instructed to hold its position until the arrival of the 3rd Battalion, approximately two miles west, and the 1st Provisional Tank Unit, which was on its way from the north under the command of Col. Rothwell Brown.

Meanwhile, Roy Matsumoto had spotted something up in the trees. He first thought it was a twig, but no twig was so straight. Climbing the tree, Matsumoto saw through the leaves a wire. He touched it. It was hot. Matsumoto had discovered the telephone line connecting the Japanese 18th Division's HQ in Kamaing with their base at Maingkwan. Scrambling down the tree, Matsumoto reported his find to his immediate superior, Capt. Rex Beach, a professor of history in civilian life, who called over Lt. Phil Piazza and asked him for his field phone handset. Matsumoto had studied electricity and the telephone system in college and knew just what to do with the handset. "It was just like a regular handset," he explained. "I used a clip pin, like an alligator clip, and clipped it on to the hot wire so I could tap into the wire. Then I unscrewed the speaker part of the handset so they couldn't hear me but I could hear them."

Matsumoto sat on a branch, the handset cradled between his shoulder and ear and a notepad and pencil in his hands. Though there were three other Nisei interpreters in the 2nd Battalion, only Matsumoto was able to understand the accents of the voices he heard. His years in California spent listening to the regional dialects of his Japanese grocery store customers were now about to bear fruit.

"I was able to get very important enemy troop movements and 18th Division orders," recounted Matsumoto, who relayed what he was hearing to Captain Beach, who then passed it on up the chain of command. So crucial was the intelligence gathered by Matsumoto that Beach ordered his interpreter to remain on his branch the whole day. "I wanted to pee but didn't want to miss anything, so I wet my pants," said Matsumoto. "They dried up in the daytime."

Initially, the chatter on the telephone wires had been Japanese officers expressing surprise and confusion about the actions of the 3rd Battalion the previous day. Reinforcements were requested. Matsumoto also learned that the enemy was using captured British maps of the area, which were the same ones used by the Marauders. The only difference was that the Japanese expressed distance in meters and the Americans in yards. "I then heard a sergeant talking to his captain, and I learned they were guarding an ammo dump," said Matsumoto. "There were only three or four of them, and the sergeant said, 'What shall we do?' Their captain said a position, and I reported this." Merrill passed this message to Stilwell, requesting an airstrike against the dump, which was duly delivered with excellent results.

The last intelligence Matsumoto picked up was also the most valuable: Forward elements of the 18th Division were ordered to withdraw south from Maingkwan. To cover this retreat, a force of Japanese troops was instructed to attack the Americans dug in on the road below where Matsumoto was eavesdropping on their conversation.

The Japanese launched their attack a short while later. It fell on the Blue Combat Team, every man of which was ready and waiting thanks to

Matsumoto's tip-off. "We crouched in our foxholes. I could feel my muscles trying to cross in cramps and the blood pounding in my face," recalled Capt. Fred Lyons. "Then the firing began in earnest. More Japs ran into view—so close you could see the bronze star shining dully on their bouncing little hats. The Tommy guns paused only for reloading, as one after the other the Japs ducked and melted away into the grass. The boys must have killed a hundred, but it was all over in a hurry."

By now, the 2nd Battalion had been without fresh water for thirty-six hours, and supplies of ammunition were dwindling. Lieutenant Colonel McGee doubted they had the capabilities to resist a second and larger Japanese assault down the road. He called Merrill by phone, explained the situation, and received permission to withdraw. Merrill felt that the battalion had "accomplished its mission." Hunter disagreed, believing the decision to pull back the 2nd Battalion to Wesu Ga was "premature," a divergence of opinion that McGee took as a personal slight. As the battalion pulled back, Jack Thornton of Mississippi cursed loudly that he hadn't had the chance to get himself an enemy scalp. Thornton's buddies knew him as "Smiling Jack," and George Rose recalled that "he was really upset and swore that he wasn't going home until he got a Jap. He made us promise to let him stay close to the machine guns in our next fight with the Japs."

By the time the 2nd Battalion arrived at Wesu Gu early in the morning of March 6, Hunter was on his way north to meet Col. Rothwell Brown and guide his tanks of the Chinese 1st Provisional Tank Group to the Marauders HQ. It was a small party that Hunter led north—just himself, Colonel Chun Lee, the 38th Division's liaison officer, and six soldiers, including two of the 1st Battalion's best scouts. Hunter had arranged to meet Brown at a small village just north of the Nambyu River at noon.

After a couple of hours on the trail, Hunter heard sounds up ahead. Melting into the jungle, Hunter watched as a Japanese heavy weapons platoon jogged south "at their admirable, steady, tireless pace." A little further on, the party reached the village, but Brown wasn't there. Hunter waited until 1230 and then probed a little farther north, but of the Chinese 1st Provisional Tank Group there was no sign. What Hunter did discover, however, was a paddy field with its grass beaten down, which "indicated to me that a large body of Japanese had flopped there briefly, possibly the night before." In Hunter's estimation, at least a battalion had camped in the paddy field on the evening of March 5. As he hurried back down the trail, sounds of distant firing from the direction of Walawbum indicated where the Japanese battalion had been headed.

★

During the night of March 5–6, the 3rd Battalion's Orange Combat Team had listened to the noises coming from the western bank of the Numpyek. In the darkness, they recognized the sound of truck engines, of tailgates being open and shut, and the slow, continuous screech of artillery pieces wheeled into position. At 0400 hours, Bernard Martin and Bill Smawley were roused by Sergeant Ballard and ordered to grab their weapons and find themselves a foxhole on the hillside overlooking the river. "We got our M1 rifles, had a fruit bar, and went up the hill," remembered Martin. They slipped into a foxhole "by a big tree—Bill on one side and me on the other."

At first light, Sgt. Andrew Pung climbed back up his tree. "Pung had a walkie-talkie radio with him," wrote Dave Richardson a few days later. "Soon he reported seeing some telephone wires and several emplacements at the edge of the grassy clearing. Then his routine report changed to an excited one. He forgot all about radio etiquette. 'Listen,' he blurted into the microphone, 'there's a bunch of Japs coming out of the jungle and into this grass across the river. A big bunch. Get ready for an attack. I'll tell you when they're near enough to open fire.'"

The Japanese were out of the jungle and advancing across the grassy clearing toward the riverbank. Riflemen clicked rounds into chambers, and BAR gunners pulled back the bolts on their weapons. Mortar men ripped open shell cases. "Minutes ticked by," wrote Richardson. "There was a tense silence."

Then the battle was joined. Martin saw three mortar explosions tear up the ground across which the Japanese were charging toward the riverbank. It was his cue to start firing. "The noise was deafening," remembered Martin. "Bill Smawley and I were numbed; we'd never witnessed anything like this. It was like shooting fish in a barrel."

Scores of Japanese never made it as far as the riverbank. They were scythed down by the lethal accuracy of their enemy's fire from across the river. "The Americans," wrote Richardson, "just lay in their holes and blasted away" as a second wave charged across the grassy clearing. Many of the Japanese carried Nambu machine guns and boxes of ammunition. Their officers ordered them on, screaming "*susume!*" (advance) and "*banzai!*," the traditional Japanese battle cry. The Orange Combat Team lined them up and shot them down until the grassy clearing was carpeted with the dead and the dying. "The Dead End Kids were happy," noted Richardson. "They yelled at their machine gunners and BAR men to 'Mow down that bunch over there boy!' and then shouted 'Atta boy,' as they concentrated their rifle fire on single targets. George Fisher Jr. of Napoleon, Ohio, spat a gob of tobacco juice every time his M1 got a Jap."

First Lieutenant Victor Weingartner, commanding the platoon in the center of the American positions, caught Richardson's eye and grinned. "Those little bastards must think we're amateurs at this jungle-fighting stuff," he yelled above the din. "*Banzai* charges might leave terrified the civilians in Singapore, but they're nothing but good moving target practice for us."

The Japanese retaliated with a salvo from their 77mm mountain guns, but their range was too long. Their mortar fire was more telling. Sergeant Pugh was almost blown out of his perch by one round. He was down from the tree before his Japanese counterpart had time to adjust his mortar team's range.

For the next few hours, desultory mortar fire was exchanged across the river. The soldiers who were dug in along the bank cleaned their weapons, reinforced their foxholes with logs, ate what remained of their rations, and wished that their water bottles were heavier. Sergeant James Ballard set off for Lagang Ga on an ammunition run, leading a mule train comprised of four skinners, one of whom was Harold Bengtson. "It was pitch dark and Japs were everywhere," he wrote later. "I know that I was scared as hell! That was the first time I realized the Japs were trying to kill me. You talk about an eerie feeling going through the jungle in the dark not knowing where the hell you are . . . [but] this shows how important discipline is. We put our trust in our Ballard and made it there and back."*

From the trees on the other side of the river, the Orange Combat Team heard the sound of more trucks arriving, the snap of their tailgates, and the bark of a sergeant's instructions. A second assault was brewing.

At 1700 hours, the sun began to dip behind the tree line away to the west. The Americans shielded their eyes as they peered out from over the rim of their foxholes. Suddenly, two heavy machine guns thumped into life. A predictable salvo of artillery shells followed. Then came the charge—two companies of Japanese infantry, screaming and shrieking, their officers' swords glinting in the evening sun. Beach told his men to hold their fire. The quickest men, the bravest men, reached the water unmolested. "Beach shouted, 'Let them get in the middle of the stream,'" recalled Bernard Martin. "The Japs ran like hell toward us, the officer screaming and yelling and waving his sword."

Then Beach gave the order to fire. A line of Japanese went down in the first few seconds. Within minutes, there were hundreds of dead and wounded. Beach had sited his guns well, placing two heavy machine guns low on the riverbank, both manned by experienced soldiers who had seen action in Guadalcanal. Between them, Earl Kinsinger and Joe Diorio fired ten thousand rounds. Dave Richardson watched one soldier, Bernie Strasbaugh, "firing as fast as he could shove magazines into his weapon. When he spotted five Japs in a group running toward a dropped machine gun, he stood up, riddled them with fire and flopped down again."

*Ballard was awarded a Silver Star for this feat.

The Japanese fire was more accurate than the morning's encounter. Martin remembered that at one moment "we all pulled our heads in and we could hear the bullets going by like angry bees." In the Orange Combat Team's aid station, Capt. James Hopkin, known as "Hoppy" to the men, was surprised how few casualties he'd seen: just three men, all lightly wounded by mortar shell bursts. At one point during the day, Hopkins received a visit from a lieutenant in search of spare ammunition. The doctor gave up his shotgun and shells.

By now, the battle had settled into a rhythm. The Japanese would send over a salvo of shells and then rake the riverbank with machine gun fire. Insults would then be heard in surprisingly good English. "Roosevelt eats shit!" was a Japanese favorite. The Orange Combat Team replied with barbs of their own. "Tojo eats shit!" The Japanese threw back: "Eleanor [Roosevelt] eats powdered eggs!" The Americans grinned and responded with: "Tojo eats corned beef!"

To the best of Bernard Martin's knowledge, it was during this verbal engagement that the men began referring to themselves as "Merrill's Marauders." "It was Lieutenant Colonel Beach who told us that the newspapers were calling us Merrill's Marauders," he said. "We liked that name better than the Dead End Kids. When we were screaming abuse at the Japs across the river, we started yelling, 'We're the Marauders.'"*

By sunset, the Khaki Combat Team of the 3rd Battalion had moved to the left flank, allowing the Orange Combat Team to concentrate on holding the right flank. Casualties were still remarkably light, and Capt. James Hopkins had momentarily left the aid station to check on the state of the men's morale. He needn't have bothered. "The spirit of the men was awe-inspiring," he said. "They seemed to ignore the bullets, the artillery, and the mortar rounds. Some stood up and shook their fists, imploring the Japanese to come on."

Not a man among the Marauders had anything but respect for the courage shown by the Japanese, but they were also baffled by their tactics. "I respected the Japanese very much—or the soldiers I did," reflected Bernard Martin. "They weren't afraid. But they had poor commanders. The Japanese always launched frontal attacks. On several occasions they could have outflanked us, but their commanders were stupid. On this occasion, this officer appeared in shiny boots and pressed pants, waving his sword and leading a charge across the river."

Darkness brought with it a new sound, an unfamiliar one that took the Marauders a few moments to comprehend. It was the sound of wooden litters being carried toward the Japanese wounded.

*From this point on in the narrative, the 5307th will be referred to as "The Marauders."

"The hours dragged on and a heavy fog set in," wrote Dave Richardson. "While some of the men peered through the mist at the field across the river, others dozed in their foxholes with their heads propped on horseshoe-type packs. The Dead End Kids weren't cocky or swaggering tonight; they were exhausted from the tension of the two attacks."

The Japanese sent over some more artillery shells from their 10mm howitzers in sporadic salvos. Some of the Marauders didn't even stir from their slumber. At 2200 hours, the shelling stopped. Shortly afterward, Lieutenant Colonel Beach received a message from General Merrill to withdraw. The general had recently welcomed the lead elements of the Chinese 38th Division, and he had confidence in their ability to finish the job at Walawbum. In the meantime, the Marauders would pull back, swing around to the east, and cut the Kamaing Road near Chanmoi in the Japanese rear.

"Okay, gentleman," said Beach, on receiving the order. "Let's go home."

★

By midmorning on March 7, the Chinese 38th Division was streaming into Walawbum in such numbers that the Marauders' mission to Chanmoi was canceled. The men remained where they were, cheering on the arriving Chinese, marveling at their clean, shaven, gleaming appearance. In hailing the operation a triumph, Stilwell boasted of the close cooperation between the Allies. "The fight for Maingkwan and Walawbum is won, and only isolated mopping-up operations remain," he declared to a circle of war correspondents. "I believe we have killed two thousand Japanese in this operation alone, which should be good news in any language except Japanese. I wish to stress the fact that Chinese and Americans fought and died side by side. They fraternized, shared their food, their comforts, and their hardships. It's not an exaggeration to say they have virtually formed a mutual admiration society."

The harmony didn't last long. An initial source of resentment on the Americans' part was the discovery that the Chinese soldiers refused to eat the K-rations. So the Northern Combat Area Command (NCAC) supplied them "canned corn beef and beans, cucumbers, onions, rice, and other fresh foods." The Marauders were denied such luxuries and continued to subsist on the detested K-rations.

Relations deteriorated when a flight of American fighters mistook a column of Chinese troops moving toward Wesu Ga for Japanese. Not long after, the Chinese suffered a similar lapse in judgment, to the cost of the C Company, Red Combat Team, 1st Battalion. "We were underway and moving south along the river east of Wesu Ga," remembered medic Richard Murch. "I was leading my mule and holding on to the tail of the mule ahead when I was violently thrown into the air, landing in a heap in a semi-dazed condition."

Murch staggered to his feet and saw that the mule in front had been "torn apart" by a mortar shell. Suddenly, a machine gun opened up. "I tried to scramble up the bank so I could hide in the bushes," remembered Murch. "But the bank was very high and steep and I started to slide down, coming to rest straddling a five-foot bush. . . . Flat on my back I watched the leaves fly away as the machine gunner lowered his range toward me. I knew I had only seconds to live, and in a panic state cried out, 'Please Lord, let me live to be fifty-three.'"

Someone close to Murch shouted out (it was actually Lt. Sam Wilson and his Chinese interpreter), and in a second the firing stopped. It had been a Chinese attack, both the mortar and the machine gun. Murch had sustained a broken arm and a torn scalp, and his right leg was peppered with small bits of shrapnel from the mortar. "For those who say there is no God, what can I say?" Murch reflected. As to why he'd chosen fifty-three as the age to which he wished to live, that was a mystery Murch had plenty of time to ponder while recuperating in the 20th General Hospital.

The Americans also discovered that the sanitation habits of the Chinese didn't match their spic-and-span uniforms. Colonel Hunter was disgusted when a Chinese detachment "bedded down in our midst and proceeded to contaminate the area thoroughly, defecating not only in the river, but all over the bivouac area as well."

For weeks, Hunter had emphasized to his men the importance of sanitation, disciplining any soldier who neglected to bury his own waste or that of the mules after an overnight bivouac. When the Marauders went into rest camp after Walawbum, they dug latrine pits five feet long and eighteen inches wide down to a depth of two feet. "In the building of the slit trench, we cut a few stakes that had a Y on one end and we drove them into the ground," remembered Bernard Martin. "Then we laid a bamboo across from one end to the other and that was our seat. You can be assured that it was so uncomfortable nobody read any newspapers. It was on and off ASAP." To clean themselves, most of the men used grass, though in the communications platoon they accorded themselves the privilege of using spare message forms. "A little rough," said Martin, "but better than nothing."

Hunter finally got to meet Col. Rothwell Brown, who apologized for missing their earlier engagement but explained he had been unavoidably detained by a force of Japanese on the trail south from Maingkwan. Though neither Brown nor Hunter knew it, it was this chance encounter with Chinese tanks that contributed to General Tanaka's change of strategy. Instead of ordering both the 55th and 56th Infantry regiments to attack the

Marauders, Tanaka directed the 56th to attack the Americans at Walawbum; meanwhile, the rest of the 18th Division would withdraw south along the Kamaing Road. In effect, the 56th's role was to engage the Americans and ensure a safe retreat for the bulk of Tanaka's army down trails that Stilwell's intelligence officer didn't know existed; Stilwell's G2 was Joe, his son. "It was a glaring deficiency in young Joe's theater intelligence not to have discovered that Tanaka's forces had constructed a route of withdrawal south and west of Walawbum," said Hunter, who appreciated quicker than Merrill the missed opportunity to inflict a crushing defeat on the enemy.

Nevertheless, though the hesitant Chinese advance had allowed Tanaka the chance to withdraw, the Marauders had killed eight hundred of the enemy, the majority dying in front of the 3rd Battalion's guns on the banks of the Numpyek River. American casualties amounted to eight dead and thirty-seven wounded. General Merrill was delighted. "General Stilwell has sent a message that he is pleased," Merrill informed his senior officers at a staff conference on the evening of March 7. "Between us and the Chinese, we have forced the Japanese to withdraw farther in the last three days than they have in the last three months of fighting . . . please convey to your men General Stilwell's and my congratulations for a fine piece of work. Get rested and re-equipped as soon as possible, and be ready to move on our next operation in three days."

★

The men of the 3rd Battalion were treated as heroes for their exploits at Walawbum. When Charlton Ogburn encountered the men, they were "keyed-up, cocky and exuberant," reveling in the joy of being alive. Up close, however, Ogburn noticed their pallor and their "feverish-looking eyes." A decent meal soon put the color back in the collective cheeks of the 3rd Battalion. Sergeant James McGuire of the Khaki Combat Team had his "first good meal in a week," consisting of rice and a donut. Then he caught up with his diary. For March 6, he wrote of how, dug in on the banks of the Numpyek, the "Japs shelled us with artillery and mortars. We got so close to their guns the concussion shook us. Shells going over our heads all day. Dug in with knife and helmets."

On March 8, the 3rd Battalion, now at Shikau Ga, feasted on eggplant and rice, all taken from the abandoned Japanese positions. The food, and the rest, revitalized the morale of the men. So did Bernard Martin's idea to tune in his radio to Tokyo Rose. "She was pleasant to listen to," recalled Martin. "Of course, she felt sad to think that we would not be alive much longer now that her army knew where we were and will bury us before the end of the week! But she played some good American music: Glen Miller,

Tommy Dorsey, Harry James, Cab Callaway, Benny Goodman, and Kay Kyser—all the top orchestras."

On March 8, McGuire wrote in his diary that he'd heard his first music in nearly two months. The following night Martin tuned into the BBC, and the men cheered as they listened to an account of their action at Walawbum and the extent of the Japanese casualties.

On hearing of the Marauders' success, Lord Louis Mountbatten, supreme commander of SEAC, sent a note to General Stilwell at his headquarters, requesting that it be issued to the American and Chinese troops operating under his command.

"Your rapid advance down the Hukawng Valley and your successes in a series of encounters with the enemy are gaining you much honor and renown," declared Mountbatten. "You are facing a formidable enemy in difficult country, but you are outfighting and out-maneuvering him and you have recently gained an outstanding victory in the Maingkwan-Walawbum area against one of the enemy's toughest, most seasoned divisions. What is more, you are pressing on, supported in strength and supplied by your colleagues in the air, secure in the knowledge that you can and will succeed.

"You who fight on the Ledo Front, pushing forward the Ledo Road, are playing a magnificent part in assuring our joint victory. During my recent visit I have seen for myself the courage and the spirit you display under the gallant leadership of General Stilwell, and I shall remember with pride the days that I spent with you."

Back in the States, the newspapers were full of glowing accounts of the success of the "first all-American penetration into Burma." General Merrill was particularly praised, with his photograph adorning the front page of the *Montana Standard*. Alongside was a description of the "39-year-old former buck private who has specialized in a study of Japanese military strategy." In New Hampshire, the *Portsmouth Herald* dispatched one of its reporters to Franconia Notch to interview Merrill's "attractive wife" at her home. Mrs. Lucy Merrill told the paper a little bit about her husband, including his difficulty in being accepted into West Point on account of astigmatism. "So he ran away and joined the army," she explained. "He went to Panama and finally worked his way up to a sergeantcy [sic]. Five times he tried to get into the Point and each time he was rejected. Finally, on his sixth time, he made it."

★

One of the few Americans to express misgivings about the outcome of the battle for Walawbum was Charles Hunter. He had recently returned from a visit to Stilwell's headquarters at Mainkwang, where the general had described his surprise at Merrill's decision to withdraw the 3rd Battalion in anticipation of a swing to the east to cut the Kamaing Road near Chanmoi. "Stilwell decided that his orders to Merrill had not been clear enough," recalled Hunter. "In saying 'use your discretion,' he had meant to keep casualties down, not 'go roaming.'" Hunter respected Stilwell's decision to shoulder responsibility for the poor communication with Merrill that resulted in the confusion, and ultimately helped the Japanese withdraw without further casualties, but he regarded it as the inevitable consequence if orders weren't issued in writing.

Hunter also blamed Stilwell's staff in the Northern Combat Area Command, a clique of individuals who in his opinion were clannish and incompetent. "War at a theater commander's level cannot be permitted to be conducted as a personal thing with responsibilities handed out on a basis of past friendships, mutual sharing of former defeats, frustrations, and hardships," commented Hunter. "The waging of war must be as impersonal as any other science in which effects follow causes in an unbroken chain of events."

CHAPTER 10

South to Shaduzup

General Frank Merrill spent March 10 discussing the Marauders' next mission with General Stilwell at his headquarters at Mainkwang. He returned to Shikau Ga the same day, arriving to find the men as he'd left them—in a state of lazy tranquility. Sergeant James McGuire wrote in his diary for March 10: "Had rice three times today. Slept most of day. Took swim."

Some of the men used grenades to blast fish out of the river. Others cut open lengths of bamboo, and the fish were then put inside the hollowed wood and baked over a fire. They tasted delicious.

On March 11, Merrill briefed his officers on their next mission. Now that the Allies had control of the Hukawng Valley, General Stilwell wished to chase the Japanese into the Mogaung Valley twenty miles south. The Japanese had established their new frontline among a series of low hills at the head of the northern end of the Mogaung Valley. At the center of this new enemy frontline was the village of Jambu Bum.

Stilwell's plan was for the Chinese 22nd Division to spearhead the advance south along the Kamaing Road toward Jambu Bum, while to the west the Chinese 65th Regiment covered the right flank. The Marauders' task was another encircling operation, swinging east of the Kamaing Road and penetrating through the jungle to the Japanese rear, where they would cut supply lines, disable communications, and sow confusion in the enemy's ranks. To "insure maximum freedom of action for the Marauders," Stilwell detailed two regiments of the Chinese 38th Division to collaborate in the American operation.

Conscious that the 1st Battalion had for the most part been frustrated bystanders during the battle for Walawbum, Merrill delegated them the lead role in the operation. Their mission was to head south along a jungle trail and establish a block on the Kamaing Road near the village of Shaduzup, ten miles south of the enemy position at Jambu Bum. The 1st Battalion would be shadowed by the Chinese 113th Regiment and an attached artillery battery.

The 2nd and 3rd battalions, under the overall command of Colonel Hunter, were to also march south and throw up blocks at the village of Inkangahtawng, a further ten miles below Shaduzup. Thus, when the Chinese 22nd Division attacked Jambu Bum from the north of the Mogaung Valley, the retreating Japanese would find their southern exit blocked by the Marauders. Annihilation would ensue.

Lieutenant colonels McGee and Beach were briefed on their mission without the presence of Osborne. McGee confessed his surprise when informed they would move the next morning, but "I understood that this rather sudden departure was due in part to his concern over the number of cases of diarrhea being experienced, particularly in the 1st Battalion, which was bivouacked much closer to the Chinese units than the other two battalions."

A cursory glance at the British maps of the region revealed to the 1st Battalion that its route south was hazardous. Just one trail skirted Jambu Bum to the east, a trail that would be well guarded by the Japanese.

The 1st Battalion departed on its mission at 0830 hours on March 12, and for the first twenty miles progress was swift. The men marched down the narrow jungle trail safe in the knowledge that the enemy was still some distance south. Many men were pleased to be on the move again, their spirits buoyed by the docile terrain and the tolerable temperature.

Toward the end of their second day on the trail, the 1st Battalion's I&R platoon began to notice signs of recent Japanese activity. There were the telltale tracks of hobnailed boots and the "cloven-hoof marks left by the canvas shoes" favored by many Japanese.

On March 14, the I&R platoon surprised a detachment of Japanese soldiers sitting around a fire just off the trail. Four were killed, and the rest fled down the trail. Alerted to the Americans' presence, the Japanese counter-attacked in such strength that Sam Wilson withdrew his men north toward the main column with the enemy close on their heels. On receiving a radio message from Wilson requesting support, Lieutenant Colonel Osborne dispatched three rifle platoons under the command of cigar-chewing Lt. John McElmurry from Oklahoma. The Americans and Japanese clashed on the banks of a river and exchanged machine gun fire and mortar rounds. The Japanese began to withdraw, slowly, but as the Americans advanced, the density of the jungle (once off the trail, men could get lost within a few feet of one another) forced them to brave the Japanese fire on the trail. Private Edward Foronoff was killed by a round in his right eye, and Sgt. James Lennon was shot in the arm.

By dusk, the Japanese had withdrawn, but Lieutenant Colonel Osborne knew he needed a contingency plan. To continue down the trail was madness, guaranteed to result in heavy casualties. But the 1st Battalion had to reach Shaduzup no later than March 24; failure to do so would have dire repercussions for the other two battalions.

There was no choice but to head cross-country, with Sam Wilson's I&R platoon blazing the trail. "The I&R led off with one of those old British maps that had large areas of unchartered land," recalled Clarence Branscomb. "It didn't even show mountains or rivers."

This land was unchartered for a reason—the British considered it impassable. But Osborne ordered his men into it, and for six days they hacked and chopped and slashed their way through the "towering, tangled, resistant vegetation that buried hillsides, valleys and ridges together." The bamboo forests were the worst. High up, the bamboo was so tightly entwined that each length, some six inches thick, had to be cut at the top and the bottom—and then pushed aside so the men and the mules could pass. Sometimes it felt like the bamboo was fighting back, lunging angrily at the foolhardy trespassers.

Platoons alternated at the head of the column, with the fresh men attacking the bamboo with machetes and curses, until exhaustion replaced expletives and the only sound audible was the dull thud of their tools. Further down the column, the recently relieved men trudged forward, the straps of their packs cutting into aching shoulders, sweat running down their bodies and into their boots.

The mules suffered from weeping saddle sores as they negotiated the tortuous route. Some stumbled and fell, breaking legs that left their handlers with no alternative but to shoot them. It was a sickening task for the muleskinners, who had developed a deep bond with animals to which they'd given pet names: Mike, Rattail, Myrtle, and Flop Ears.

Supplies began to dwindle. Hunger and thirst were constant companions. Mules could eat bamboo leaves, and though the men could extract water from the bamboo, it wasn't enough. "Thirst had got so bad that one time I came across an elephant footprint and just moved the mosquitoes aside to fill up my canteen cup to get a drink of water," recalled Robert Passanisi.

Once out of the worst of the bamboo forests, Lieutenant Colonel Osborne called up an airdrop. It was scheduled for March 16, but when the transport planes arrived overhead they couldn't locate the battalion because of the forested terrain. The men on the ground gazed mournfully skyward as aircraft crammed with supplies passed overhead; it was a peculiar form of torture.

Osborne and his men spent the rest of the day improving the drop zone. The next morning at 0730 hours, they tried again. This time the resupply was effective, though not all the bundles were retrievable.

Resupplied and reinvigorated, the battalion pressed on, but the jungle soon began sapping the morale once again. Dysentery was now among the men. The Americans blamed the Chinese and their sanitary habits.

On March 19, the battalion bivouacked in a clearing, the routine for such a procedure by now well established. One of the most important tasks, after posting guards, was dividing the water source with colored markers: the furthest marker upstream for drinking, then midstream where the animals watered, and farthest downstream for bathing.

★

The 1st Battalion was now encountering frequent Japanese patrols. On March 20, the lead platoon ran into a Japanese machine gun nest, a skirmish that left one Marauder dead and two wounded.

Two days later, another enemy ambush cost a Marauder his life and left several more wounded. There were flurries of firefights for the rest of the day. Each one was a new delay, another reason for Osborne to fret.

On March 25, it took the battalion three hours to cover a mile. The work was morale-sapping and backbreaking. Osborne had already informed Merrill that the terrain and the enemy were delaying their advance; now he began to fear that the entire mission was in jeopardy if they couldn't reach Shaduzup in a matter of days. Remembering what Orde Wingate had told the Marauders all those months earlier about "acting with vigor according to the situation confronting them," Osborne came up with a cunning plan. He ordered Lt. John McElmurry's platoon to strike out northwest along the trail and attack the Japanese along the Kamaing Road. This diversionary attack might fool the enemy into believing a major attack was in progress and allow the rest of the 1st Battalion to advance unmolested toward their objective.

The plan worked. McElmurry's patrol surprised two Japanese soldiers mapping trail, killing one and letting the other escape to spread word of an American incursion. Soon mortar rounds were raining down on the jungle. As McElmurry's platoon diverted Japanese attention, the rest of the 1st Battalion headed southwest toward the Kamaing Road.

The first Marauder to spot the road was Lt. Phil Weld, describing it from his vantage point at the top of a tree as "a fold in the forested range across the valley." With the road found, it took only an hour more to locate the Chengun River.

Sergeant Clarence Branscomb described the Chegun as a "small stream." His I&R platoon, led by Sam Wilson, had reached it ahead of the rest of the 1st Battalion. "We figured by following it downstream we were bound to find the main river—and Shaduzup," said Branscomb.

Branscomb by now had grown to admire and respect Wilson, even indulging his irrepressible enthusiasm. "Sam was a good soldier, never afraid to ask for advice," recalled Branscomb. Together they were a formidable team: the hard-nosed Pacific veteran and the young, instinctive outdoorsman who, idealistic as he might have been, wasn't the kind to squander their lives in pursuit of glory. On one occasion, they had been advancing cautiously down a jungle when Wilson detected the faint whiff of fish heads and rice. Looking into the undergrowth, he spotted "the slight discoloration in the leaves of the branches" and knew that meant only one thing: the enemy was concealed within.

In the late morning of March 27, Branscomb was moving noiselessly along the shallow waters of the Chengun when he saw ahead its confluence with the Mogaung. The Mogaung was a proper river, perhaps fifty feet wide, the sun sparkling off its muddy water. Branscomb and the other lead scout, John Sukup, suddenly stopped. There were voices up river.

Wilson sent a runner back down the Chengun and then, as he often did, consulted Branscomb. "We spread the I&R out up and down the [Mogaung] river along the mountain facing the river," reflected Branscomb. He and Wilson then went forward along the bank to ascertain whether the voices belonged to a patrol or something more permanent. The pair hadn't gone far when "four or five Japs came down to the water on the other side about 150 feet away." Wilson and Branscomb ducked out of sight and watched as the men began washing their clothes. "Sam and I then withdrew and went looking for Lieutenant Colonel Osborne," said Branscomb. "We found him sitting on a rock thoroughly bushed after our long push. He told Sam to take some of the I&R and cross the river and see how many Japs there were."

Branscomb thought the idea was crazy. "It's about 3 p.m. and the sun is shining and the river is armpit deep," he said. The Japanese were around, and if they were washing clothes they were clearly encamped and not just passing through on a patrol. "I told Sam I wasn't going," remembered Branscomb. "This didn't shake him up too much. He just took off his pack and grabbed his carbine [and], along with one other person, started out."

The soldier who volunteered to accompany Wilson was twenty-year-old Sgt. Perlee Tintary. Branscomb watched the pair slip into the river without regret; his common sense had got him through Guadalcanal, and he was damned sure it would get him through Burma. Wilson and Tintary waded into the river, their carbines held over their heads as they scanned the opposite bank. Branscomb's gaze was also riveted on the south side of the river, but from where he lay he could see further up the bank, beyond the bushes that lined the edge. Suddenly, a Japanese patrol ambled into view. They were in no great hurry, but all the same they were headed in Wilson's direction. Branscomb looked back to Wilson. He was oblivious to the grave danger approaching. Branscomb silently willed his young officer to glance around, as he'd been doing at regular intervals, relying on his sergeant's greater field of vision. Look at me, Sam, screamed a voice in Branscomb's head. Wilson turned. Branscomb began "frantically pumping my fist up and down." Wilson gestured to Tintary, and the pair powered through the water as the Japanese patrol approached. All that separated the two enemies was a group of bushes. The two Americans reached the bank and threw themselves in the undergrowth "only a minute before the patrol passed."

Unfazed by their near-fatal encounter with the patrol, Wilson and Tintary slithered out of the water and crept through the jungle. Up ahead, they saw a Japanese encampment. Wilson sketched in his mind the strength and disposition of the enemy position before withdrawing back across the river without further mishap.

Osborne thanked Wilson for his gallant endeavor and began devising his plan of attack. First, the battalion's mules were moved back up the Chengun to avoid their braying giving away their position, a maneuver that Branscomb remembered creating "a lot of swearing and confusion." Osborne then assembled his officers and briefed them on their role in the upcoming engagement.

At 0300 hours, Lt. Phil Weld's platoon began crossing the Mogaung in the vanguard of the White Combat Team. They reached the west bank undetected. A little over an hour later, the rest of the Combat Team were across, damp but alert and in position. At 0430 hours, the attack commenced. The Japanese never knew what hit them. Some were killed while still half asleep, and others were shot dead as they stumbled from their bivouacs.

With the camp in their control, the Marauders began establishing a block on the Kamaing Road that led from Kamaing, in the south, to Shaduzup.

Daylight brought a swift riposte from the Japanese. Their artillery opened up on the Americans in an attempt to unblock the road so they could get supplies north to their comrades at Shaduzup, which was now under attack from the Chinese 22nd Division. Late in the morning, word reached 1st Battalion HQ that a telephone line had been spotted in the trees close to the road. Osborne ordered Nisei interpreter Grant Hirabayashi to see what intelligence he could glean from the line. Hirabayashi, not the tallest of men, entered the Mogaung with his heart beating fast. "As we crossed the river, the water was shoulder deep," he recalled. "I placed my carbine in my right hand and held it over my head while I lifted the pouch with dictionaries and maps with my left hand, and I struggled because the pouch was obstructing my view. When we reached midstream, I heard three shots."

The sniper who failed three times to shoot Hirabayashi paid for his profligacy. "I later heard that when the sniper opened up, those who were providing cover for us opened up with all the automatic weapons on hand," recalled Hirabayashi. "And the firepower was so great that it cut down a tree and they found the sniper tied to the tree."

Hirabayashi reached the road only to learn from the officer in charge that the line had been found to be dead. "But my river crossing was not in vain," recalled the interpreter. "The enemy . . . retreated leaving behind their breakfast. I had a feast with rice and a can of sardines!"

★

The Japanese artillery intensified at dusk, the shells landing among the Marauders dug in on the east banks of the Mogaung River. Medical teams worked by candlelight in the dark, unable to evacuate the seriously wounded down the Chengun until dawn. "We spread out . . . facing the river and prepared for a bad night," recalled Branscomb, "and were not disappointed."

During the day, the Japanese had brought up additional artillery pieces; in the evening, they brought the guns to bear on the Americans—first the arched projection of 70mm howitzers and then the flat trajectory of the 77mm mountain guns, a terrifying weapon whose shells arrived with a "sudden shriek." The unlucky ones died without really knowing what hit them. The lucky ones, if they could be called that, cowered in foxholes and willed themselves to endure.

Sam Wilson's I&R platoon was positioned on a forward slope of the east bank and bore the brunt of the Japanese bombardment. "They pounded us all night," recalled Branscomb, who lacked a buddy in the platoon with whom to share the ordeal in a foxhole. "I dug a post hole and sort of stood up, leaving a very small opening at the top." Entombed in the soil, Branscomb watched the barrage creep closer to their positions until shells were "hitting so close that I could hardly hear."

Branscomb's luck held, but others' ran out. A shell landed in a foxhole containing two unrelated soldiers named Dervis Allen and Eugene Allen. Dervis was blown to bits. Eugene, "Young Allen" to his buddies, was left with terrible wounds. Branscomb "heard Young Allen calling for me." Without a moment's hesitation, Branscomb wormed his way out of his post hole and crawled into the darkness in search of a medic. More shells landed. Branscomb crawled on. Either his luck would hold or it wouldn't. "It seemed like forever, with many encounters with thornbushes and other people's foxholes," Branscomb remembered. At each foxhole he encountered, Branscomb asked if there was a medic inside. At last he found one. The medic handed over some morphine, and Branscomb set off. "In the total darkness, I reached in and found Young Allen," he recalled. "What I felt almost made me sick."

Branscomb gave Young Allen a shot of morphine. A figure appeared at the rim of the foxhole. "We're pulling back," he told Branscomb, out of range of the Japanese guns. Branscomb remained where he was. Young Allen was too badly wounded to move, but it didn't seem right to leave him to die alone. Branscomb stayed to the end, listening to Young Allen call for his mother in his last moments of life. Then he scrambled out of the foxhole and rejoined the rest of his unit.*

Not long after dawn on March 29, four Chinese howitzers attached to the 113th Regiment opened up on Japanese artillery. Soon, Chinese infantrymen appeared. The 1st Battalion's ordeal was at an end.

As the Marauders rested by the banks of the Chengun, they learned of events elsewhere—the Japanese retreat from Jambu Bum and from Shaduzup. Estimates as to how many Japanese the Chinese had killed were unknown, but the 1st Battalion put its own tally at three hundred enemy dead at a cost of eight Marauders killed and thirty-five wounded.

The men would remember their dead comrades in time, but for the moment they lay back in the grass and luxuriated in what Phil Weld described as the "pure 100-proof delight of being alive."

Clarence Branscomb was awarded a Silver Star for his courage this night.

CHAPTER 11

The Deadly Jungle

The 2nd and 3rd battalions had marched south from Shikau Ga on the same day, March 12, as the 1st Battalion. Their objective was the village of Inkangahtawng, ten miles below Shaduzup, where blocks would be established prior to the main Chinese attack on Jambu Bum.

The two battalions set off in good spirits, determined to crush the enemy on what would be their final mission before the "dry" season ended. Colonel Hunter recalled that "we freely discussed where we would be and what we would do when the rains came." In Merrill's opinion, they would "hole up" in Shaduzup during the monsoon season; the men liked the sound of that. "Operation Hole Up" became a favorite topic of conversation.

At the end of the first day's march, Sgt. James McGuire of the 3rd Battalion wrote in his diary: "Moved out 10:30am. Got a Large pack, 5 days rations. It weighs 45lbs. Be glad when our mission is over. We have 5 days to reach objective. I really was wet with sweat when we reached bivouac area."

On March 13, the Marauders covered fifteen miles and feasted on rice pudding for supper. The next day, they made fourteen miles before selecting a large sandbar as a drop zone for a resupply. The aircraft came in at 1600 hours, and the men were soon cramming three days' worth of rations into their packs.

One reason for the speed with which the Marauders marched south was the presence of Jack Girsham, a forty-nine-year-old big-game hunter born in Burma to a British father and Burmese mother. Girsham knew the Asian jungle better than any other white man; he had grown up in it, killing his first tiger at the age of sixteen and gaining a reputation as a skilled marksman and fearless tracker. The reputation wasn't quite warranted, as the modest Girsham was always quick to point out. One creature terrified him—the king cobra. The closest he'd come to death was when he disturbed a twelve-foot cobra enjoying the sun. The snake reared, spread its hood, and "swayed gently from side to side," staring at Girsham with its small, chilling eyes before lowering its head and vanishing into the elephant grass.

Girsham feared the cobra and hated the Japanese. His wife and son had died in the jungle along with thousands of other Burmese refugees fleeing toward India in 1942, and Girsham wanted revenge. Commissioned initially as a second lieutenant in the British Army, Girsham was headhunted by the Americans as he lay in a hospital recovering from a bad knee sustained during a game of rugby. Merrill interviewed Girsham at Stilwell's headquarters at Shingbiyang, and the pair hit it off straight away. "He was particularly interested in my stories of elephant and tiger hunting," recalled Girsham, who agreed to act as Merrill's guide when he returned on a big-game hunt after the war. Girsham also liked what he saw of colonels George McGee and William Osborne, calling them "great field commanders," while Charles Hunter was one of "the finest officers you could want . . . much like Merrill, but with more of a temper, and not at all hesitant about stating his opinion when the higher-ups blundered."

Girsham's role on the march toward Inkangahtawng was to guide the Marauders "along the narrow valley of the winding Tanai Hka," flanked east and west by mountains and carpeted in dense jungle.

The trail on March 15 rose and dipped and steadily became muddier as the rain intensified. Captain James Hopkins, one of the 3rd Battalion's medical officers, noticed an increase in the number of soldiers succumbing to dysentery, while another menace now began to appear in the damp and humid conditions. "We started to find leeches everywhere," remembered Roy Matsumoto. "Our legs was the most common place to find them but I found some in my boots." Vincent Melillo discovered leeches trying to squeeze into his boots through the eyelets, while one of Logan Weston's I&R scouts required a native guide to extract a leech from the inside of a nostril using a pair of bamboo tweezers.

Captain Fred Lyons loathed these "horrifying grayish-brown parasites that bury their heads in your veins and suck till they are bloated several times larger than normal size with your blood." The average leech was about an inch long with suckers in their mouths that bit into human flesh. A chemical was then released that prevented coagulation of the victim's blood, enabling it to flow into the leech. The parasite sucked out the blood until its body doubled in size and then dropped off on its own accord. At first, the Marauders assumed the way to deal with a leech was just to rip it away, but that wasn't the answer. The body might have gone, but the head was still under the flesh, which would cause "open wounds about the circumference of a grapefruit." The Marauders devised alternative methods of attack.

"I began every morning with an examination to see how many leeches had been living off me through the night," recalled Lyons. "Once there were nine, swelled to the size of half sausages with my blood. Some of the boys got them into their ears and noses, and then the medics made use of a special technique. It seems a leech will reach down to put its tail in water that's near, so the medics would hold a cupful of water under a leech sufferer's nose or ear. As the leech reached down, the medic would tie a loop of string to the tail and pull tight. Then he would touch the end of a burning cigarette to the leech, and it would immediately come loose."

As they moved down the trail, Girsham identified tiger tracks at several of the small streams crossed by battalions, while the guide pointed out to the soldiers the difference in size between the bigger front paw prints and the hind prints. There were other animals, too, that the Marauders encountered. "Saw a few tame elephants," wrote Sgt. James McGuire in his diary on March 16. There were seven in all that lumbered down the trail, each holding the tail of the one in front with its trunk as if they had come straight out of the pages of a Rudyard Kipling adventure story. The Kachin guides enlisted the beasts in the Marauders with a warning to the Marauders that elephants and mules couldn't stand the sight of each other. The joke among muleskinners was that their beasts had an innate suspicion of "an animal that hangs down at both ends." Nonetheless, on March 17 McGuire noted excitedly in his diary that the elephants had helped transport bundles at an airdrop.

Elephants weren't the only curious encounter the Marauders had deep in the jungle. As they approached the village of Naubum, the lead scouts saw a white man wearing a plumed bush hat "leaning against a tree and calmly chewing on a twig." He introduced himself to Colonel Hunter as Father James Stuart, an Irish missionary who was fluent in Kachin and willing to act as a guide. Hunter was happy to have him, and so were the men who took communion and listened enthralled to some of Father Stuart's stories. He'd been born in Derry, he told them, ordained in 1935, and sent to Burma the following year along with seven other priests to civilize the Kachins. Stuart was the only priest still in that part of Burma. He was allowed to remain by the Japanese, who believed the Irishman when he insisted his enemy was the British. It was no such thing, and for over two years he had been passing information to the Allies.

In the weeks that followed, Father Stuart remained with the Marauders, hearing confession and even baptizing one or two soldiers. He also enjoyed teasing them, reminding those men who complained about their lack of furloughs that "in my branch of the service, we spend ninety-six straight months without leave in the jungle."

Once at Naubum, the Marauders contacted a unit of Detachment 101 of the OSS, led by an American captain who sported the most extravagant auburn beard Hunter had ever seen. The unit was composed of three hundred Kachins, all eager to kill the Japanese because of atrocities perpetrated on their families—and because the OSS paid them with drugs. "The Kachins were a very easy, quiet, and likeable race. They could not do enough for us," said Bernard Martin. "And we lousy Americans rewarded them with dope . . . and they loved it like candy."

Opium was the drug of choice for the Kachins. Traditionally, they had harvested it from Burma's poppy fields, but the war had drastically restricted the drug's availability, so the OSS ensured a ready supply in return for the Kachins' fidelity.* Captain James Hopkins remembered that Merrill had among his possessions "a ball of raw opium about four inches in diameter," which was to be used to pay Kachins if and when required.

★

March 18 was a day of rest for the 2nd and 3rd battalions. They were encamped at Weilangyang, approximately fifteen miles due east of Shaduzup, a peaceful spot where the men could sleep or swim in the Tanai. Some of the Marauders began to convince themselves that the Chinese advance had made their continued presence in Burma redundant. "Don't know if we'll stay here today or not," wrote James McGuire in his diary, the day he learned that he had been promoted to staff sergeant. "Our mission accomplished . . . had a good rest."

The lull was temporary, a brief pause while General Stilwell considered the news from Lieutenant Colonel Osborne that the 1st Battalion had fallen behind schedule because of the ferocious terrain they were encountering en route to blocking the Kamaing Road south of Shaduzup. On March 19, Stilwell issued fresh instructions to Merrill, which he kept to himself on the short but exhausting march north to Janpan. Light relief was provided by the elephants, particularly the calf that crossed the fast-flowing Tanai completely submerged but for the tip of its periscope trunk. Going up and down the hills, the men watched with childish delight as the elephants hauled themselves up by curling their trunks around trees and then slid down the other side on their bellies, legs splayed and tails twitching.

On arriving at the village of Janpan on March 20, Merrill had a *basha* built so he could hold a staff conference. First he briefed his officers on the general situation in the Mogaung Valley: The Chinese were pushing south toward Shaduzup while the 1st Battalion under Lieutenant Colonel Osborne, supported by the Chinese 113th Regiment,

---

*It's estimated that the British and Americans "dispensed at least twenty kilos a month [of opium] for at least 24 months of the second and third Burma campaigns."

were headed just south of the same objective. According to the latest intelligence reports available to Merrill, the Japanese had between five hundred to six hundred troops at Jambu Bum, another three hundred at Shaduzup, and approximately two thousand soldiers further south. Then Merrill issued his orders, which again were verbal. The Orange Combat Team of the 3rd Battalion was to remain in the Janpan area, prepared to move at short notice and ready to counter any Japanese infiltration in conjunction with the OSS 101 Detachment. In addition, a radio team (Bernard Martin's) was "to report to the command group with SCR 284 radio to work the OSS information net."

The 2nd Battalion together with the Khaki Combat Team of the 3rd Battalion were placed under the command of Colonel Hunter, who was instructed by Merrill "to cut the Kamaing Road some distance south of Shaduzup in an effort to suck Japs away from that area and to block any movement into Shaduzup from the south." Hunter was told he could use his discretion in deciding the best point to block, so long as it was "that portion of the road between Warazup on the north and Malakwang on the south— roughly five miles apart."

Aware that McGee might object to his men being placed under the command of Colonel Hunter, Merrill saw the 2nd Battalion commander alone. "I know that you can do the job," Merrill told McGee, "but one and a half [battalions] of the outfit is involved, and after all this is what Hunter is here for and he might as well get started."

McGee reluctantly accepted the orders, though he told Merrill he resented having Hunter as his superior for the operation. Prior to the staff conference, McGee's last sight of Hunter had been of him attempting to get the Marauders' elephant troops to retrieve bundles on the drop zone. It was, in McGee's opinion, "an exercise of no current or future significance."

Hunter's problem was that he still had no clearly defined role within the Marauders. For the first four months of the unit's existence, he'd been its commander. Then Merrill was appointed over his head by Stilwell, and Hunter was reduced to the 2 I/C. So what was his function? The three battalions were led by capable and experienced officers, and Merrill rarely sought his tactical advice. Hunter had rank but no influence; he was a jungle paper tiger.

McGee knew this, but he had no sympathy for his fellow West Pointer. "Up to this point in the campaign, he had no command responsibilities nor even demanding duties," said McGee of Hunter. "His principal function had been in regard to routine airdrops, and in that capacity I had little contact with him." McGee made his opinion known to Merrill, who showed "regard for my feelings," but the pair agreed "it was indeed time for Hunter to get his feet wet operationally."

It wasn't an ideal way in which to embark on an operation deep into enemy territory—the second-in-command bitter toward his superior. Some of the officers must have sensed it, for rumors began to circulate about McGee's "jealousy," although Jack Girsham had no doubts that "everyone was committed to doing the job."

CHAPTER 12

Sixteen Banzai Attacks

Hunter led his force south from Janpan a few hours after receiving his instructions from Merrill. The Blue Combat Team of the 2nd Battalion was in the vanguard as they marched along the mountaintop trail toward their objective forty miles to the southwest. They bivouacked for the night in the village of Nhpum Ga, nearly three thousand feet up in the mountains. The 2nd Battalion's Green Combat Team, and the Khaki Combat Team of the 3rd Battalion, encamped four miles north of Nhpum Ga in the village of Hsamshingyang. "It really was hot today," wrote Staff Sgt. James McGuire that evening. "Walked 12 miles all day. Never had any water. Really hurt for water. Hit village where they're [sic] is water. Plenty of food in packs. The villages here are occupied by women and children. Kachins have kept Japs out of hills."

Early the next morning, March 21, Hunter and the main force passed through Nhpum Ga and continued on to Auche five miles south. The trail between the two settlements "was along the crest of a narrow ridge, its precipitous sides covered with rank growth." "Camped in village," McGuire wrote in his diary. "Heard music on radio. I'm supposed to be in charge of 6 mortars. I hope this is [the] last mission."

Hunter organized a resupply at Auche and struck a deal with the Kachin headman: In return for allowing their village to be used as a drop zone for a resupply, they got to keep the parachute cloth, a precious commodity in the weaving of garments.

At the same time, Hunter took a message from Merrill over the radio. Jambu Bum had fallen to the Chinese, and the Japanese were withdrawing. Stilwell had ordered Merrill and his men to "come fast now." Consequently, Merrill informed Hunter that the block must be in place thirty-six hours earlier than originally planned. Merrill added that he'd instructed the

Orange Combat Team to head south from Janpan and block the trails south around Auche.

Hunter was disturbed by the change in plan. He now had to ask his men to march thirty miles and throw caution to the wind in doing so. "Our air photos had failed to arrive," reflected Hunter. "There would be no time for reconnaissance and selection of a site or to rest the men and animals prior to actual occupation of the area selected for the roadblock." There was also the formidable obstacle in their path of the Mogaung River, the same forty-foot-wide stretch of water that the 1st Battalion was approaching.

★

On March 22, General Merrill and his headquarter staff at Janpan "spent much of the day enjoying a celebration that was put on in their honor by the village." A feast was held in their honor, a cornucopia of local specialties, and the Americans "marveled at the ceremonial dresses" worn by the Kachins.

Further south, Colonel Hunter and his men were battling with a cruel landscape. Having struck out from Auche at 0700 hours, the Marauders headed toward Manpin, ten miles southwest, a route that took them off the three-thousand-foot ridgeline and down through a steep jungle trail to the banks of the Nampana River. On reaching the river, the men turned downstream and followed the course of the Nampana for the next eight miles. "Maneuvering through that riverbed was a nightmare," said George Rose of the Green Combat Team's heavy weapons platoon. "The water was about waist deep in the deepest parts. We'd hold on to the bank for a little way, then when there was no more room we'd struggle across to the other side, often sinking up to our chins. Some of us would not have made it if it had not been for the mules to hang onto. Back and forth we waded until we lost count of the number of times we crossed that damn river." One soldier did keep count, however, informing Hunter "that we had crossed the Nampana a total of fifty-six times."

They reached Manpin in late afternoon. Hunter called in another resupply by air, restocking the men's backpacks with three days of K-rations and a much cherished donut. Hunter then instructed McGee to push on with the 2nd Battalion to Sharaw, five miles northwest through the flat Mogaung Valley, and the 3rd Battalion's Khaki Combat Team followed soon after. "Marched until 11pm," noted the diary of Sgt. James McGuire, who ended the day thoroughly wet. "It rained cats and dogs."

On March 23, the 2nd Battalion was now six miles southeast of Inkangahtawng, the site selected by Hunter for the roadblock. He issued his final instructions to McGee, telling him to block the road between Inkangahtawng and Kamaing, to the south. He would have the Khaki

Combat Team in reserve, and the whole operation would be complemented by the 1st Battalion's block a few miles to the north.

McGee's force left for Inkangahtawng just after dawn on March 23, with the I&R platoons of the Green and Blue Combat teams leading the way. Vincent Melillo, who was in the latter, was now one of the Marauders' most experienced scouts. "I relied on sight, sound, and smell equally," he reflected. "You had to be on the lookout everywhere, even in the trees, and we were always listening for sounds of their presence. And you could smell the Japs, pick up a scent of whatever they were cooking with."

★

The trail covered in the morning of March 23 by the two I&R teams began muddy, became marshy, and then wound through tall elephant grass. The Green Combat Team penetrated as far west as the Mogaung River. "The Mogaung, from bank to bank, was about 250 feet wide, but the water itself was only about 150 feet wide," recalled George Rose. "The banks of the river were rather steep, eight to ten feet high. Fortunately, it was the dry season and the water level was low and ran very slowly."

Meanwhile, Lt. William Grissom and his Blue Combat Team were reconnoitering the village of Ngagahtawng at approximately 1600 hours. "Our platoon was walking down a trail checking fire lanes and clearing the trail," said Melillo. "I was out front and saw some Japs, so we all hit the ground, opened up, and started firing. The Japs did the same thing."

As Melillo returned fire, he saw Grissom crawling through the jungle with a grenade clutched in his hand. "Lieutenant Grissom was a ballplayer," said Melillo, "and he threw it at the Japs like you'd throw a baseball."*

With the Japanese now alerted to their presence, McGee decided to ford the Mogaung River and establish blocks on the road to the west. The animals and mortars were left on the east bank as the men hurried across the water and advanced toward their objective. "Nearing the Jap road where we planned to throw in the second roadblock, we were moving carefully and quietly," recalled Capt. Fred Lyons of the Blue Combat Team. "Once again came that tense feeling of nervous expectancy."

Lieutenant Ted McLogan of the 2nd Battalion's Green Combat Team was also apprehensive as he waded across the Mogaung at 1700 hours. "We dug in with our back to the river and our front to a clearing at another little village, hoping we hadn't been observed," he remembered. The Khaki Combat Team,

---

*Some previous accounts of the 2nd battalion's action in March 23 stated it was the Green Combat Team's I&R platoon that had the first contact with the Japanese. Melillo says this is incorrect, and it was Lieutenant Grissom's Blue I&R team.

under the command of Major Edwin Briggs, remained on the east bank of the Mogaung with the animals and established a strong perimeter with the 60mm and 81mm mortars to cover the 2nd Battalion's rear.

Hunter and his staff of six men had spent the day at Sharaw, overseeing the evacuation of a number of sick men. He also received a message from Merrill informing him that the 1st Battalion was still behind schedule and unable to be in position by March 24. This disclosure posed a serious threat to McGee. If Osborne didn't lay the block before the enemy became aware of McGee's presence, the Japanese could attack the 2nd Battalion from the north and south. Hunter communicated this information to McGee as he settled down for the night three hundred yards east of the Kamaing Road deep inside Japanese territory. There was an additional problem that neither Hunter nor McGee knew about: The Chinese 22nd Division had stopped its advance south. McGee was now dangerously isolated.

★

By nightfall on March 23, the Khaki Combat Team had established a strong perimeter on the east banks of the Mogaung. "Marched in rain until noon, really muddy and slippery up and down hills," wrote Sgt. James McGuire in his diary. "Went to river, where roadblock was put in. Got there about dark. Heard a lot of Jap trucks moving up and down the road."

From their position three hundred yards east of the Kamaing Road, the 2nd Battalion could not only hear the trucks, they could hear the men on them. "We knew we were going to get hit at dawn because all night long . . . we could hear them getting off trucks, jabbering away," recalled Lt. Phil Piazza. "They were very noisy soldiers. They were good in some respects but were always very noisy, whereas we always stressed discipline and quietness because when operating behind enemy lines like that, you had to be very quiet."

Piazza was close to McGee in his command post, as was Capt. Fred Lyons, who, as the night wore on, began to think of the western movies he'd watched as a kid. "We circled into our wagon wheel and dug the holes for the coming scrap," he said. "We knew it was coming, for all night long on the road we could hear the bang of truck tailgates and the thud of feet landing on the ground. Every bang meant another truckload of Jap soldiers unloading."

Companies F and G were dug in on the western perimeter, and George Rose—a member of G Company's heavy weapons platoon—was in a gun pit about twenty yards to the left and rear of an abandoned bamboo shack. To the right of the shack—and about eight feet from Rose's pit—was Harry Hahn and his machine gun. "I could see the trees on the other side of the field and knew that was the direction from which the Japanese would attack," said Rose. "Our perimeter was formed in a half-circle leading back to the river on each end."

Rose and Hahn listened to the sounds coming from the darkness a few hundred yards to their front. Neither liked what they heard. "It sounded like ten thousand of them," recalled Rose. "All we could do was sit at our guns and wait."

Phil Piazza appeared late in the evening, surveying the terrain for the mortar section, and at around 0200 hours Colonel McGee arrived on the perimeter. "With him was my good friend Roy Matsumoto," said Rose. "I walked over and asked Roy if any of those Japanese were his kinfolks. He replied, 'I hope not.'"

Matsumoto was his usual phlegmatic self, sharing in Rose's joke and appearing unconcerned at the battalion's predicament. But like all the Marauders' Nisei interpreters, he had special reason to feel apprehensive. Since the Rape of Nanking in 1937, when the Japanese murdered an estimated three hundred thousand Chinese civilians over the course of six weeks, the Emperor's army had a well-justified reputation for barbarity. Throughout the South Pacific and Southeast Asia, the Japanese had committed widespread atrocities, killing and raping civilians and brutalizing its prisoners of war. To the Japanese military mind, a soldier who surrendered his weapon also surrendered his honor and therefore forfeited his right to respect. Matsumoto knew that if he was captured by the Japanese, he would be put to death in a manner that didn't bear thinking about. "There was always a chance of being captured," he reflected. "Therefore, I carried two hand grenades—one for the enemy and one for me."

After McGee and Matsumoto had returned to the battalion CP, Rose and the other members of the heavy weapons platoon were left alone in their foxholes. In this part of northern Burma, on this morning, there was no mist, just a persistent rain that began during the night and continued after dawn. But daylight brought no Japanese assault.

Lieutenant Ted McLogan of F Company was in his foxhole close to the perimeter when McGee's runner arrived with a message. "Maggie wants to see you," the runner told McLogan. "Maggie" was the enlisted men's name for McGee. The officers were more deferential, calling him "Colonel." McLogan followed the runner to the battalion CP, where he found his commander squatting in the rain, drawing on the ground with a stick "an outline of our position and where certain of our units were." As McGee continued to draw, he started to talk, his eyes fixed on the ground. "Mac," he said, "I should have had the battalion on the road two hours ago, but I'm not going to put them in a situation I know so little about." McGee paused momentarily, then continued. "And that's where you come in. I want you to take your platoon and go to the road."

With his stick, McGee showed McLogan the route to take to the road, going through the perimeter held by 2nd Lt. Hessel Witten's platoon. Once McLogan reached the road, he was to continue on toward the village of Inkangahtawng and radio back "everything of importance" he found to the CP. McLogan looked at his commanding officer. "I said, 'And after that?' Then he finally looked up and said, 'And after that we will come and rescue you.'"

McLogan returned to his platoon, pulled the men off the line, and briefed them on what they must do. His thirty-nine men had been reduced to thirty through sickness, but Sgt. Paul Michael, the unflappable West Virginian who had fought with McLogan at Vella Lavella, was still there. McGee came over, wished the men luck, and told McLogan he would "have twelve rounds of [mortar] ammo fired to your front. That will keep their heads down long enough for you to move out."

The mortar rounds began coming over as McLogan's platoon moved up toward the perimeter. One . . . two . . . three . . . four . . . McLogan looked around and noticed that most of his men were having one final furious drag on a cigarette. They looked as apprehensive as he felt. "This is just like Hollywood," joked McLogan, trying to muster a smile. There was no reaction from his men. When the eleventh mortar round landed close to the road, McLogan said a silent prayer, and in the aftershock of the twelfth explosion, he led his men out toward the village of Inkangahtawng

"We were in a skirmish line and your heart is pumping and the palms of your hands sweating so you can hardly hang on to your rifle without dropping it," remembered McLogan. The men scanned the trees and the elephant grass, looking for a movement, a glint, an unnatural color. As the platoon emerged from the elephant grass, they saw a small bridge ahead. They also saw the enemy. "We bumped right into a Japanese patrol, maybe a dozen or so," recalled McLogan. The Marauders dropped to the ground, firing as they went, their eyes fixed on the enemy. "First thing that came to my mind was why the hell do I have to be a lieutenant and find some way to get out of this mess," reflected McLogan. "I spotted Sergeant Michael and in a whisper I said, 'Take the first squad and hit them from flank,' and off he went with a dozen men."

With his squad, Michael carried out McLogan's instructions, and the moment they began pouring enfilade fire into the Japanese, the rest of the platoon scrambled to their feet and launched a frontal assault. The Japanese withdrew. McLogan pushed forward. The Japanese opened fire from a new defensive position. McLogan and his men fell flat and returned fire. McLogan felt a tap on his arm. It was his radioman, holding out the receiver. McGee was on the end of the line. "What's going on out there?" McGee asked. "I can hear all this firing." McLogan gave his commanding officer a situation report, including their mounting casualty list. "Okay," said McGee, "pull back."

McLogan's platoon withdrew to the perimeter without further incident. George Rose watched them return from his foxhole. It was now around 0730 hours, and still the Japanese hadn't charged. Rose began unwrapping some of his rations. "Suddenly someone yelled, 'Fire for effect! Fire for effect!'" Rose heard the sound of the incoming mortar round and ducked down in his hole. "The ground erupted like an earthquake, tossing us around in our slit trenches and foxholes," he recalled. Rose likened the sound of the explosion to "a thousand church bells" ringing in his ears. Then he saw Hahn stagger from his slit trench, hands pressed to his ears, screaming that he'd gone deaf. Rose leapt from his foxhole and hauled Hahn back under cover. Rose was aware of more screams coming from another slit trench nearby. Ellis Yoder, a twenty-year-old from Pennsylvania, was almost hysterical as he hollered, "The gun won't fire and Avery is dead!"

Rose scrambled over to the slit trench. Yoder had the wild-eyed look of a madman, and Darrell Avery was lying dead in the trench. "A piece of shell had pierced his helmet and went right into his head," remembered Rose. "His brains were scattered all over the place." Rose calmed down Yoder, and the two of them pulled the corpse out of the way and examined the M1919 Browning.

The bolt had been damaged. That was the bad news for Rose, who kept glancing westward across the field knowing that if the Japanese launched a *banzai* charge with the gun out of action, they were "dead meat." The good news was that Rose always carried an extra bolt in his pocket. In less than three minutes, Rose had stripped down the weapon, replaced the bolt, and reassembled the .30 Browning.

Still, there was no sign of the Japanese. Rose and the men of G Company waited, chewing slowly on a stick of a gum, as was the habit of Browning machine gunners. One piece of advice passed on by the combat veterans of the 3rd Battalion was always to have some gum on hand—good for plugging bullet holes in a Browning's water jacket if they ran out of bandages.

Further up, the men of the perimeter F Company were staring across fifty yards of field at a wall of eight-feet-high elephant grass. Another salvo of mortar rounds came over. The Marauders curled into balls, let the explosion pass, and then poked their heads up over the rims of their foxholes. Someone shouted that he could see the Japanese creeping through the elephant grass. There was more mortar fire—it was coming at regular intervals. The Marauders shouted encouragement to each other from foxhole to foxhole. The attack was about to be launched. And then from the grass came a roar, a hundred screams of *"banzai"* merged into one fearful shriek. The Japanese emerged from the elephant grass, their rifles thrust forward, bayonets pointing at the men deep in their ground.

On the extreme north flank of the American position was Cpl. James Phillips, alone in his foxhole with a Thompson submachine gun. A Japanese officer waving a sword and holding a pistol ran straight for Phillips. He waited until the officer was fifteen yards away and then fired a short burst as he'd been trained. The advancing Japanese was hit by the bullets, but still he kept on. Phillips fired a longer burst and the officer stumbled and fell, his head coming to rest on the lip of the foxhole. Two thoughts came to Phillips: one, he needed more ammunition; two, the sword would make a great souvenir. Jumping from his foxhole, Phillips dashed back the ten yards to his squad leader's position, grabbed a handful of magazines, and turned to return to his position. As he did, Phillips saw one of his buddies crouched over the dead officer, stripping him of his sword and depriving Phillips of his souvenir.

Company G bore the brunt of the second *banzai* charge, but unlike their comrades in the first wave of attack, the Japanese launching themselves at George Rose and his buddies did so over 175 yards of exposed ground. Captain Fred Lyons was crawling up to support Company G when the assault began. "They were big Japanese marines, fully six feet tall, wearing yellowish khaki uniforms that seemed to envelope them like gunny sacks," he recalled. "There's not much expression to a Japanese face, but I could plainly see the strained look about them that turned to shock and surprise as our machine-gun fire hit. One Jap's rifle seemed to fly like a spear as he fell. Another sank to the ground, hit in the stomach. I crawled on toward the perimeter and moved into a new foxhole."

The second attack ended as the first charge had, with a jagged line of Japanese corpses lying in the field under the morning drizzle. But the assaults kept coming throughout the morning, one after another with only a brief respite. "I had bodies piled up so high in front of my machine guns that I had to get out and kick the bodies out of the way so we could fire our machine guns," remembered Phil Piazza. He, like the rest of the Marauders, was torn between respecting the bravery of their enemy or ridiculing their stupidity. "One thing about them, I have to hand it to them, their courage was exceptional," reflected Piazza. "When they attack, it's an honor for them to die. As far as Americans are concerned, we try not to let our men die."

On one occasion, a Japanese succeeded in breaching the wall of fire and getting in among the Americans. Bounding into the first foxhole he saw, the soldier came face to face with twenty-three-year-old Pvt. Len Wray from Mississippi. Lyons watched as Wray lunged at the intruder. "They wrestled, straining and pulling to break each other's grip," he recalled. "No one dared shoot at the Jap for fear of hitting [Wray]." Then the American ripped the rifle from his opponent's grasp, and for a moment the Japanese stood and stared in bewilderment. "Divested of his arms, he leaped upward to get out of the way," said Lyons. "As he jumped, a hail of machine gun slugs caught him."

The scene had been witnessed by the Japanese, and their retaliation was swift and savage. A salvo of mortar shells arced through the sky. One exploded in the foxhole containing Jack Thornton, "Smiling Jack" to his buddies. Thornton had left Walawbum complaining that he hadn't had the chance to kill any Japanese. Now they had killed him before he got his chance.

After lunch, the Japanese changed their point of attack to the southern perimeter of the Marauders' position, slipping in close to the river under the cover of mortar fire. Lieutenant Phil Piazza went forward to act as an observer for the Americans' mortars. "I was outside the perimeter directing mortar fire to my men and a machine gun got me in the head," he recalled. One of the medics ran forward and dragged Piazza back within the perimeter, and together with another soldier he carried the wounded officer as far as the river. Sergeant Salvadore Rapisarda of the 3rd Battalion's Khaki Combat Team waded across the river with a litter over his shoulder. "He was bleeding like a sieve, with blood coming out from all over," he recalled of Piazza's condition. Rapisarda helped carry Piazza over the Mogaung and deposited him into the care of the 3rd Battalion medical team, convinced there was little they could do to save Piazza.

Another of the 2nd Battalion carried across the river out of harm's way was Virginian Jim Breeden, who'd been shot close to George Rose's foxhole. Rose, who was first on the scene, discovered that the bullet "penetrated the [right] thigh, came out of the back of the thigh, passed through the left calf, breaking bone, and then wounded a toe." Before Rose had time to evacuate Breeden, the Japanese launched a fresh charge. Rose dashed back to his hole and raked the enemy with machine gun fire. Breeden "had to lie there in his foxhole for over an hour," recalled Rose. "I kept talking to him and telling him to use his belt as a tourniquet to stop the flow of blood." Rose eventually managed to help evacuate Breeden from his hole and hand him over to the battalion's surgeons.

Rose stayed where he was, sharing his foxhole with a growing pile of empty ammunition boxes. He counted ten, but he had several more full boxes ready to repel the next wave of Japanese. "Each attack was made with ten to forty men, never with more than forty," reflected Rose. "If they had charged with all their men at once, they could have overrun us." By midafternoon, Rose was almost numb with fatigue. At one point, he shifted position in his foxhole and discovered he'd been lying in the remains of Darrell Avery's brain. "I was so busy, I never gave it a thought," he noted.

★

Back at Sharaw, Colonel Hunter's radio had developed a fault. He could receive messages but not send any, so while he was aware of McGee's predicament he

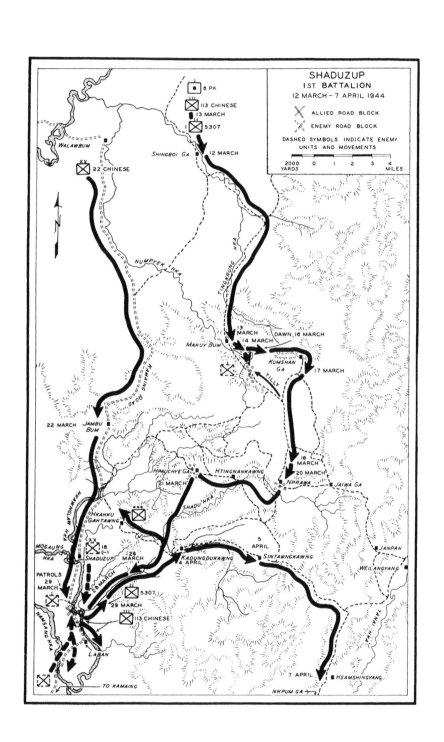

SHADUZUP
1ST BATTALION
12 MARCH – 7 APRIL 1944

ALLIED ROAD BLOCK
ENEMY ROAD BLOCK
DASHED SYMBOLS INDICATE ENEMY
UNITS AND MOVEMENTS

2000 YARDS   0   1   2   3   4   MILES

6 PK
113 CHINESE
13 MARCH
5307

WALAWBUM
SHINGBOI GA   12 MARCH

22 CHINESE

NUMPYEK HKA

TINGKRUNG HKA

MAKUY BUM
13 MARCH   DAWN, 16 MARCH
14 MARCH
KUMSHAN GA
TILLY   17 MARCH

22 MARCH   JAMBU BUM

18 MARCH
HPAUCHYE GA   HTINGNANKAWNG   20 MARCH
21 MARCH   NPRAWA   JAIWA GA

HKAHKU GAHTAWNG
SHADU HKA

MOGAUNG HKA
18 (–)   5 APRIL
SHADUZUP   26 MARCH   KADUNGDUKAWNG   SINTAWNGKAWNG   JANPAN
PATROLS   4 APRIL   WEILANGYANG
29 MARCH
5307
29 MARCH
113 CHINESE
LABAN
TO KAMAING   7 APRIL   HSAMSHINGYANG
NHPUM GA

couldn't issue instructions. McGee had intercepted a message sent from the 1st Battalion to General Merrill at Janpan in which Osborne informed his commander of their late arrival at Shaduzup. It was the first McGee had heard of the news, and he now fully appreciated the danger he faced.

McGee sent a message to Merrill advising that the battalion was running low on ammunition and that casualties were beginning to mount, with two dead and at least twelve wounded. The return message from Merrill instructed McGee to withdraw the 2nd Battalion to the east side of the Mogaung because "a captured map showed two Japanese battalions moving to outflank our blocking force." McGee immediately sent a message to Maj. Edwin Briggs, commander of the Khaki Combat Team on the other side of the river: "I plan to withdraw from this side to the east bank when I get fighter support. Be prepared to support me with all you have. Cover the riverbanks on my sides so they do not catch us from the flanks."

At approximately 1545 hours, a flight of P-51 fighters attacked the Japanese positions, guided on to their targets by Lieutenant Dallison, the Army Air Force liaison officer attached to the 2nd Battalion. As the aerial assault ended, the Khaki mortars opened up a barrage on the Japanese. McGee ordered the 2nd Battalion to pull back across the Mogaung River. "The water was a welcome relief," said George Rose, "as it washed away the mess that covered my clothing and me."

The battalion's soldiers were practically out on their feet by the time they reached the village of Ngagahtawng. "The men were dead tired; they hadn't slept probably in several nights," recalled Ted McLogan. Sergeant James McGuire of the Khaki Combat Team described in his diary the events of March 24 on the east bank of the river: "Jap artillery shelled us for about ½ day. They shelled the hell out of us. Very few hit home, hit within 30 yards of me. Shrapnel hit close to me, some hit knife and helmet. Air force saved the day for us. We had seven wounded, none killed.* Japs charged our machine guns, they must have been doped up. Killed over 200 Japs. We pulled out, we destroyed a lot of equipment. Had to carry everything."

McGee's force didn't rest long in Ngagahtawng. At 0500 hours the next morning, March 25, they pulled out with a sense of urgency. Overnight, a message had been received from General Merrill, warning McGee that a unit of three hundred heavily armed Japanese were moving north. The Orange Combat Team had been dispatched to intercept them, but it was further evidence of the number of Japanese in the vicinity because of the slow progress being made by the Chinese.

The rain was torrential throughout the morning as the 2nd Battalion trudged east. "We had to cut holes in the litters we were carrying to let

*In fact Khaki Combat Team lost one man, Pvt. Raymond Bratten.

the water drain out," recalled McLogan. Lieutenant Phil Piazza was one of the litter cases. Aware of the "abominable" conditions his stretcher-bearers were enduring on his behalf, Piazza ordered them to strap him to a horse.

As the 2nd Battalion hurried toward Sharaw, Colonel Hunter was still ignorant of their situation because of his faulty radio, which could send but not receive. In frustration, Hunter summoned an L-4 liaison plane at first light and took off to see the situation for himself.

The aircraft headed north, following the trail toward Inkangahtawng. Hunter caught sight of the 2nd Battalion, and to his "surprise" they were moving south. "Urging the pilot to get down on the deck, I could tell it was McGee and that he had been in a fight," recalled Hunter. "I could see one man, a blood-soaked bandage on his head, riding a horse, as well as several wounded being carried on improvised litters."

Hunter told the pilot to fly on, but there was no sign of the Japanese in pursuit. Returning to his command post at Sharaw, Hunter told his radioman to request several litter-bearing L-4s so that McGee's wounded could be evacuated the moment they arrived.

★

When the 2nd Battalion arrived at Sharaw, Hunter asked McGee to debrief him on the previous forty-eight hours. He wasn't pleased with what he heard. Why had McGee ordered McLogan's platoon on an aggressive patrol toward Inkangahtawng, contrary to his orders? Hunter also queried why McGee had tried to block the road close to the village when his instructions had been to select an uninhabited area. But Hunter's strongest criticism was reserved for McGee's decision to withdraw based on an intelligence message sent by Merrill that a captured map showed two Japanese battalions moving to outflank his position. "In my opinion this message should not have been sent," said Hunter. "It transmitted unverified information from a source that could easily have been a plant. If I were being outflanked by a force close enough to endanger my mission and didn't know it, I should have been relieved and sent back to the infantry school for a refresher."

McGee wasn't much interested in what Hunter had to say. Over the previous twenty-four hours, he had taken his orders from Merrill, not Hunter, whose communication problems reinforced McGee's amateurish opinion of him. If Hunter had been so concerned about lines of communication, why hadn't he moved up to Inkangahtawng instead of remaining back at Sharaw? "I told him bluntly that my orders were coming from General Merrill," recalled McGee, ". . . [that] the 2nd battalion was moving without delay, in accordance with my current orders, to Manpin, and on to the Auche-Warong ridgeline."

Hunter agreed, reluctantly, admitting that "since communication with Merrill had been sporadic and difficult, I could not do otherwise but agree to his concept of this change in command relationship."

Hunter nevertheless considered that the 2nd Battalion had been withdrawn prematurely as a result of the messages that had passed between McGee and Merrill. In Hunter's view, the 1st Battalion had been left exposed by the withdrawal of the 2nd Battalion. But in McGee's estimation, had they remained in position on the west bank of the Mogaung, they would have run out of ammunition and probably been annihilated.

McGee didn't appreciate Hunter's insinuation that he had withdrawn his men in undue haste. The 2nd Battalion had repelled sixteen *banzai* attacks and killed an estimated two hundred Japanese, and at a staggeringly low cost to themselves. They had pulled back in an orderly and disciplined fashion, despite their exhaustion, their hunger, and the dozen litter cases. It was, said Phil Piazza, "an exceptionally fine action in that Colonel McGee was able to withdraw the troops . . . pull back across the river by leapfrogging without the Japanese knowing that we eventually had the whole battalion across the river."

The atmosphere between McGee and Hunter was tense on the evening of March 25 as the 2nd Battalion and the Khaki Combat Team bivouacked. Sergeant James McGuire described the day in his diary, noting the effort of marching up and down a muddy trail in the rain carrying wounded men on litters. "Japs hot on our trail," he added. "Be glad when we get out of here."

At 1000 hours on March 26, McGee led his men back down the trail toward Auche, fifteen miles to the east along the trail. Hunter followed once he'd seen the last of the wounded evacuated by air.

They arrived at Manpin—five miles southeast of Sharaw—at midday, and there was a further confrontation between Hunter and McGee as they argued over the next course of action. It was McGee's wish to continue on the trail to Auche, but Hunter wanted him to help clear a field for an airdrop. "He was fairly stubborn," remembered Hunter, "but after some strong advice on my part he agreed to resupply his battalion before his departure."

As soon as the bundles were down and distributed, McGee pushed on down the trail at 1700 hours and marched for a further three hours up a rocky riverbed before bivouacking for the night in a narrow river gorge. "Tonite makes total of 70 miles we have covered in last four days," recorded the battalion diary.

Hunter had remained at Manpin with Lieutenant Colonel Beach and the 3rd Battalion, the Khaki Combat Team now reunited with their comrades from Orange. Among the latter was Capt. James Hopkins, who had arrived at Manpin with his medical detachment the previous day. He was uneasy at their predicament. "The possibility of being surrounded and cut off in enemy territory seemed to be likely," recalled Hopkins. "The jungle was wet, and the atmosphere was foggy and humid, all of which helped to create a sense of anxiety and depression."

Shortly after McGee had headed north, an OSS agent with the code name "Skittles" arrived at Manpin with news for the Marauders. His contact in Kamaing, the man who supplied milk to the Japanese garrison, had reported "that a large force" left the town in trucks at noon headed north along the wide Warong-Auche trail. As Hunter digested the intelligence, a patrol of P-51 fighters arrived overhead on dusk patrol. He called them up, relayed the news of the Japanese column, and invited the fighters to strafe them, which they did with much "glee."

Far from being disturbed by the large Japanese force advancing from the south, Hunter saw it as an opportunity to attack Kamaing, to act with the vigor advised by General Wingate.* He radioed Merrill and requested permission to advance south with the 3rd Battalion and capture the lightly held town of Kamaing. "I was disappointed when instead of getting permission to attack I was told to withdraw," remembered Hunter. "This golden opportunity should have been seized and exploited with all resources available."

Hunter and the 3rd Battalion moved north in the tracks of the 2nd Battalion toward Auche, with the large Japanese force from Kamaing in hot pursuit. Between them and Hunter was Logan Weston and his I&R platoon.

---

*Wingate had been killed two days earlier when his aircraft, en route from Burma to India, crashed in the jungle-covered hills of northern India.

CHAPTER 13

Merrill Goes Down

Weston had come south from Janpan several days earlier, travelling along the well-worn trail through Auche and Nhpum Ga. At Manpin on March 25, Lieutenant Colonel Beach had instructed Weston's I&R platoon to set up a block at Poakum, seven miles north of Kamaing. Simultaneously, Beach ordered a rifle platoon under Lt. Warren Smith of K Company, Orange Combat Team, to perform a similar task on the Warong–Tatbum road, south of Warong.

By the afternoon of March 24, Weston's block was in place among the thick shrub of the trail that led from Kamaing to Poakum. His forty-two men—including a mortar section and some .30-caliber machine guns—were positioned on a slope with their flanks well protected and a withdrawal route plotted. Weston was in communication with Merrill and had knowledge of the 2nd Battalion's engagement on the west bank of the Mogaung River. He guessed that the Japanese would attempt to outflank McGee by coming up the trail he was now blocking and attacking from the east.

Sure enough, up the trail appeared a twelve-strong Japanese patrol. Weston's men wiped them out. Next, the Japanese sent scout dogs down the trail to sniff out the enemy. The dogs were killed, as were many of the soldiers who followed. The Japanese now tried to blast the Americans out of the jungle with mortar rounds, but Weston's men were too well protected in their foxholes. Night fell, a gloom illuminated by the odd spray of tracer and the flash of an exploding mortar round. "Every muscle in our bodies tensed as we peered into the pitch darkness," recalled Weston. "We could hear the muffled sounds of the Japanese moving in the darkness, regrouping for another inevitable attack."

The I&R men strained their ears to detect the slightest sound from out in front. Grenades were the most effective weapon, lobbed gently down the hill, exploding in the faces of the Japanese who crawled through the jungle.

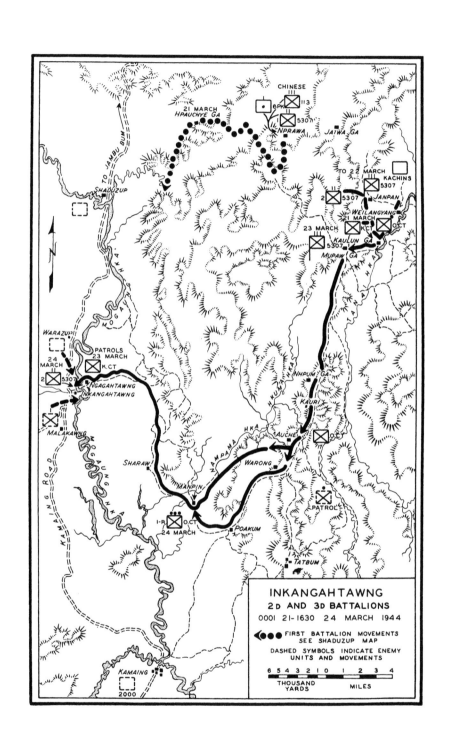

CHINESE

6 PK 113

5307

TO JAMBU BUM

21 MARCH
HPAUCHYE GA

NPRAWA

JAIWA GA

TO 22 MARCH   KACHINS
5307

SHADUZUP

2   5307   JANPAN

WEILANGYANG
21 MARCH

MOGAUNG HKA

23 MARCH   K.C.T   O.C.T

KAULUN G.
5307

MUPAW GA

WARAZUP

PATROLS
23 MARCH

24
MARCH

2   5307   K.C.T

NGAGAHTAWNG
INKANGAHTAWNG

NHPUM GA

KAURI

MALAKAWNG

MOGAUNG HKA

KAMAING ROAD

SHARAW

AUCHE   O.C.T

NAMPAMA HKA

WARONG

MANPIN

PATROL

I-R   O.C.T
24 MARCH

POAKUM

TATBUM

INKANGAHTAWNG

2D AND 3D BATTALIONS

0001 21-1630 24 MARCH 1944

FIRST BATTALION MOVEMENTS
SEE SHADUZUP MAP

DASHED SYMBOLS INDICATE ENEMY
UNITS AND MOVEMENTS

6 5 4 3 2 1 0   1   2   3   4

THOUSAND   MILES
YARDS

KAMAING

2000

At first light on March 25, the Japanese attacked up the slope in greater numbers and under heavier mortar fire. Weston's radio was hit, cutting them off from the rest of the force, and there were signs the enemy was trying to outflank them. Weston withdrew his men north, encountering Lieutenant Smith's platoon about half a mile up the trail. Weston asked Smith for some of their ammunition, and he also used his radio to call Lieutenant Colonel Beach and request permission for Smith "to protect my withdrawal route and for me to fight a delaying action from my present position until joining his platoon at Warong."

With permission granted, Smith led his forty-five men east to prepare defensive positions on the Warong trail, while Weston's I&R platoon readied themselves for another furious engagement with the Japanese coming up from Kamaing. The night was a "tense and sleepless" one for Weston as he lay in his foxhole listening to the Japanese working their way through the jungle. He estimated their strength at a thousand, and ominously they were to their north and their south.

At dawn on March 26, West pulled back toward Smith but almost immediately encountered three enemy soldiers trying to work their way around the Americans. "If these soldiers had managed to move in behind us, then we were nearly surrounded," reflected Weston. "We needed help, and quickly."

Weston reached Smith's position without further incident, and the two officers agreed that they should continue to block the trails to ensure the safe withdrawal to Auche of the 2nd and 3rd battalions. There were a couple of brief skirmishes during the day, but to the relief of Weston there was no *banzai* charge. During the night, however, it was obvious that the enemy was preparing for an all-out assault at first light. Weston ordered his men to vacate their positions, leaving behind their wounded mules and starting a couple of campfires before they pulled back. By now, recalled Sgt. Alfred Greer, they were "beat to a pulp. The physical exhaustion of marching through and over the mountains, mud, and water, disease, insufficient provisions, little sleep, biting insects, and always in enemy territory was brutal and gnawed away at our bodies and nerves." Only the presence of Weston, his calm, softly spoken instructions, and his unshakeable faith "gave us the will to go on."

The assault came an hour later, with the Japanese charging at the campfires from the north and south. As Weston's men dug, they heard the screams of the dying as the Japanese from the north clashed with their comrades attacking from the south. It was several minutes before the Japanese realized their mistake.

On the same morning, Lieutenant Smith and his men ambushed a company of Japanese soldiers advancing down the Tatbum Trail. Twenty-eight of the enemy were killed and the rest fled into a small valley, where Weston's mortars inflicted further damage. But by 1100 hours, the main body of Japanese had located their prey and were attempting an encirclement. Weston ordered a full-scale withdrawal toward Auche with the two detachments leapfrogging one another as they went. The enemy gave chase. At one point, as Weston coordinated his left flank with Smith's right flank, he saw a movement to his left. He glanced up just as the Japanese soldier hurled the grenade. "I dove for cover behind a fallen banana tree," said Weston. "A split second later I heard a hiss, then a muffled thud. I looked over the banana tree and saw the grenade lying there in two halves. It would have blown me to kingdom come had it not been a dud." Weston noted the look of surprise on the Japanese soldier's face, and then shot him.

Weston and Smith arrived at the hilltop village of Auche in the afternoon of March 26. No time was wasted in establishing defensive positions to the south so they could protect the 2nd and 3rd battalions due to arrive shortly on the trail that led east from Manpin.

Smith and Weston between them had held up a Japanese battalion for three days, allowing their comrades precious time to complete their withdrawal from Manpin. But for their actions, the 2nd and 3rd battalions—still unable to call on support from the slow-moving Chinese to their north—might have been attacked in their rears. Realizing the seriousness of the situation, General Merrill had moved his headquarters south from Janpan to Nhpum Ga, four and a half miles above Auche, on March 24.

★

Nhpum Ga consisted of four or five *bashas* in a clearing 400 yards long (north to south) and 250 yards wide (east to west) surrounded by dense jungle. Nearly three thousand feet above sea level, the village lay on a precipitous ridge between the Tanai River, two miles to the east, and the Hkuma one and a half miles to the west. Nhpum Ga was in fact a junction, situated on the main trail running north to south, with secondary trails leading down slopes covered in thick bamboo and large hardwood trees to the rivers 1,400 feet below.

When Merrill and his staff arrived at Nhpum Ga, they found the collection of *bashas* on a small knoll just off the trail junction leading west toward the Hkuma River. To the east of the huts, the ground sloped up to a height of about fifty feet, while westward, overlooking the junction, was a thin hill running parallel to the main trail.

Merrill's staff considered it a charming spot. Captain John Jones sat and watched some of the local Kachin children "play the same games as they do in New York or Centerville." One game bore a passing resemblance to bowling, and the Americans tried their hand at rolling a large brown nut at the target, their lame endeavors eliciting "a hearty laugh" from the children.

Merrill's HQ was still at Nhpum Ga when Weston's force reached Auche on the afternoon of March 26. Early the following morning, Lieutenant Colonel McGee led the 2nd Battalion into Auche, arriving at 1000 hours, whereupon they dug in southward to await the arrival of the 3rd Battalion. When they showed up in the afternoon, Lieutenant Colonel Beach received orders from Merrill to continue north to Nhpum Ga in what remained of the daylight. Once at Nhpum Ga, the 3rd Battalion was instructed by Merrill to head four miles further north to Hsamshingyang, a trek that involved continuing "up and down for one and a half mile until a gradual descent" into a valley which, in the words of Colonel Hunter, "was the key terrain feature of the area." Hsamshingyang was 1,500 feet beneath Nhpum Ga and, although marked on the old British maps used by the Marauders, it wasn't a village; it was more a flat, ten-acre clearing favored by several local villages as a rice-growing area. In short, it was ideal for an airstrip, and the 3rd Battalion was ordered to prepare such a facility on arriving at Hsamshingyang.

But the first thing the 3rd Battalion did on reaching Hsamshingyang was rest for the night. Sergeant James McGuire, who had been recording the battalion's total mileage since entering Burma, wrote in his diary for March 27: "Walked 428 mi so far in Burma. Crossed same river 50 times. Went up that dreaded hill, 3100 ft. up. Took 2 hrs to go up it. By passed B [2nd] Bn. and bivouacked for night."

★

The 2nd Battalion spent the night eight miles south of Hsamshingyang in the village of Auche. The Japanese were not far behind, so McGee roused his men early on March 28, and at 0600 hours the battalion began filing out along the narrow ridgeline for Nhpum Ga. "The Green Combat Team was moving out, and as I was passing, Colonel McGee was standing on the trail with a couple of other officers beside him," remembered Sgt. Warren Ventura, a member of the heavy weapons section. "He noticed me with a machine gun on my back and directed me to set that machine gun up right in the trail and stay there until the area was clear of all troops."

Ventura wasn't too happy with the position chosen by McGee; it was in the center of the trail with little protection. "So after the troops had moved out, I directed my two men—Lester Weddle and J. D. Young—to a position about forty feet behind us, north of us, just off the trail, about five or six feet."

While Weddle and Young dug and camouflaged the gun pit, Ventura stayed on the .30-caliber M1919 Browning heavy machine gun, staring intently down the trail for the Japanese battalion he knew to be in pursuit. When the pit was dug, the three Americans set up the gun and waited. "It seemed like a rather long time," recalled Ventura, "but finally the Japanese came along. I don't believe that we could see four or five of them at most when we opened fire."

Having killed the scouts, Ventura and his two men picked up their gun and ran back up the ridge to a position they had previously scouted. "I figured this was the best field of fire we were going to find," said Ventura. "So on the ridge we set up position, and there was another gully behind us through which we could withdraw without the Japanese catching us flat-footed."

The Japanese advanced up the trail, and another burst from the Browning accounted for several of the enemy. This time, however, instead of withdrawing, Ventura and his two men remained where they were. "The Japanese having seen that we'd withdrawn so fast from the first position most likely thought we were going to continue to just run," Ventura said. "Well, we surprised them. Ten or twelve came into view and we opened fire, and I'm quite certain we killed every one of them."

For a few minutes, there was silence. Ventura, Weddle, and Young waited. Off to their left they spotted a movement, "so we put a heavy burst of fire into the brush traversing back and forth," Ventura said.

The three withdrew again, sprinting half a mile up the trail, their tired, underfed bodies protesting against the sudden burst of activity. "We found another position where we could wait and have a means of escaping again," said Ventura. "But this time we did not have such a good field of fire, and when the Japs came into view there were only three or four of them. We fired and withdrew immediately."

This time Ventura, Weddle, and Young didn't stop, but kept on the trail toward Nhpum Ga. Further ahead, the main column was struggling up the steep razorback ridge that led north from Auche, the ankle-deep mud churned up by thousands of boots and hooves, making progress treacherous. It was now 0700 hours, an hour since the column had started its march and a few minutes since the last burst of gunfire from Sergeant Ventura's Browning.

Suddenly, they heard another sound, that of an artillery gun from the direction of Warong. The Japanese 70mm shell exploded with a "deafening impact" about two hundred yards off the trail. Seconds later, another high-velocity shell landed, this time a little closer. Some of the men scrambled for cover. The next shell exploded toward the rear of the column, wounding one soldier and some of the animals. The mules began to buck and bray, and their panic spread to the men. "We were on top of the ridgeline, and the only way to go was straight ahead," said Lt. Ted McLogan. "So we ran."

As the men ran, they fell, some slipping in the mud, others thrown off their feet by the blast waves of exploding shells or the shrapnel from rounds hitting trees. T5g Hugh McPherson was killed instantly in one blast, and others staggered off the trail wounded.

Some of the men thought they should stop running. "When the word was passed down to double time, which was an all-out run under artillery fire, I could not understand why we did not stop and fight," recalled Pvt. Gabriel Kinney.

Amid the disorder were several individual acts of cold, hard courage. Private Ed Kohler, Company F of the Green Combat Team, was near the rear of the trail when he glanced back and saw T5 Bill Henderson on his hands and knees.

"Let's go, Bill!" shouted Kohler, who was suffering from a bout of recurrent malaria contracted on Guadalcanal.

Henderson looked up, despair all over his face. "I can't move." Shrapnel had ripped through both knees.

"I told him to drop his equipment and throw it in the brush," recalled Kohler. "He told me I should move back and he would hold them off as long as he could."

Kohler was in no mood for heroic sacrifices. "Get ready," he snapped at Henderson. "You are going back with me."

Kohler hoisted Henderson over his shoulders in a fireman's lift "and took off." The Japanese were only a few hundred yards to their rear. "We didn't get very far when an artillery shell burst real close to us and knocked us both to the ground," remembered Kohler. "I picked Bill up again and despite the artillery and rifle fire we made it to Nhpum Ga."

Kohler handed Henderson to one of the medics and "just passed out," spent with the effort of carrying a wounded man up a hill while running a fever of 104.

★

Between Kohler and the Japanese was Sgt. Warren Ventura and his machine gun team. The three men brought up the rear of the struggling column and were the last men to reach the trail junction at Kauri, an abandoned settlement a mile south of Nhpum Ga. There they encountered Lt. Brendon Lynch and a couple of machine gun teams. "They had been sent back to take up positions at Kauri to try and delay the Japanese [and] to give the battalion time to dig in at Nhpum Ga," recalled Ventura who, with his two men, continued north on the undulating trail.

The 2nd Battalion began streaming into Nhpum Ga at 1000 hours, several carrying wounds, although not all were physical. One soldier was shaking violently. "I'm not afraid, damn it," he protested. "I tell you, I'm not afraid. I just can't stop shaking."

Major Bernard Rogoff, together with captains Henry Stelling and Lewis Kolodny, established an aid station in front of a *basha* situated between two hills near the center of the village. Merrill and Hunter, the latter having arrived at Nhpum Ga with the 3rd Battalion the previous day, listened to McGee's tale of woe. He himself had narrowly escaped death from a "tree burst which wounded several men of his headquarters," and in his estimation it wouldn't be long before the Japanese attacked.

Merrill asked McGee if he'd left a combat team at Auche. McGee replied in the negative and "told him that I had not as my orders were to move the battalion." He did add that Lieutenant Lynch and his machine gun teams had been sent to Kauri to delay the enemy advance.

According to Hunter, Merrill was "surprised" to see the 2nd Battalion at Nhpum Ga, and he mentioned to McGee the "possibility of holding at Auche" with just a combat team. McGee ruled this out, emphasizing to Merrill the strength of the Japanese force headed their way.

"Can Nhpum Ga be held?" Merrill asked McGee.

"Yes, we can hold Nhpum Ga," replied McGee.

"Good," said Merrill. "Hold Nhpum Ga. I am going down the trail to Hsamshingyang [to] get out of your way. I will send you further instructions from there."

There was a reason why Merrill wished to get out of the way other than to establish the unit CP out of the line of fire. In the previous couple of days, he had been feeling increasingly unwell. He might, perhaps, have identified the symptoms to those he'd experienced two years earlier trekking north through Burma with Stilwell. Merrill left Nhpum Ga looking pale and withdrawn. When he reached Hsamshingyang, he was leaning on the arms of his staff for support. Soon after, Merrill suffered a mild attack. "I had no warning of Merrill's approaching illness," recalled Hunter. "He had not undergone any violent exercise in the last few days to have placed a strain on his heart." The only clue to Merrill's condition was his daily dose of "thick purplish medicine" to combat what he claimed was dysentery.

Hunter had his suspicions. None of the detachment's doctors had prescribed the medicine, and on the small vial was a label printed in what Hunter believed was Hindustani. According to Capt. James Hopkins, one of the 3rd Battalion doctors who examined Merrill at Hsamshingyang at lunchtime on March 28, "we all agreed that he probably had had a heart attack . . . no one was aware that he had suffered a previous heart attack."

On the evening of March 28, Orange Combat Team radio operator Bernard Martin received a visit from his battalion commander, Lieutenant Colonel Beach. "He said, 'We're shipping out the general tomorrow,'" recalled Martin. "'He's having problems with his chest.' That's the word he used, *chest*.' He didn't say anything about a heart attack. So I was told to send a message to base requesting an L-5 as fast as possible at first light. I sent it in clear text: 'General is hurting. Plane.'"

Merrill selflessly refused to be evacuated on the morning of March 29 until after those Marauders wounded in the retreat from Auche. With Merrill gone, Colonel Hunter assumed command of the Marauders, and a message was sent to the three battalion commanders apprising them of the fact.

With Merrill in the air and on his way to the 20th General Hospital in Ledo, Hunter trekked the four miles to Nhpum Ga. From the north, the trail to where the 2nd Battalion was situated "came around a bend along the slope with high ground rising on the right," wrote Hunter. "To the left was a rather deep ravine which, curving some hundred yards to the south, ended at the rear and downhill from the village."

Once in Nhpum Ga, McGee gave Hunter a tour of his position, pointing out that the "perimeter had to have a figure-eight-shaped boundary to hold the high ground and include a slow-flowing water hole situated under a promontory on the north-east corner."

Hunter was impressed with how McGee had deployed his men. They occupied all the available high ground, with platoons positioned on the two hills either side of the trail at the rear (north) of the village. The animals were picketed at the northernmost point in Nhpum Ga, close to the trail from Hsamshingyang, and the aid station had been moved to the sloping ground at the rear of the village, partly protected from enemy fire by a small knoll. The medical team was well prepared for casualties, having spent several hours digging foxholes large enough for a doctor to be able to treat a man lying on a litter.

The Blue Combat Team was dug in on the southern and eastern perimeters of Nhpum Ga, closest to the trail leading from Auche, while the Green team was defending the northern and western sides.

McGee told Hunter that the previous day the battalion had come under sporadic but heavy artillery fire, during which a number of their two hundred horses and mules were killed. P-51 fighters from the 51st Fighter Group had in response strafed the Japanese during the afternoon of March 28, an attack that reduced the intensity of the artillery fire and delayed the enemy advance north.

McGee had at his disposal nine hundred men. In addition to their individual weapons, the 2nd Battalion possessed seven .30 M1919 Browning heavy machine guns, six light machine guns, seven 81mm mortars, and ten 60mm mortars. They had fired the last of their 81mm rounds, and only a small number of 60mm rounds remained.

With the battalion also running low on food, Hunter called in an airdrop. The resupply began at 1040 hours and continued intermittently until 1400 hours. The men were delighted with what fell from the sky: ammunition, mortar rounds, clothes, new boots, and, best of all, an abundance of rations and, as a special treat, chicken, bread, apple turnovers, jam, and milk. "Christmas in March!" roared Sgt. Robert Sobczak as he surveyed the goodies.

Before Hunter departed at 1530 hours, he instructed McGee to site a machine gun at the rear of the position in order to keep open the trail that led north to Hsamshingyang and ensure that the Japanese didn't try to come up through one of the ravines. McGee did as instructed, ordering George Rose to position his Browning at the top of the trail. Hunter informed McGee that he would run twice-daily patrols from Hsamshingyang to Nhpum Ga to maintain a supply and communication link between the two villages.

When Hunter arrived back at Hsamshingyang, he sent a message to Colonel Osborne at Shaduzup ordering him "to move on Hsamshingyang by easy stages." The communication reached the 1st Battalion shortly after they had been relieved by the Chinese 113th Regiment on the bank of the Chengun, and the men were still imbibing the "pure 100-proof delight of being alive."

The men of the 3rd Battalion were less sanguine than their comrades. Earlier in the day, patrols to the north of Hsamshingyang had encountered a force of Japanese soldiers trying to outflank their position. That night, Sgt. James McGuire confided to his diary: "Our clothes are torn, shoes no good and to think the USA is well equipped. We are a sorry looking bunch."

CHAPTER 14

Besieged and Bombarded at Nhpum Ga

Vincent Melillo spent the night of March 29–30 in a foxhole in Nphum Ga with Eddie Eiksant for company. The pair had been buddies for three years in the 33rd Infantry Regiment, and Melillo trusted the Virginian "with my life." The two men of the Blue Combat Team were dug in on the southeast perimeter of Nhpum Ga overlooking a steep ravine.

They passed a peaceful night, reminiscing about the old times with the 33rd, prizefighting with the San Blas Indians in Panama, riding the *chivas* to the clubs in Panama City, and the day they were inspected by President Roosevelt in Trinidad.

In the wee small hours, as Eiksant slept at the bottom of the foxhole, Melillo kept awake by singing songs under his breath, one of his favorites being a tune he'd learned from the British in India:

There's a troop ship leaving Bombay
Off to the land I adore.
There'll be no promotions, this side of the ocean
So cheer up my lads,
Bless them all.
Bless them all, bless them all
The long and the short and the tall.
Bless the kind sergeant who puts you to bed
And pours ice water all over your head.

Also embedded in the south perimeter were privates first class Gabriel Kinney and Milton Goldman, two southern boys from Alabama and Mississippi, respectively. Kinney was one of his platoon's four BAR men (each squad contained a BAR), and he took a certain amount of pride in the responsibility. Not all GIs liked the BAR—some found it longer to load a magazine than to empty it at the enemy—but it had yet to let Kinney down since he'd started carrying one on Guadalcanal. The Browning Automatic Rifle fired six hundred rounds per minute, and each magazine contained twenty rounds. "I always tried to fire short bursts," remembered Kinney, "no more than three rounds a burst, although that was quite hard to do with the trigger."

The Japanese made their first attempt to seize Nhpum Ga at dawn on March 30. They started with artillery, then followed up with mortars and finally a frenzied *banzai* charge up the ravine toward the eastern perimeter. Melillo and Eiskant opened fire with their M1s, cutting down the enemy as they dodged between the hardwood trees below. The Japanese returned a withering fire. One bullet hit the stock of Melillo's weapon, splitting it right in half. The enemy fell back, the artillery fire intensified and then slackened, and the infantry came again, this time attacking the perimeter further north.

Kinney had soon fired so many rounds from his BAR that the barrel glowed red, scorching the wooden fore end beneath. Next to him in his foxhole, Milton Goldman kept him supplied with fresh ammunition, although one of the advantages of the BAR was that its rounds were compatible with the M1 rifle and .30 M1919 Browning.

Once again the Japanese were beaten back, but some men had gotten close enough to the hilltop to spot the American mortar positions on the reverse side of the hill at the rear of Nhpum Ga. Soon the Japanese artillery was ranging in on the 2nd Battalion's mortars, inflicting damage and killing a number of the mules picketed not far away at the rear of the village.

The Japanese had two artillery guns, one of which the Americans contemptuously nicknamed "Big Bertha." Its whistling 105mm shell allowed the Marauders time to take cover. The high-velocity 70mm gun—the same one that had inflicted so much damage on the trail between Auche and Nhpum Ga—was the one the battalion feared. It had been brought up to within a thousand yards of the village, so close that there was hardly any time delay between the shell exiting the barrel and hitting its target. "We called him 'Pistol Pete,'" said Melillo. "He would fire at the same time every day, and he was firing so close to our position."

By the afternoon of March 30, "Pistol Pete" had blown away the top of the hill that shielded the 2nd Battalion's mortar section. Casualties were starting to mount among the Marauders. "They were constantly shelling us, making the treatment of the wounded a large problem," recalled Capt. Lewis Kolodny, surgeon of the Green Combat team. A soldier was carried to the aid station having had the "top of his skull sheared right off exposing the brain." Kolodny and all the other battalion doctors were skilled surgeons, but they didn't have the equipment or facilities to treat such a wound. "There was absolutely nothing we could do for him," said Kolodny. "So I brought him into the hole with me—and he was unconscious, of course—and just kept him there until he died."

At one point during the day, during a lull between *banzai* attacks, Lt. Brendon Lynch and Cpl. Louis Black of the Blue Combat Team crept out of the perimeter on a reconnaissance, penetrating the jungle to check on the whereabouts of the enemy. It was a brave deed, but on their return the pair erred by approaching the village from a different direction to which they had left. The tired, nervous Marauders who were bunkered down in their foxholes in this section of the perimeter weren't aware that two of their number had been out reconnoitering the enemy. They saw movement through the trees, opened fire, and killed the two Marauders.*

Night fell over Nhpum Ga, but the Japanese continued to lay siege to the hillside, sniping from the east, west, and south at the slightest sound. Coughing, digging, and reloading all became dangerous activities in the inky blackness.

The accidental deaths of Lynch and Black heightened the tension at night. Men didn't want to leave their foxholes. They preferred to stay where they were, even if it meant using their helmet as a latrine and burying the waste just over the rim.

Daybreak on March 31 was a gruesome affair. The blotted carcasses of dead mules and horses had split during the sultry heat of the night, spilling intestines and creating a nauseous aroma that hung like a blanket over the village.

At 0530, the Japanese attacked with mortars and artillery. An hour later, the infantry charged up the eastern ravine. They died in their droves, but their courage secured a vital prize: control of the only fresh source of water in Nhpum Ga. Now, recalled Lt. Ted McLogan, the "enemy covered the waterhole with mortar fire, and snipers ringed the tall grass and jungle growth that overlooked the trail leading to it."

Elsewhere on the morning of March 31, the Japanese took other measures to cut off supplies to the 2nd Battalion. As a patrol from the 3rd Battalion's Orange Combat Team approached Nhpum Ga on the trail from Hsamshingyang, they encountered a Japanese block. The two forces

Black was killed instantly; Lynch died of his wounds.

exchanged fire before the Marauders withdrew north in the face of the enemy's superior firepower.

Some P-51 fighters appeared at midday, strafing whatever Japanese they could see down below through the jungle. Later in the day, some P-40s appeared overheard, dropping bombs through the trees, desperately trying to destroy "Pistol Pete." Lieutenant Colonel McGee launched an attempt to unblock the trail north with a reinforced platoon, but "within 200 yards of the perimeter it ran into prepared enemy positions."

McGee subsequently sent a series of messages to Colonel Hunter at Hsamshingyang, each one brief but blunt in its description of their worsening plight.

> We have been hit on three sides. Platoon from Orange was cut off and are making their way back through the jungle.

> My rear is blocked. I cannot withdraw north. Something has to come up to take the pressure off.

> Casualty report today, three dead nine wounded.

> Will need sixty and eighty one [mortar] ammo tomorrow badly.

At sundown on March 31, the 2nd Battalion war diary noted: "Animals are taking a beating. Shrapnel and stray bullets are mowing them down."

By now, McGee had ordered everyone into a foxhole, even his headquarters staff and the muleskinners. The Marauders spent an uncomfortable night in the ground, trying to block out the stench of their dead and ignore the taunts of the enemy living. The Japanese knew the name of their enemy's commander and shouted the fact through the trees, cackling: "Where's McGee?" Lieutenant Ted McLogan and his Green Combat Team platoon were dug in on the small hill in the northwest of the village, what Ed Kohler described as "the hot spot on the hill." He could hear them talking and laughing, as if they were egging on one another like naughty children. "Babe Ruth eats shit," one would shout. "We're coming to get you, Yank," yelled another.

★

Colonel Hunter spent March 31 at Hsamshingyang absorbing the news that the Japanese had blocked the trail leading to Nhpum Ga. Determined to reopen the crucial supply line, he drew up plans for a mule train to leave on April 1 supported by the Orange Combat Team. Meanwhile, the

Khaki Combat Team would continue to patrol the immediate vicinity to ensure that the Japanese didn't attempt to swing around wide and attack Hsamshingyang from the north. Hunter was in discussions over the radio with Major Hancock, the Marauders' supply officer at Ledo, about the feasibility of dropping two 75mm howitzers, an idea of General Merrill's as he lay on a stretcher in Ledo following his evacuation.

The imminent arrival of the howitzers was a boost for the Marauders' morale; so too was the first mail from home in two months. Private Harold Bengtson was stunned to receive his draft notice. He took the notice to Lieutenant Colonel Beach, and with a broad grin on his face requested permission to return to the States to report to the draft board. Beach told Bengtson where he could shove his draft notice.

Along with the mail were the latest editions of *Yank* magazine and *CBI Roundup*, the latter the Armed Forces newspaper in the Far East, known affectionately among the GIs as the "Fishwrapper." Dave Richardson's article about his experiences at Walawbum was featured prominently in *Yank*, while the Fishwrapper also carried a glowing account of the unit's first action. "The CBI and Yank has big write ups about us, but also pictures," wrote McGuire in his diary.

There was much whooping and cheering as the 3rd Battalion read what the *CBI* had to say about their stand at Walawbum. They were "tough, battlewise veterans of the Southwest Pacific"; they were "devil-may-care volunteers"; they were "the roughest, toughest bunch of Infantry our Army's ever molded together." The paper described their triumph at Walawbum, when they beat off two thousand Japanese during a three-day ordeal that enabled the Chinese 22nd Division to advance south and seize Maingkwan.

Some of the reporting was less well received, though the men laughed all the same. "Decorations are a dime a dozen in this novel outfit," declared *CBI*, a statement that couldn't have been further from the truth. And their description of General Merrill as "energetic" drew an ironic laugh.

★

It began to rain heavily during the morning of April 1. In Nhpum Ga, the men in their foxholes gathered what they could in their ponchos. The stench was as toxic as ever, made worse by the Japanese corpses rotting in the ravine among the bamboo and hardwood trees. Apart from the odd salvo of shells, the day was quiet—no infantry attack, but no sign of supply aircraft or fighter support because of the low cloud draped over the ridgeline.

In his command post, a chain of two-man foxholes chiseled out of the red clay and rock of Nhpum Ga, Lieutenant Colonel McGee received a message from Colonel Hunter informing him that two 75mm howitzers would be dropped the next day on Hsamshingyang; they would be in action within hours of their arrival. Hunter radioed another message to Nhpum Ga late in the afternoon of April 1 telling McGee that the "Nips [are] running like hell from Shaduzup." There were too many dead to be counted, added Hunter, who said the victory was in no small part due to the 2nd Battalion's block at Inkangahtawng. The message ended: "Expect your friends to pull out tonight or tomorrow morning. Mortar the hell out of them."

April 2 was a day of bitter fighting north and south of Nhpum Ga. The previous day, the Orange Combat Team had fought its way up two of the four miles that separated Hsamshingyang from the 2nd Battalion before withdrawing in the face of well-fortified Japanese blocks on the trail. Leroy Brown had been killed and several men wounded in the fierce clashes.

On April 2, it was the turn of the Khaki Combat Team, which advanced on a zigzag trail up the hillside, the terrain rising, then flattening, in a series of small plateaus. The sun had replaced the rain, but the men of L Company creeping south were shut off from its rays by the mass of towering bamboo on either side of the trail.

The Marauders peered through the murk, their eyes scanning the dense undergrowth for an enemy they knew to be there. It was a painstaking progress—a couple of yards forward, pause, observe, listen, advance another two yards. Corporal Edgar Robertson was the lead scout, Cpl. Frank Graham the second. Graham was first to spot the machine gun nest, twenty yards ahead and to the right of the trail. He shouted a warning and dived to his right. Robertson went to his left—and was shot dead. Another machine gun opened up. Graham took a round in his right shoulder, and Sgt. John Ploederl was shot in both legs. One of Ploederl's buddies crawled through the jungle, grabbed him by the ankles, and began dragging him down the slope. Another burst from the machine gun caught Ploederl in the chest.

Word reached Capt. James Hopkins and a litter party a hundred yards back down the trail that two men were dead and Graham was lying trapped with a wound to his shoulder. "I went forward with a litter and aid men to help the wounded," remembered Hopkins. "When our little group had almost reached Graham, a Japanese machine gun opened up and we made a hasty retreat on our bellies." Despite the wound to his right shoulder, Graham continued to blaze away with the machine gun as he slithered his way away from trouble and into the arms of the aid team.

Every yard was a vicious struggle, where the terrain as much as the Japanese repelled the Americans and made a mockery of their sobriquet—"Marauders." It was a lethal slog.

★

Back at Hsamshingyang, on April 2, the long-awaited howitzers were dropped on the end of double parachutes. Waiting to unpack them was Sgt. John Acker of the 3rd Battalion, erstwhile with the 98th Field Artillery in New Guinea. He cursed when he discovered that the guns were minus their aiming circle, the instrument used to set the two guns to fire parallel to each other. Acker's equanimity returned when one of the men produced a compass so he could set the guns parallel at a distance of thirty feet apart.

"Colonel Hunter had asked me, as soon as we got the guns [unpacked], to come over and talk to him," remembered Acker. "He was across the rice paddy in an area under some brush there with his tent. . . . Soon as I made the statement 'Sir, the guns are already to fire,' you could see the delight in his eyes as he realized that maybe he had more dependence on us now than he had before."

Hunter rose from his chair and unfurled a map on the card table that served as his desk. Pointing out Nhpum Ga, Hunter then moved his finger south to the Japanese 70mm gun sited at Kauri. It was a challenge for Acker and his hastily formed gun crew; to knock out the Japanese gun, they would have to fire over the heads of the beleaguered 2nd Battalion trapped on the hill.

Hunter called up McGee on the radio and asked if anyone in the 2nd Battalion had experience in ranging artillery fire. Someone was found, an ROTC artillery graduate, whose unenviable task was to position himself in the center of the perimeter and adjust the fire of Sergeant Acker's two howitzers.

Acker recalled that Hunter "was very thrilled and had a lot of confidence in us" when the gun crews began firing. The hill was measured to be approximately six thousand yards from the two artillery pieces, but targeting the guns proved a problem without an experienced crew and observer. Acker ordered the crews to fire the first two rounds the howitzer's maximum range of 8,500 yards. He also removed one of the four bags of gunpowder in the shells, which "would let us fire high enough to clear our troops on the hill, yet fall short enough to hit near our targets."

The guns fired and the 2nd Battalion's observer reported hearing "a faint noise to the south." Just then some P-40s appeared overhead, so Hunter asked the flight leader to act as a spotter as they fired a salvo of smoke rounds. Using the coordinates given by the flight leader, Hunter and Acker plotted a new path that was described by the observer on Nhpum Ga as "on line" but "way over." After another minor adjustment, the two howitzers now had the range of the Japanese positions around Kauri.

★

Most of the 2nd Battalion men dug in on the perimeter of Nhpum Ga were unaware of the two howitzers. From first light on April 2, they had been under constant attack, from both artillery fire and infantry assaults. On the eastern perimeter, the Blue Combat Team held off a sustained charge up the ravine. A growing number of soldiers were reporting sick, most with dysentery, though one or two were going out of their mind. But in general, the Marauder spirit was alive and well. Vincent Melillo watched in disbelief as Eddie Eiskant crawled out of their foxhole, "over the cliff to retrieve a watch from a dead Jap." It was a good watch, Eiskant told Melillo, a souvenir to show the folks back home.

In the foxhole he shared with Milton Goldman a few meters south, Gabriel Kinney was thirsty and tired but otherwise well, his morale as replenished as his BAR magazines. "The thought of being overrun was always there," he reflected. "But I thought if they could keep us in ammunition, we could hold."

The 2nd Battalion received a much-needed airdrop in the afternoon, hauling in supplies of ammunition and rations. Among the items dropped was some reading matter, though not old copies of newspapers or *Time* magazine. Instead, some joker back at base had thought it a hoot to include a romantic French novel, a pocketbook of etiquette, and a children's picture book on wild animals. The men of the 2nd Battalion took the prank well, even delivering one of the books to Lewis Kolodny in the medical station—a gynecological guide.

But the one essential that was still missing from the resupply was water. On April 1, Lieutenant Colonel McGee had radioed Major Hancock requesting as a matter of urgency five hundred gallons of water. Hancock was on the case, wrestling with the challenge of safely dropping water by air, but every hour that passed without water was agony for the 2nd Battalion.

"We cleared the bamboo inside the perimeter and cut open the joints, getting as much as a cup of water from each joint," said Capt. Fred Lyons. "But the bamboo didn't last long with a thousand men."

With no more bamboo to hack open, Marauders did whatever was necessary to acquire water. They drank rainwater scoped from elephant tracks and sterilized with a couple of halazone tablets and flavored with a dash of lemonade powder from their K-rations. But when the rain stopped and the sun emerged, the elephant prints dried up, leaving only one source of water for the 2nd Battalion. "It was a patch of swampy ground that rain seeped into," recalled Ted McLogan. "But it had the bodies of twenty-five mules and they were covered in maggots and flies." Men, who a few weeks earlier had groused about conditions in India, now risked their lives to crawl down to the swamp at night and fill their canteens with the fetid water. "They were tough days," reflected McLogan. But they were also revelatory ones, as men drew on depths of resilience most never knew they possessed. Some of the soldiers even found humor in their dire predicament, joking that there was nothing quite like a cup of dead-mule-flavor coffee in the morning to set oneself up for the rest of the day.

In one foxhole on the eastern perimeter, a member of the Blue Combat Team woke from a slumber to be told by his buddy: "You look wonderful this morning. Who's your undertaker?"

CHAPTER 15

"This War Is Hell"

April 3 was an awful day for the 2nd Battalion, one that for a small number of men exhausted their well of endurance. It was the Japanese shelling that withdrew the last drops. Men who could fight off one *banzai* charge after another with utter disregard for their own safety shook in terror as shells churned up Nhpum Ga. They fell to the north of the village, to the east, to the west, and in the south. Some found a victim, most didn't, but each shell drew a little more on that well. To fight as an infantryman, in a hand-to-hand struggle, was what young men always imagined war would be like; not to cower passively in a foxhole, waiting to be crippled or killed by a random shell.

Lieutenant Colonel McGee remained as steady as ever, at least on the surface. Inwardly, this tough, uncompromising commander was distraught at the damage being done to his battalion. In midmorning, he sent a calm but blunt message to Hsamshingyang:

> Situation getting critical. Took heavy artillery attack this morning. 3 killed, 12 wounded. Japs working around to our west. Animal losses heavy. Detailed report later. General health of command only fair. Much diarrhea and stomach disorders. You must push on.

The rear of the camp where the mules were picketed now resembled an abattoir. Flies and maggots swarmed over the dead, and the stench made men wretch. Muleskinners who for weeks had showered harsh affection on their beasts now led the crippled animals to one side, shot them, and covered them as best they could.

Conditions for the wounded men were marginally better but still hellish, not helped by the tenacious if wayward sniper taking potshots at doctors Henry Stelling and Lewis Kolodny, "which of course we did not appreciate." Kolodny asked one of the bazooka men to silence the sniper. With that threat eliminated, Kolodny got down to the task of treating the wounded, improvising as best he could in the circumstances and reverting to the most primitive methods of treatment. Seeing the maggots feasting on the dead horses gave Kolodny an idea. "Rather than do surgery on the [wounded] leg, we would clean it up and put plaster on the entire thing and leave it there," explained Kolodny, who relied on the plaster skills of one of his sergeants. "Maggots would get into the wound, and the maggots would eat the dead tissue, leaving the live tissue alone." The treatment worked, though it couldn't be performed on the more seriously wounded men. "There were a couple of patients who did have to have amputations, and that was done literally with a bayonet," recalled Kolodny.

Kolodny and Stelling performed these operations "almost standing on one's head on the edges of foxholes in which the patients lay," conscious that they were within range of any sharp-eyed Japanese sniper. But by now in Nhpum Ga, acts of uncommon valor were commonplace. Medics braved shellfire and snipers to retrieve the wounded from foxholes, and muleskinners helped dig more holes in which to accommodate the litter cases.

But on April 3, the aid station was approaching a crisis point. There was barely enough water left to make plaster casts or to administer sulfadiazine for the wounded. "Some of the men became delirious from thirst, and all suffered marked dehydration," recalled Stelling, who also found it increasingly "difficult to recognize one's closest associates by looks and because of personality changes due to the physical and mental strain of the siege."

Marauders whose wounds were not sufficiently serious returned to their foxholes once their wounds were dressed. *Endurance* became the battalion watchword.

Gabriel Kinney had shrapnel wounds to his leg and back, as well as a dent in his helmet from a sniper's bullet. None tormented him as much as his parched mouth. "The sniping and shelling we could fight; the thirst we could not," he reflected.

Hunter strove to relieve Nhpum Ga. On learning from McGee the full extent of their plight, he called up an airstrike and arranged for a resupply. He also sent the 2nd Battalion a message: "Make Plans to fight your way out to the northwest tomorrow. Will give you all possible assistance. Suggest 0600 as best time. Allies not in sight. Destroy all excess equipment and shoot animals if necessary. Adjust our artillery on west flank."

McGee appreciated the message but replied that a fighting withdrawal northwest was impractical because of the state of the men; six soldiers had now died in the day's fighting, and the aid station was overflowing with wounded.

Hunter thanked McGee for his honesty and organized an airdrop and an attack on the Japanese positions by the 51st Fighter Group. Hunter then called a staff conference in his tent at Hsamshingyang. The situation on the hill four miles to their south was grim, he explained, and there was a possibility that the 2nd Battalion would be overrun if not relieved in the next few days. Hunter informed his officers that he had spoken to Lieutenant Colonel Osborne, and his 1st Battalion was now embarked on a forced march from Shaduzup to aid in the lifting of the siege, but that they wouldn't arrive for five days. The earliest they could expect any Chinese troops was in eleven days. In short, the burden of relieving the men trapped on Nhpum Ga fell to the 3rd Battalion.

"Gentlemen," announced Hunter, "in the morning we will start an attack that will drive through to the 2nd Battalion. It may take two or three days, but we will get through. All troops except the sick and the muleskinners will be withdrawn from the airstrip. All large patrols will be called in and Kachins substituted wherever possible."

Hunter then outlined the plan of attack for the following day, April 4. The Orange Combat Team would launch the initial assault due south along the trail. Once the enemy was engaged, the Khaki Combat Team, having followed Orange south to within four hundred yards of the Japanese positions, would swing west and hit them on the flank. The two howitzers would be hauled up the trail and used to fire point-blank into the Japanese positions. Hunter set zero hour for 1200 hours.

★

Colonel Hunter and Lieutenant Colonel Beach moved up to the jumping-off position to wish the men luck as zero hour approached. Delays in moving men and howitzers up the trail had pushed back the start of the assault to 1600 hours, but there was a steely determination about those members of the 3rd Battalion that Hunter encountered. "We've been attacking up this goddamned hill for four days now," he told one group. "Today, let's take what casualties we have to, to get the job done."

The attack began with a barrage of mortar and artillery fire. The men of the Orange Combat Team pressed themselves flat as the shells rushed over their heads. Ahead of them, hidden along a 150-yard front, were scores of well-armed Japanese peering down from their camouflaged positions. Dan Carrigan, one of Logan Weston's I&R platoon, who wore a long, red goatee that he had been growing for weeks, muttered, "I hope the mortar gang leaves some for us."

As the barrage lifted, Weston and his men advanced up the hill, "scrambling, crawling, worming their way through the thick growth of jungle." There was no sign of the enemy as Weston hauled himself through the carpet of rotting vegetation. To his left was the trail, and to his right the bulk of his men. He noticed that the skirmish line had become crooked, "so I went over to straighten things out." They climbed higher. Still no contact. The Japanese were patient. When the Americans were within thirty yards of their frontline, the firing began. The first burst killed Dan Carrigan and wounded Jean LeBrun in his chest and arm.

The Orange Combat Team returned fire, seeking out an enemy so close that they could practically smell them. Except for the power of the weapons, the fighting harked back to an earlier age when soldiers relied not on technology but on courage, initiative, and cunning. Inman Avery's sword was his BAR, which he wielded with deadly precision. He shot six of the enemy before a sniper winged him in the right shoulder. Grinning to Weston as he went back down the hill for treatment, Avery pointed to his left shoulder and said: "On New Georgia they got me here. Now they got me here, almost identical. They got me bracketed."

To the west of the Orange Combat Team, Staff Sgt. James McGuire and his comrades in the Khaki Combat Team were forcing their way through the jungle in an outflanking maneuver. "Tough going," McGuire would write. "Everything hand carried and trail had to be cut." Mortars, heavy machine guns, and flame-throwers had been discarded in the desire to move as quickly and as quietly as possible, leaving the men feeling exposed and vulnerable.

"We should not be doing this," whispered lead scout Ed Nichols to his platoon leader as they crept through the still, sunless jungle. Seconds later, a bullet passed through Nichols' helmet and into his brain. Gunfire now came from all directions. The Marauders dived behind trees and into hollows. Bullets chipped bark from trees and chopped down bamboo. McGuire was one of the lucky ones. "We got hit," he told his diary that night. "Nick [Nichols] got killed, 4 others got wounded, Sutterfield hit badly . . . 2 Jap machine guns did all the damage. Japs in behind us. We killed one and another got away. We pulled out. Had to carry litter cases 5 mi and cut trail."

T5G Luther Sutterfield, a twenty-three-year-old from McCurtain County, Oklahoma, idolized by his four sisters, was carried into the aid station with a bullet wound to the right side of his skull. Sutterfield had been trying to reach Nichols and the other scout, Paul Fields, a buddy of his with whom he'd fought on Guadalcanal. Captain Milton Ivens, the Combat Team surgeon, fought a frantic battle to save the young man. Sutterfield received two units of blood plasma, but the trauma to his skull was too severe for him to survive.

A short while later, Pvt. Kermit Busher was brought to the aid tent having been shot just after Sutterfield. "It was a light machine gun," he recalled. "And I must have got about fifteen or twenty bullets . . . they blew out my leg completely. I lost the bone and it was just hanging there." Hopkins believed there was a chance that Busher's leg could be saved if he was evacuated immediately. An L-4 aircraft was requested, and when it arrived on the small airstrip at Hsamshingyang, Busher was loaded on board. For takeoff, recalled Busher, "they tied the tail down to something that would hold it and then they let the engine rev up as much as possible. They chopped the rope holding the tail, and it had a catapult action. We didn't get to rise that quickly because I remember looking off to the side and there were monkeys looking around before we got above the trees." A day after being shot, Busher underwent surgery in the 20th General Hospital.

As the wounded continued to be brought down the trail to the aid station, the bloody fighting intensified with the enemies trying to outflank one other. Bernard Martin and his radio team had moved south to take up position at the rear of the 3rd Battalion. They were the link between Lieutenant Colonel Beach and Hunter, who was now back in his new CP at Mahkyetkwang, a little further north up the valley. Bill Smawley and another man were in the radio pit while Martin and the rest of the team were dug in around. "The transmitter generator was grinding up a storm that could be heard all the way back to base," recalled Martin.

Suddenly, one of the radio team's muleskinners spotted some movement in the trees to their right. "I told him to go to Colonel Beach and have him send a couple of BAR men," recalled Martin. "He took off, and I got the other two muleskinners and radio operators all together and we had our rifles ready. Pretty soon, the BAR men came and listened and said, 'Colonel Beach says there are no Allied troops behind us.' Then they got in the hole with us and he said, 'When I give you the signal fire at least two to three feet above the ground. . . .' I shot about eight or nine clips before I gave up. We sat back and waited and the BAR man took off, crabbed across the field, and came back with a smile on his face saying, 'Well, we got a few of them.'"

★

In Nhpum Ga, the men of the 2nd Battalion lay in their foxholes listening to the sound of battle to their north. It sounded real close. By the end of the day, a radio message from Hunter informed McGee that the 3rd Battalion was now just a mile from the perimeter. But it was still a mile, and in that mile were scores of Japanese dug in on a plateau overlooking the trail. On the south side of Nhpum Ga, hundreds of Japanese and several artillery pieces were still wreaking havoc on the 2nd Battalion. The stench of death was unbearable, and the sights and sounds of the dying were so ghastly that they became embedded deep in men's souls. The battalion diarist recorded the suffering in short, stark prose. "One man lay to the southeast just outside the perimeter with his entire frontal lobe exposed," was the entry on April 4. "The medics tried to get at him all night but the Japs threw up flares and opened fire whenever there was a sound in that vicinity."

McGee sent Hunter a radio message describing events. He ended with a simple request: "Please hurry."

At dusk, the Japanese launched attacks against the north, east, and western perimeters of Nhpum Ga. Each one was resisted, but the soldiers were now close to exhaustion. "Men so weak with stomach ailments they couldn't stand up but lay against the boxes and bales," remembered Capt. Fred Lyons, who that day had been fired on as he repaired a line of telephone wire. "I wriggled and twisted, pulling my wire with me," he said. "Still another puff. Five times the sniper, concealed in a tree somewhere near the clearing, shot at me, and five times he missed."

The forte of the Japanese soldier wasn't sniping; it was the *banzai* charge that required no skill but great courage. In the early hours of April 5, the Japanese launched another such assault, rushing from the jungle and hurling themselves at the western perimeter defended by Company G of the Green Combat Team. The Browning heavy machine gun covering the trail up the hill from the Hkuma River killed dozens, but the Japanese were in a frenzy this night. They kept coming. A bullet hit the Browning's water cooler. The gun overheated, stopped firing. Albert Wankel and Robert Thompson had no chance. Nor did Ellis Yoder, the twenty-year-old from Pennsylvania who'd had a narrow escape at Inkangahtawng. This time there was no George Rose to come to his rescue, as hordes of screaming Japanese stormed the gun pit.

The Japanese were eventually repulsed, but not before they had killed the three Marauders and made off with the Browning machine gun.

On the western side of the perimeter, Ed Kohler was sharing a foxhole with Sgt. Roy Matsumoto. Both men were sick by April 1—Kohler with malaria, Matsumoto with the same dysentery that had cut a swathe through the 2nd Battalion. Of the four Nisei interpreters assigned to McGee, two had been evacuated with dysentery before the trail to Hsamshingyang had been blocked by the Japanese. A third suffered so much that he could barely leave his foxhole.

Lieutenant Colonel McGee had ordered Matsumoto up to the frontline in the hope he might be able to hear some of what was being said by the Japanese. They were dug in among the jungle just thirty yards from where Matsumoto and Kohler huddled in their foxhole. "About all I could get out of Roy was 'Don't let them get me,'" remembered Kohler. "He was pretty much afraid of getting captured, and for good reason. It would have been rough on him."

The Japanese thought they were smart hurling insults at the Americans, but they were being outsmarted by Matsumoto. He could hear a lot of what was being said. Already he had pinpointed his enemy's accent, the Fukuoka dialect spoken in southern Japan. If he'd wanted to, if he'd been naive, Matsumoto might have fired a few insults back in their own tongue. That would have given the game away. Matsumoto kept quiet—and kept listening.

An enemy officer began issuing instructions to his men about which section of the perimeter to next attack. Matsumoto passed the commands to Lt. Ted McLogan, who redeployed his men to counter the threat. Twice more during the nigh, the Japanese threw themselves at the western perimeter, but the Marauders were waiting, eager to avenge the death of their three buddies. "They lined up in a line and attacked," said Kohler. "When the line was all killed, another one would come in. They kept this up all night. When daylight came, we had dead Japs everyplace. I shot an officer and he fell so close to my foxhole that I got his sword without getting out of my foxhole."

Early on in the siege, Kohler learned how to spot if an enemy assault was imminent. Above the smell of the decay that lingered over the hilltop wafted the sweetish pungent scent of opium. "This would tell me we are going to get hit again pretty soon," recalled Kohler.

★

April 5 was a quieter one for the 2nd Battalion. They took another airdrop of ammunition and food, but still there was no sign of water. For the 3rd Battalion, the fighting to the north was even fiercer than the day before. The Japanese diverted troops from the south of Nhpum Ga to repel the Americans' push toward the plateau at the top of the trail.

The attack began with another barrage from Sergeant Acker's two howitzers. Captain James Hopkins watched from his forward aid post as the men of the Orange Combat Team trooped forward, many depositing their packs at his feet. Hopkins put on a brave face, wishing them luck and telling them he'd see them again soon. It was a charade. As a doctor, he acknowledged that he and his medical staff would never be "able to say that we understood their courage, or their mental and physical strength, as they on this morning prepared to advance into almost certain death or injury." A few hours earlier, Hopkins had moved among the infantrymen as they ate breakfast, discreetly suggesting they shouldn't go into battle on a full stomach. "I was thinking that with their stomach and intestines empty, they would have a better chance of survival if they had abdominal wounds," he admitted.

Once again, Lt. Logan Weston and his I&R platoon were to the fore when the barrage lifted and the infantry moved forward toward the plateau. They took more casualties, and the word reached Hopkins at his aid station that he was required up the trail. He arrived to discover Weston crouching over his platoon medic, Joe Gomez, the man who carried everything in his bag. Gomez had been hit in the head by a fragment from an American mortar shell that had burst in a tree fifteen yards away. As Hopkins examined Gomez's wound, the "fragment of bone driven into his brain," Weston held the hand of his wounded comrade and together they said a prayer.*

Hopkins saw that Weston had been wounded in the right ankle by the same mortar burst that had felled Gomez. Despite the injury, Weston refused to abandon his men. So while Hopkins organized the evacuation of Gomez, he told the new medic—Dan Hardinger—to bandage Weston's ankle. Hardinger was known as "Swede" among the Orange Combat Team. A big, powerful man, he was a genuine gentle giant, a Seventh Day Adventist and conscientious objector who refused to carry a weapon. Hardinger had served under Hopkins on Guadalcanal, and the doctor considered him "brave, caring, and capable."

By sundown on April 5, the 3rd Battalion had seized another three hundred precious yards of jungle. The Marauders searched enemy dead for intelligence, checking the fly of their breeches where soldiers' names and unit were written in India ink. Besides intelligence documents, they hoped to find cigarettes. Among several brands recovered were a number of popular American ones, but to the disappointment of the Marauders, they turned out to be poor-quality Japanese imitations. They were smoked all the same.

On one corpse was a note from a platoon leader to his company commander in which he apologized for withdrawing further up the hill. The American shelling was just too intense. Other retrieved information revealed that the Japanese were a "reinforced battalion from the 114th Regiment of the 18th Division." Some scrawled lines on a scrap of paper were found on another corpse, lines of a poem that were translated by one of the Nisei interpreters:

> With the blood-stained flag of the Rising Sun, I'd like to conquer the world.
> As I spit on the Great Wall of China,
> A multi-hued rainbow rises above the Gobi Desert.
> On the Ganges River at the foot of majestic Himalaya Mountains,
> Sons of Nippon look for some crocodiles.
> Today we're in Berlin,
> Tomorrow in Moscow,
> Home of snowbound Siberia,
> As the fog lifts we see the City of London,
> Rising high, as the ceremonial fish of Boys' Day does.

*Gomez was airlifted to hospital in Ledo where he made a miraculous recovery.

Now we're in Chicago, once terrorized by gangsters,
Where our grandchildren pay homage to our memorial monument.

★

In his position on top of the hill at the northwest corner of Nhpum Ga, Lt. Ted McLogan could hear an unusual amount of chattering from the Japanese frontline on this particular evening. For some reason, despite the horror of their situation, the noises reminded McLogan of "a theater letting out." He called for Matsumoto, and the Nisei interpreter crawled up to his officer's foxhole. Masumoto strained his ears but shook his head. "Can't make it out," he told McLogan. But something was definitely up.

Matsumoto handed McLogan his carbine and began unfastening his ammunition belt. McLogan asked what he was doing. Going to find out what it was that had the enemy so excited, replied Matsumoto. Stuffing two grenades into his pants, the interpreter told his foxhole buddy Ed Kohler of his intention. Kohler called him "crazy." Matsumoto asked Kohler to make sure he didn't shoot him when he came back. They agreed on a password, and then he was off.

Matsumoto was scared as he crawled down the slope. The night was so black that he couldn't see his own hand in front of his face. He could literally bump into the enemy. He prayed what he called his "ABCD" prayer—to Allah, Buddha, Christ, or the Devil. Anyone who would listen. Matsumoto wriggled to within a few feet of the Japanese. He was close enough that he could almost reach out and touch them. "The Japanese were talking in their foxholes just as soldiers do," he said. Girls, food, family. Matsumoto remained motionless, listening for a clue as to what had them so animated. Then it came: an anxious soldier asking his buddy if he reckoned their dawn attack would finally break the Americans.

"He was gone for twenty minutes before he came back," recalled McLogan. "He said, 'Mac, you're not going to like this. They are going to be hitting full strength on your platoon in the morning, and the orders are it must be taken.'"

McLogan radioed the information to McGee. "I want you to vacate your foxholes, but booby-trap them first, then move back one hundred feet up the hill," McGee ordered. "That will give you a longer field of fire when they come in the morning." In addition, McGee temporarily reinforced McLogan's platoon with BAR men, and Capt. Thomas Bogardus ordered his Browning heavy machine gun team onto the hill.

The attack unfolded just as the Japanese had unwittingly revealed to Matsumoto. McLogan watched as the Japanese charged from the jungle and leapt into the empty foxholes to bayonet the helpless Americans. The booby traps detonated. From the top of the hill, the Marauders poured a withering fire onto the confused enemy below. "There were probably seventy-five of them in the charge, and we shot a lot of them," recalled McLogan. Matsumoto looked over the top of his carbine and saw the second wave of enemy soldiers hesitate, unsure whether to go on or fall back. Matsumoto had studied Japanese infantry tactics as a cadet in Hiroshima. He knew the order to now issue. "Prepare to charge,'" he yelled in perfect Japanese. He paused, then hollered, "Charge!"

Sergeant Warren Ventura was in the trench not far from Matsumoto, having just repaired a problem with his machine gun. "By the time I had fired five or six shots, the attack was over," he recalled. "Then on my right flank about thirty-five yards away from me, I hear someone yelling and he's yelling in Japanese. I look and it's Roy Matsumoto, standing there, fully exposed above the ground, with a carbine and firing away at the Japanese and ordering them in Japanese to charge."

With impeccable discipline, the second wave of Japanese infantry obeyed Matsumoto's instructions. They ran up the hill and onto the guns of the Marauders. "My machine gun had a good field of fire," said Ventura, "[but] how Matsumoto lived through this attack . . . the man led a charmed life."

The Americans counted fifty-four dead on the slope beneath their position. Matsumoto felt no sadness as he surveyed the carnage. "I was happy," he said. "They had tried to wipe us out, but we had wiped them out."

Five minutes later, McGee appeared "to congratulate the guys on the job they'd done." The body count delighted him. Suddenly, the Japanese opened up from the jungle, raking with heavy machine gun fire what was now called "McLogan's Hill." McLogan and McGee dived into a small defilade. "I could literally see the bullets striking all around me, hitting leaves and trees," said McLogan. "There was a stick about the size of my thumb, about ten inches long, just in front of my chin, and it disappeared just like that."

George Rose, who had been enlisted to help in the defense of McLogan's Hill, recognized a familiar sound through the maelstrom—the Browning machine gun that had been captured the previous evening. "I could recognize the clanging sound of the damaged gun's water tank anywhere," he recalled.

McGee didn't appear too perturbed by the storm hail of bullets; it was simply the Japanese venting their anger. They were riled, upset, and that pleased McGee.

He was still in good spirits a few hours later when he updated the battalion diary. Apart from a salvo of five shells, the morning had been peaceful in Nhpum Ga. To the south he could see black smoke rising from Japanese positions after an airstrike by P-51s, and to his north he could hear the 3rd Battalion "hammering out there now . . . they are not far out." They'd received a resupply in the early afternoon, though one plane had kicked out its bundles of rations way beyond the 2nd Battalion's perimeter. "Guess he is feeding the Nips," noted McGee. Then at 1640 hours, he added in the diary: "Plane just finished dropping water."

It had taken Major Hancock a couple of days, but the supply officer for whom no obstacle was insurmountable had devised a way to drop water. Down from the sky came five hundred gallons of water in plastic casks with aluminum screw tops, the first fresh water the battalion had received for over a week. "When I saw those dangling, sausage-like bottles come floating down the parachutes, I breathed a fervent prayer of thanks," recalled Capt. Fred Lyons. There was more than just water this day. One bundle contained hundreds of cigarettes, the cartons donated by a variety of American Legion posts and civic clubs. "It made us feel for a while that there was such a place as the United States," said Lyons.

The transport planes came over again, and the "kickers" on board waited for the hand signal from their pilots before launching their bundles out the door. This time, as the trapped men on Nhpum Ga looked up, they saw floating down dozens of small boxes. For a few moments, they watched in bemusement. Then, when the first boxes began landing among the corpses and craters, the cry suddenly went up: "fried chicken." "It was a strange sight to see a bunch of battle-worn GIs elbowing one another to be first for the leg or the breast," recalled Lyons. "Just as the feast was being passed out to the second line, Jap artillery fire began lobbing in and the boys scattered. In the next lull, those who returned found somebody had risked his life for one more taste of that chicken, for there was none left."

★

Morale among the men at Hsamshingyang on April 6 was also higher than it had been for a while. The Chinese had made good progress in the previous couple of days and were now just ten miles north, wiping out the last pockets of Japanese troops who threatened the 3rd Battalion's rear. Colonel Hunter and Lieutenant Colonel Beach had planned for this new day a fresh offensive, an artillery barrage from the two howitzers preluding the infantry assault. The previous day, some of the dead Japanese had been found wearing the boots and carrying the weapons of dead Marauders. There was a whiff of vengeance in the air as the Khaki Combat Team moved up into positions

By sunset on April 6, only five hundred yards separated the 3rd Battalion from the sloping ground in the northeastern corner of Nhpum Ga. To the besieged men, this was known as "Maggot Hill" because of the larvae growing fat on the dead animals. Someone had even gone to the effort of scrawling the name on the side of a ration box. Nearby was a mortar emplacement with a similar signpost announcing "Fort Sad Sack."

For some of the 2nd Battalion trapped in the village, the proximity of salvation only exacerbated their misery. They were within shouting distance of relief, yet for all the immediate good it was doing them, their 3rd Battalion buddies might as well have been in Bombay.

Captain Henry Stelling, one of the battalion doctors, was growing concerned with the mental state of the men. "They began to look like skeletons, haggard and worn, and very thin from severe battle exhaustion due to prolonged and almost constant enemy fire and bombardment," he noted. They had food, and now water, but the lack of sleep and the constant stress, the gnawing tension of never knowing where the next shell might land or when the next *banzai* charge might start, was wearing them down. The indefatigable McGee was still at his command post, like the captain on the bridge of his foundering ship not even countenancing the possibility of abandonment, but "most of the men and officers began to have the hopeless look of despair." Over the previous week, the dead and dying had been numbering on average twenty a day—too many for the medical team to deal with. The muleskinners dug as fast as they could, but the dead were now covered with only a light smattering of earth.

★

April 7 was a Friday, and as McGee wrote up the 2nd Battalion diary at 1745 hours, he realized it wasn't any old Friday. "Today was Good Friday," he wrote. "Boy, we never realized Easter is almost here." So was salvation, although McGee and his men didn't yet know it. Forty-five minutes earlier, at 1700 hours, Lieutenant Colonel Osborne had led the 1st Battalion into Hsamshingyang after an epic thirty-mile march in five days across brutal, enemy-infested terrain. "After we pulled out of Shaduzup, we headed to a prearranged destination for an airdrop," remembered radioman Robert Passanisi. "We were out of rations and low on ammo. Before long, we were informed that the drop site was moved and would be a day later. This scenario was repeated for the five days it took to get to Hsamshingyang."

The eight hundred men were exhausted. More than two hundred were suffering the effects of acute dysentery. Some soldiers had cut a hole in the rear of their pants so that they wouldn't have to drop out of the column when struck by stomach cramps but could simply march on toward their buddies in the 2nd Battalion. Charlton Ogburn delicately described their uniforms as being encrusted with mud and blood when they arrived at Hsamshingyang. They were soiled with more than just that.

As the 1st Battalion soldiers gorged on their first food in thirty-six hours, Colonel Hunter called a staff conference in which he formulated the attack for April 8. Khaki Combat Team would continue to assault the trail to Nhpum Ga, while Orange attacked from the east. Meantime, Hunter instructed Osborne to muster all his fit men and strike the Japanese positions southeast of Nhpum Ga. Osborne sifted through his ravaged battalion and selected 254 men, placing them under the command of Capt. Tom Senff.

Passanisi recalled that during the five-day march to Hsamshingyang, there had been "lots of griping and everybody was dragging ass" as the men toiled through the jungle. But now, asked to rescue their buddies on Nhpum Ga, no one demurred. "We all knew there was a major problem, and groups from the different platoons who could just went along," said Passanisi. "The men seldom had to be told what to do. They generally were told what had to be done, and they just did it."

Hunter had finally acquired some aerial reconnaissance photos of the village and, placing them on his desk, "outlined to Senff the mission of executing a flank attack around the high ground on the right (west) side of Nhpum Ga."

"I hope this is over quick," wrote Sgt. James McGuire in his diary as his Khaki Combat Team waited for the attack to begin. His platoon had been whittled down from thirty-four men to sixteen, and he feared for the sanity of some of the survivors. "Boy in plt [platoon], his nerves broke and another one is as bad," wrote McGuire. "This war is hell."

★

Colonel Hunter's field order for April 8 was brief and to the point: "Nhpum Ga will fall today." It didn't, despite more heroic efforts from the emaciated and exhausted Marauders. The I&R platoon of the Khaki headquarter company bore the brunt of the carnage, suffering nine casualties among its twenty-two soldiers as it fought through the forest of bamboo that guarded Nhpum Ga. T5g Ted Gilmore, a Missouri boy, was shredded by grenade fragments as he covered the advance of a flamethrower. With blood pouring from wounds to his head, arms, and legs, Gilmore called out to his platoon leader, Lt. George Hearn, "How about charging the yellow bastards?"

The Japanese were now fighting dirty, "extracting a slug from a cartridge and reinserting it with its butt end forward," recalled Hunter. Medics also found that an increasing number of Marauders had been shot by rounds in which the ball had been removed and replaced with "a pointed hand-carved hardwood substance." At least it meant that the enemy's supply lines were blocked.

The gun crews had now moved the two howitzers to within a few hundred yards of Nhpum Ga. The weapons were carried on the backs of a twelve-strong mule train with the gun barrels and tailpieces making the beasts rock and sway as they negotiated the trail. The muleskinners spent a considerable amount of time adjusting the saddles on the mules for the challenge of transporting the artillery pieces, another demonstration of the dynamic teamwork within each battalion.

"We found a place about one thousand yards from Nhpum Ga," recalled Acker. "There was a nice bend in the trail to the left with a deep ravine to the right and Nhpum Ga hill directly in front of us. This was an ideal location for our gun position. The enemy, with their flat-trajectory guns, could not fire low enough to hit us. Their shells would hit the hill in front of us. If they raised their elevation to clear the hill, their shells would go over our heads and into the ravine behind us."

Once the howitzers were dug in, Acker's problem was ranging the two guns, a conundrum solved by the courage of Robert Carr. He volunteered to creep forward and act as an observer even though the I&R man had no experience. "But I know what to do," he told Acker. Dave Richardson, the war correspondent for Yank magazine, watched Carr advance up the hillside carrying a couple of grenades and a walkie-talkie. "When I started to crawl up the hill, we were firing hot and heavy and fast," remembered Carr. "I couldn't keep up, so I would get up and run, then go prone when the shells hit."

A few minutes later, Carr's voice came through on the walkie-talkie. "Jap position approximately seven hundred yards from guns," he said, then added the coordinates. "Fire a smoke shell and I'll zero you in."

The howitzers fired half a dozen smoke shells with a slight pause between each as Carr adjusted their range. Then he came back on the walkie-talkie to tell Acker that the guns were zeroed in on the Japanese positions. The sergeant ordered his crew to fire five rounds. A minute later, Staff Sgt. Henry E. Hoot, the gun crew's radioman, received a message. "Holy smoke!" he told Acker. "Some infantry officer is on the radio. He's excited as hell. Says you're right on the target. And get this, he wants us to fire 'Battery 100 rounds.'"

Acker laughed at the message. "Okay, boys," he told his crew. "Open those shell cases fast. Gun crews, prepare to fire at will."

Carr gave a running commentary over the radio throughout the onslaught. The shells are hitting the trees too high, he informed Acker at one point. Acker ordered his men to put in a delayed fuse, which allowed the shells to strike the trees and explode a second later as they hit the ground.

Seconds after the first delayed fuse had been fired, Carr came on the walkie-talkie: "Move over ten yards . . . and if you don't hear from me, you know you've got too close."

"In the next 15 minutes, the jungle hills rang as the two pack howitzers threw 134 shells into the Jap perimeter," wrote Dave Richardson. "The crews had been a bit slow two days before because they hadn't seen a howitzer in seven months, but now they performed as artillerymen should."

Frank Merrill had a weak heart and weak character, but it still brought him fame at the expense of the Marauders' real leader—Col. Charles Hunter.

Clarence Branscomb grins for the camera as he marches down the Ledo Road toward Burma, unconcerned by the ominous sign at the roadside: "God Be With You, Welcome to Borderville."

A Marauder patrol stands over a dead Japanese soldier. Note the height of the elephant grass on either side of the trail.

Captain Henry Stelling, one of the 2nd Battalion doctors, and his legendary backpack, which contained more than one hundred pounds of medical supplies.

Marauders shoot the breeze with the Chinese 1st Provisional Tank Group, commanded by Col. Rothwell Brown, after their arrival at Walawbum.

Lieutenant Colonel William Osborne, commander of the 1st Battalion, briefs his officers prior to the Shaduzup operation.

Marauders watch as a C-47 pilot drops supplies on the end of color-coded parachutes. Pilots would often approach the DZ at four hundred feet, risking a stall as they lowered the front of the aircraft and raised the tail, which made it easier for the kickers to heave out the bundles.

A patrol from the 1st Battalion returns from a scouting mission during the march toward Shaduzup. The bamboo forests were a serious impediment to the battalion's progress south.

The jungle was so dense in places in Burma that a man could vanish from sight if he stepped three feet off the trail. Here, a member of the communications platoon carries on his back a sixty-five-pound SCR 300 radio, a portable radio transceiver also known as a walkie-talkie.

A Browning heavy machine gun crew of the 3rd Battalion in action close to Nhpum Ga on April 6, 1944. Three days later, the siege was finally lifted.

Hsamshingyang, seen here from a supply aircraft, was the village four miles north of Nhpum Ga from where the 3rd Battalion made a series of gallant attempts to relieve the besieged 2nd Battalion.

Foxhole buddies Tech Sgt. J. C. Price (left) and Sgt. George E. Feltwell of the Blue Combat Team. The pair celebrated their birthdays together during the 2nd Battalion's epic engagement at Nhpum Ga.

The indomitable Lt. Col. George McGee, 2nd Battalion commander, is greeted by Lt. Col. Charles Beach (left), C.O. of the 3rd Battalion, shortly after the liberation of Nhpum Ga.

"His leadership was the main reason for our survival at Nhpum Ga," said one 2nd Battalion veteran of Lt. Col. George McGee, seen here shortly after the siege.

"McLogan's Hill" at Nhpum Ga was named after 1st Lt. Ted McLogan, who together with Roy Matsumoto outwitted the Japanese to devastating effect. *Ted McLogan*

Staff Sergeant Roy Matsumoto (right) and Sgt. Akiji Yoshimura were two of the Marauders' fourteen Nisei interpreters who performed such courageous and invaluable work in Burma.

Jack Howard helps bring in a wounded comrade from the 3rd Battalion's Orange Combat Team during the bitter fight to lift the siege at Nhpum Ga.

On April 9, 1944, Easter Sunday, the Marauders kneel in prayer at Hsamshingyang, shortly after the men of the 3rd Battalion broke through to their 2nd Battalion buddies at Nhpum Ga.

Taken at Hsamshingyang on April 20, 1944, this photo shows the ethnic mix of the Marauders. Back row, left to right: Harold Stevenson (Irish), Stephen Komar (Ukrainian), George Altman (German), Carl Hamelic (Dutch), Jose Montoya (Spanish), A. E. Quinn (Anglo-Burmese), D. G. Wilson (Anglo–Burmese), Joseph Yuele (Italian). Third row, left to right: Kai L. Wong (Chinese), Chester Dulian (Polish), Caifson Johnson (Swedish), Louis Perdomo (Cuban), Jack Crowley (American). Second row, left to right: Russell Hill (English), Werner Katz (Jewish), Miles Elson (Swedish), Francis Wonsowicz (Polish), Edward Kucera (Bohemian), Bernard Martin (French), Bill Smawley (English–Irish). Front row, left to right: Father James Stuart (Irish), N'Ching Gam (Kachin), Li Yaw Tank (Maru), Purta Singly (Nepalese), Hpakawn Zau Mun (Atzi).

Colonel Charles Hunter (right) briefs two of his officers shortly before he leads H Force on the punishing but ultimately successful march on the vital airstrip at Myitkyina.

Staff Sergeant Robert Passanisi of the 1st Battalion was a super radio operator whose skills were much in demand in Burma. His barber skills less so.

The march up the 6,100-foot Naura Hkyat Pass in the Kumon Mountains was a brutal test of endurance for Marauders and animals. Note that the horse in this photo is caring only a saddle and a few blankets, unlike the mules, which could bear up to two hundred pounds of equipment.

1. T/Sgt. Dave Richardson (Yank Magazine), 2. Capt. Clancy Topp, 3. T/Sgt.Warren Bechlen, 4. Sgt. David Quaid, 5. Cpl. William Safran, 6. Pvt. Joseph Razkowski, 7. Pvt. Daniel Novak, 8. Tillman Durdin (N.Y. Times).   Myitkyina Airstrip, May 19, 1944.   Photo by B. Hoffman

Myitkyina Airstrip on May 19—the press corps shelter from Japanese sniper fire. Dave Richardson of *Yank* magazine, far left, was with the Marauders every step of the way in Burma, while newsreel photographer David Quaid (4) marched with them over the Kumon mountains.

Three Marauders grab a well-earned rest, using a poncho as shelter from the heavy rain they often encountered. The improvised lean-to affords no protection against Burma's legion of insects.

The Marauders' defensive positions at the Myitkyina airstrip in July 1944 needed to be deep and secure to protect against the daily pounding by Japanese 157mm artillery.

Above the hellish din, Carr reported that the enemy soldiers were "squealing." An hour later, Acker crawled forward to survey the damage from Carr's vantage spot. "There were Japanese dripping out of the trees, parts of body falling out at times," he remembered. "We'd actually dug them out of the foxholes with delayed fuses."

★

As the 3rd Battalion attacked from the north and east, Capt. Tom Senff led his 254 men from the 1st Battalion west, down into the Hkuma Valley and along the riverbed. The trek was too much for five men, who dropped out from exhaustion, but the rest headed south to outflank the Japanese. At 1800 hours, the force turned north. They were less than a thousand yards from Nhpum Ga. They could hear firing from above, see fresh boot prints on the muddy trail, smell the stench hanging over the valley. Then to their front they spotted three enemy soldiers. Shots were exchanged, but no casualties incurred. Senff ordered his men to establish a block near the trail that linked Nhpum Ga to Kauri, while blocks were also set up on the narrow paths used to resupply the Japanese troops closest to the village. Then the 1st Battalion bivouacked for the night. Just 850 yards lay between them and the 2nd Battalion.

★

"Today is Easter," wrote Lieutenant Colonel McGee in the battalion diary on Sunday April 9. "Activity very slight. In fact we tried to stir some up."

North of Nhpum Ga, the Khaki Combat Team sent out an early-morning patrol. They encountered a lone enemy soldier, ragged and wild-eyed, an object clutched in his grasp. The Americans shot the Japanese. Then they saw what he'd been carrying—a human arm. Was it cannibalism, or had the soldier tried to fulfill the Japanese tradition of removing a body part from a fallen comrade (if the removal of the entire corpse wasn't possible) so that it could be burnt and the ashes sent to the Yasukuni Shrine?

★

At 0700 hours, transport planes appeared over Nhpum Ga and began dropping supplies into the village.

At 1000 hours, a patrol from the 3rd Battalion advanced up the hill after a sustained artillery and mortar barrage and reported "dead Japanese everywhere."

At 1100 hours, a patrol from the Orange Combat Team pushed toward the western perimeter of Nhpum Ga. An enemy machine gun opened fire, killing T5g Alfred Finn.

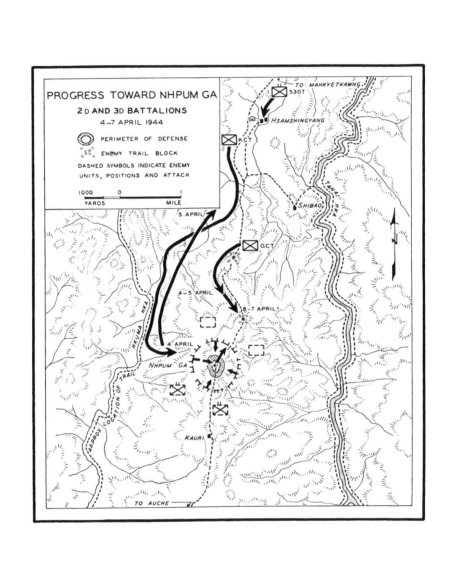

PROGRESS TOWARD NHPUM GA

2 D AND 3 D BATTALIONS

4–7 APRIL 1944

PERIMETER OF DEFENSE

ENEMY TRAIL BLOCK

DASHED SYMBOLS INDICATE ENEMY
UNITS, POSITIONS AND ATTACK

1000   0   MILE
YARDS

TO MAHKYETKAWNG
5307

HSAMSHINGYANG

KCT

SHIBAO

5 APRIL

O.C.

4–5 APRIL

6–7 APRIL

4 APRIL

NHPUM GA

KAURI

APPROX LOCATION OF TRAIL

HKUMA HKA

TANAI HKA

TO AUCHE

At 1200 hours, 2nd Lt. Winslow Stevens of the Orange Combat Team led his patrol toward the northern perimeter of Nhpum Ga. He was desperately close to the village, and it preyed on his mind that he could be shot by his own side.

Stevens thought he saw three figures through the undergrowth, just a glimpse, enough to see that they weren't dressed in tan. He started to curse at "the top of his voice" in a way no Japanese could ever hope to imitate.

Stevens paused before a thick patch of undergrowth, unsure of whether he should risk plunging inside. A few feet away on the other side of the undergrowth, George Rose lined up his Browning machine gun. "The three scouts ahead of my gun came back in line with me and said someone was coming through there," he recalled. "I set up the machine gun in position, and they lined up beside me."

Rose readied himself, waiting for the *banzai* charge, the next inevitable onslaught. "All at once, I could hear clear out of the blue a man cussing, and I knew no Japanese could cuss like that," said Rose. Stevens broke through the undergrowth and stood before Rose and his Browning machine gun. "I had witnessed some horrible sights at the back of my machine gun," recalled Rose. "That morning before noon, April 9, Easter Sunday, I witnessed the most wonderful sight I have ever seen."

For a moment, neither man spoke. Stevens stood and stared at the four pitiful figures in front of him, their green fatigues coated in red from the village clay. Rose spoke first. "Being Easter Sunday and all," he said, "I wasn't quite sure whether you were the Second Coming or not. But you sure look good to me."

"[3rd] Battalion broke through 1200," wrote McGee in the diary. "Boy, good to see them."

★

The bulk of the Japanese had withdrawn south during the night, scared away by the arrival of the 1st Battalion on the western flank and by the news that the Chinese 38th Division was fast approaching from the north. Demoralized and defeated in their attempt to retake the Hukawng Valley, the Japanese retreated to Kauri. Though they continued to fire a few resentful artillery salvos at Nhpum Ga for a further thirty-six hours, the battle for the small hilltop village was over.

The Americans counted four hundred Japanese bodies rotting outside the perimeter. Ed Kohler remembered recoiling in horror at the sight of "more than a hundred bodies stacked between two trees like cordwood."

The cost to the Marauders of holding Nhpum Ga was 52 dead and 163 wounded, a light casualty list compared to the Japanese. But it discounted the diseased, the exhausted, and the men whose minds, if not their bodies, had been shattered by the experience.

Throughout the afternoon of Sunday, April 9, and into Monday, the 1st and 3rd battalions trekked up the trail leading from Hsamshingyang to Nhpum Ga. They wished to see for themselves the site of their comrades' magnificent stand. Charlton Ogburn, leader of the 1st Battalion communication platoon, thought that the landscape surrounding the last thousand yards of the trail resembled a forest flattened by a tornado.

To others, the desolation put them in mind of the photographs of No Man's Land they had seen from the First World War battlefields. What few trees remained had been reduced to lacerated stumps. The dead were everywhere, courageous in life, grotesque in death. As Colonel Hunter strode up the trail accompanied by Master Sgt. Joe Doyer, he came across "the lower half of a bloated body looking forever like a pair of football pants stuffed with gear packed by a high school player for an out of town game." Elsewhere, Hunter saw evidence of cannibalism, of Japanese corpses minus arms and hands, or with the flesh "stripped from the bones as it were a glove."

Nhpum Ga was a small circle of hell. "The first thing I saw when I got in there was all these dead mules and horses, and dead Japanese corpses and billions of bluebottles," recalled Capt. James Hopkins. "It was an absolutely horrible situation."

Bernard Martin remembered "the bodies more than anything, mules and men crawling with maggots. It was a real mess. I had sort of got numb to it all, but seeing those bodies, swelling up . . ."

Some of the relieving force staggered to one side and threw up, their sense overwhelmed. Ogburn likened the sight of scores of dead bloated animal carcasses to a field of giant melons. Hunter, inspecting closer a wounded horse whose gray hair appeared odd, was "stunned to see that every inch of his body was covered by a mass of inanimate gray flies gorged into lifelessness from chewing on the helpless animal."

The survivors rose from their holes in the ground like the living dead. Ogburn remembered that they "looked at us out of red-rimmed eyes that were unnaturally round and dark, with death in them."

Some of the 2nd Battalion, wrote medical officer Henry Stelling, reeled around as if in a trance with a "hopeless staring attitude." Others talked loudly and incessantly, slapping their buddies on the back and breathing in the rank, foul air as if it were the sweetest perfume on earth. It was, remembered Lt. Ted McLogan, "the thrill of being alive."

As the survivors of the 2nd Battalion shuffled north down the trail toward Hsamshingyang, they were given a two-gun salute by John Acker and his crew. George Rose was so weak from dysentery that he was barely able to carry his weapon. "I was passing blood real bad, as most of our men were doing who had dysentery," he said. Rose, whose weight had dropped from 148 to 108 pounds, was among the seventy-seven men from the 2nd Battalion evacuated in the immediate aftermath of Nhpum Ga on account of sickness.

The 1st and 3rd battalions replaced the comrades in Nhpum Ga, and once flamethrowers had incinerated the carcasses, the village was doused with five hundred pounds of chloride of lime flown in on the orders of Hunter.

Dead Marauders who had been buried were they had fallen were uncovered and buried in three cemeteries, one for each battalion. Lieutenant Logan Weston organized the internment of the 3rd Battalion's dead. Over each grave, a bamboo cross was placed and then Weston conducted a memorial service. "Tears streamed down the faces of those battle-weary, rugged men," he recalled, as he read from Job 14: 1–7, which ended thus: "For there is hope for a tree, if it be cut down, that it will sprout again, and that its shoots will not cease."

Later, Weston wrote letters of condolence to the families of his men lost in action. To the family of Dan Carrigan, killed on April 4, he began: "This is a hard letter to write because the loss of my buddy, your son, is keenly felt."

Weston then described the events leading up to the death of Carrigan, the march of the Marauders through northern Burma, and the struggle to take the unnamed hilltop. He recounted the moment that Carrigan had been killed. "Know that your son gave his life nobly and unselfishly for that which we hold high and sacred to our hearts." Weston finished by describing the remote and peaceful cemetery in which Carrigan, a native of Chicago, had been laid to rest.

"If a man dies, shall he live again?" Yes, in the next life, but also in our memories. We picture him, much as you last saw him, only with a long red goatee. He had been growing it for over three months. And, really, it gave him a rather dignified appearance.

At Hsamshingyang, the remnants of the 2nd Battalion lay in the paddy fields under the sun, sleeping, eating, and smoking. Fresh uniforms were dropped, and they received their first mail in two months. Ted McLogan received so many letters—most from his sweetheart, Beatrice, back in Washington—that he hid them so that the men who got no correspondence wouldn't feel down.

Also flown in to Hsamshingyang was Capt. James W. Parker, a dentist, who showed scant sympathy for the men of the 2nd Battalion despite their recent ordeal. "They had one of those grinding machines that was operated by hand," remembered Vincent Melillo, a patient of Parker's. "It was a drill machine which they used to work on my teeth. They had to take a hammer and chisel to get one of my teeth out."

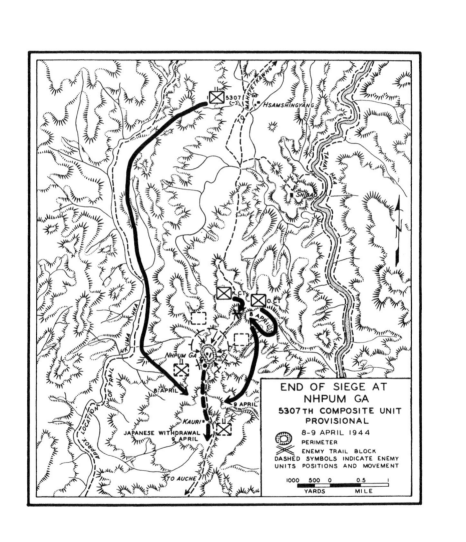

END OF SIEGE AT
NHPUM GA
5307TH COMPOSITE UNIT
PROVISIONAL
8-9 APRIL 1944

PERIMETER
ENEMY TRAIL BLOCK
DASHED SYMBOLS INDICATE ENEMY
UNITS POSITIONS AND MOVEMENT

1000 500 0   0.5   1
YARDS   MILE

CHAPTER 16

End Run to Myitkyina

Three weeks before the siege of Nhpum Ga began, the Japanese had launched an offensive to capture Imphal, the strategically important Indian town close to the frontier with Burma. Imphal was crucial to the Allies, a base containing supply dumps, airfields, and the Assam-Bengal railway, all of which supported Northern Combat Area Command's operations in both India and Burma.

The British were surprised by the offensive and unable to stem the initial Japanese advance into India. By March 29 the Japanese had severed the Imphal to Kohima road, leaving Imphal cut off from the outside world except by air. Once more, Stilwell cursed his British allies. If the Japanese succeeded in capturing Imphal and the British garrison at Kohima, he "would be isolated in Burma, all his effort and his hopes brought to nought with no outlook but another humiliation and no escape but another walkover, over the Hump to China itself."

On April 3, Stilwell met Adm. Louis Mountbatten and Field Marshal William Slim, commander of the British 14th Army, at Jorhat, an air base in Assam, to discuss the perilous situation in India. Stilwell offered to withdraw the 38th Chinese Division from northern Burma to help in the defense of Imphal. The British declined the proposal. Slim was confident his army could turn back the Japanese (Slim's soldiers would fight magnificently, repelling the Japanese during months of bloody fighting that climaxed in their victory at Kohima in June 1944), while Mountbatten recoiled at the political ramifications of allowing Chinese troops to fight in the last major outpost of the British Empire.

Stilwell flew back to his headquarters (now at Shaduzup) relieved that the situation around Imphal was in hand. True, the necessity of resupplying the British forces meant a reduction in the tonnage being flown over "The Hump" into China, but on the plus side Stilwell would not be required to deplete the strength of his forces in Burma in order to help out Slim.

Stilwell also saw an opportunity to humiliate the British while at the same time boosting the volume of supplies flown into China. His plan was to seize the airfield at Myitkyina from the Japanese, thereby denying their fighter planes the base from which to attack American cargo aircraft flying over the Himalayas. This in turn would allow the transport planes to fly a lower and more southerly course, increasing the monthly tonnage of resupply to China from 12,000 to 20,000 tons.

Stilwell now had five Chinese divisions under his command (the 50th had been added to the 14th and 30th) as well as the 3rd Indian Infantry Division, better known as the Chindits, which had been placed under his control following the death in an air accident on March 24 of Major General Wingate.

The Chindits, operating in twenty-six columns of four hundred men each, had flown into Burma in March and set up blockhouses deep in the jungle south of Myitkyina to prevent rail and road supplies reaching the Japanese 18th Division based at the airfield and nearby town. By April 21 Stilwell had devised the plan that he knew to be a "desperate gamble." With a combined force of Chinese and Marauders, he would capture Myitkyina by marching over the Kumon Mountains. The plan was a gamble because of its route—across terrain that the Japanese considered impassable. The Kachins themselves hadn't used the mountain trails over the Kumon Range for a decade or more. There were tales of giant snakes, man-eating tigers, and a sickness that cut down all but the toughest. And there were the mountains themselves.

But Stilwell had faith in the Marauders. "Galahad is OK," he wrote blithely in his diary, insisting on referring to them by their out-of-date title. "Hard fight at Nhpum Ga. Cleaned out Japs and hooked up. No worry there."

★

In the days after the lifting of the siege at Nhpum Ga, dozens of men were evacuated to the 20th General Hospital. By April 16, more than one hundred soldiers of the 2nd Battalion had been flown out while suffering from amoebic dysentery, malnutrition, skin diseases, and fevers. While the doctors tended to the physical needs of the Marauders, Charles Hunter set about restoring their spiritual well-being.

He organized the Marauders' answer to the Kentucky Derby, a race staged at Hsamshingyang between two of the unit's fastest mules. He ordered supplies of the cherished 10-to-1 rations. He arranged for a church service to be held by Father Thomas Barrett, the Marauders' chaplain who recently had arrived at the airstrip. Hunter permitted each soldier to send two V-mail letters saying they were in Burma. And he dreamed up a practical joke to play on Maj. Edward Hancock, the supply officer, who arrived to survey the site of the now-famous siege.

As Hancock bivouacked for the night in a Nhpum Ga foxhole, the Japanese suddenly attacked the village from the south. "*Banzai!*" they screamed as they came through the jungle. Only they weren't Japanese, they were Marauders, all in on the joke. Even Hancock saw the funny side. Eventually.

On April 18, Hunter judged that the time had come to have the three battalions assemble on the parade ground. "Believe it or not we are having close order drill 4 miles from Japs," an incredulous Sgt. James McGuire told his diary.

Lieutenant Sam Wilson recalled that initially the men thought Hunter "crazy" in ordering them to parade deep in the jungle. "Then it dawned on us that he knew exactly what he was doing," said Wilson. "He was reestablishing the military nature of the organization, an organization that had been spread all over Hell's half acre and was about to come apart. By lining us up and standing at attention, saluting, and making guidons out of colored parachutes and so on, he hammered us back into shape."

As the Marauders drilled, they became aware of rumors passed from company to company, platoon to platoon, squad to squad. The gossip "persisted like a mosquito, whining around your head." The men weren't pulling out of Burma, as they'd been led to believe. Rather, they were going to seize the airfield at Myitkyina. That was the rumor, at least, though there was no official confirmation.

As astonished as every other Marauder, Sam Wilson likened Stilwell to "a guy at the gaming tables who was going to make one last, big splurge when he should have known that he had spent all his luck." What had kept them going during those bleak preceding weeks was the thought of weeks of R&R in India at the end of it all, "a chance to put on a little weight, to loll around in the sun, to drink some Bullfighter brandy and Rosa rum, and to chase Indian girls." But no, they were to be thrown back into the fray.

Hunter first learned of Stilwell's intentions when Col. Henry Kinnison, one of the general's staff officers, had flown into Nhpum Ga shortly after the end of the siege. At that stage, Stilwell was only considering the possibility of marching the Marauders across the Kumon Mountains to Myitkyina. Hunter knew that once Stilwell had an idea, he usually carried it through to fruition. In anticipation of the operation, Hunter consulted the guide, Jack Girsham, and an Irish missionary, Father James Stuart, as to the feasibility of blazing a trail through the mountains. Complementing their advice with the knowledge of local Kachins, Hunter dispatched his intelligence officer, Capt. William Laffin, to survey the route.

Based on all this intelligence, Hunter drafted a "staff study" of the proposed operation, explaining that any advance on Myitkyina would entail a twenty-mile backtrack north and then a seventy-mile march on a trail that hadn't been used by the Kachins for ten years.

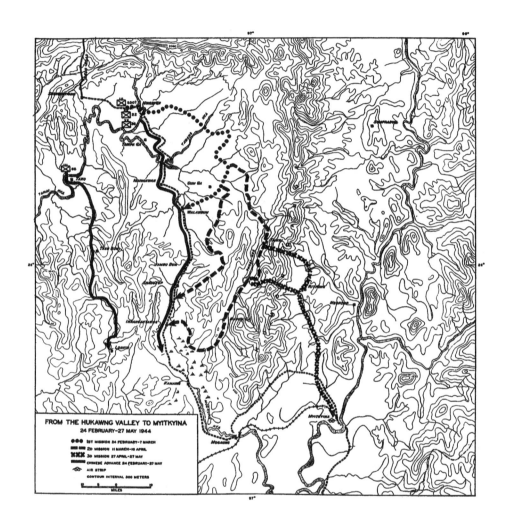

FROM THE HUKAWNG VALLEY TO MYITKYINA
24 FEBRUARY–27 MAY 1944

●●● 1ST MISSION 24 FEBRUARY–7 MARCH
▬▬ ▬▬ 2D MISSION 11 MARCH–10 APRIL
✕✕✕ 3D MISSION 27 APRIL–27 MAY
▬▬▬▬ CHINESE ADVANCE 24 FEBRUARY–27 MAY
⌂ AIR STRIP
CONTOUR INTERVAL 300 METERS

MILES

Ordered by Stilwell to send a staff officer to his HQ, Hunter dispatched his adjutant, Louis Williams. He returned a couple of days later with confirmation that they were indeed to march on Myitkyina. Williams also informed Hunter of a curious incident with Frank Merrill. The general was feeling much better after his heart trouble, asking for news of the Marauders and declaring his pride when he learned of their victory at Nhpum Ga.

Merrill was also interested with Hunter's staff study, so much in fact that he took it away to study in greater depth over lunch. A few hours later at the staff conference, Merrill "presented to General Stilwell a plan for the capture of the airstrip." It was a thorough plan, one that elicited warm praise from Stilwell, who admired its thoroughness. The only oversight on Merrill's part was his failure to tell Stilwell the name of the study's real author.

The orders carried by Williams for Hunter instructed him to lead the Marauders to Naubum, approximately twenty-five miles north along the trail and close to the jumping-off point for the march toward Myitkyina. The men began moving out on April 22, just as the monsoon season gave notice of its approach with a shower that deposited "drops as big as dimes" on the men's heads. The monsoon traveled north from the Bay of Bengal, carried on a wind that slapped into the barrier of the Himalayas. Unable to surmount these towering peaks, the rain fell on northern Burma, turning the region from May to September into one of the wettest places on earth. Some days it could rain as much twenty-five inches.

There were other ominous signs, too, as the Marauders began once more to make demands of their bodies. On April 24, the 3rd Battalion marched eight miles and saw five men drop out in what Sgt. James McGuire described to his diary as the "hottest day I've hiked yet." They reached Naubum on April 26 to discover General Stilwell waiting to greet them. "I guess it's another mission," McGuire wrote in his diary, adding the next day: "Got our mission, it's Myitkyina."

When he arrived at Naubum, Hunter described it as "alive with activity" with many new *bashas* under construction close to the airstrip. Hunter shook hands with Merrill and was then introduced to several staff officers who constituted Headquarters Myitkyina Task Force. Hunter was informed that he would command the task force in the field, which comprised the Marauders, the 150th Infantry Regiment of the 50th Chinese Division, and the 88th Regiment of the Chinese 30th Division.

Though Hunter had been appointed commander of the six thousand-strong Myitkyina Task Force, the unit was to operate as three separate entities—H Force, K Force, and M Force. K Force, commanded by Colonel Henry Kinnison, comprised the 3rd Battalion, the 88th Chinese Infantry Regiment (approximately 2,500 strong), and the Marauders' two howitzers.

Hunter was in charge of H Force, composed of the 1st Battalion and the Chinese 150th Regiment, including a battery of 75mm pack howitzers. M Force, led by Lieutenant Colonel McGee, comprised his 2nd Battalion and three hundred Kachin guerrilla fighters.

The mission allocated to K Force and H Force was to march northward from Naubum to Taikri and then wheel east into the Kumon Mountains, climbing through the 6,100-foot Naura Hkyat Pass and down to Ritpong. Once at Ritpong, approximately forty miles north of Myitkyina, the forces would split and advance on the airfield in a two-pronged drive. The role of M Force was to patrol the Senjo Ga-Hkada Ga area, blocking any attempt by the Japanese to advance from the south and also diverting enemy attention away from H Force and K Force.

Once Merrill had outlined the mission, he promised that once the airstrip had been seized, the Marauders "would be relieved and flown to an already selected site where a rest and recreational area would be constructed." He mentioned a sum of money that had been set aside for this express purpose. In short, concluded Merrill, though he appreciated that the Marauders were pretty beat up, what was required was one final effort, what Stilwell termed the "end run" to Myitkyina.

★

As K Force prepared to lead off the Myitkyina Task Force, it received a new recruit, an Army cameraman named Sgt. Dave Quaid. Quaid was a twenty-four-year-old from New York City with a 1-A physique but 4-F eyesight. Having been rejected by the infantry, Quaid joined the 161st Signal Photo Company and trained as a motion picture cameraman. The military had been slow to appreciate the propaganda benefits of filming frontline action, of allowing the folks back home to see for themselves the courage and superiority of their boys, but eventually, in January 1944, Quaid and his Bell & Howell Eyemo camera were posted to India, from where he made his way to Burma, arriving at Maingkwan shortly after news broke of the Marauders' stand at Nhpum Ga. Intrigued, Quaid set out to film the Marauders. "The first thing I did at Naubum was to find out where I could find General Merrill," recalled Quaid. "He was sitting on the steps of a *basha* hut. I walked up to him, said my name is Sergeant Quaid, a photographer, and that I wanted to join him on his next mission. He said that would be great, and I could come along."

Merrill, never slow to exploit an opportunity for publicity, invited Quaid to take some footage of himself in earnest discussion with General Stilwell. "The two Generals conferred in the middle of the strip [and] I was able to make some very good close-ups of the two generals," said Quaid. As luck would have it, a C-47 was making its last resupply run as Quaid filmed the two men, a dramatic backdrop to the auspicious occasion.

With the filming over, Quaid was told to attach himself to the radio unit of K Force, which was Bernard Martin and his crew from the Orange Combat Team. "They were very gracious and made room for me around their bamboo campfire," recalled Quaid. Martin also found some space for Quaid's camera and his twenty-four rolls of motion picture film on one of their mules. In return, Quaid told the radio team about the fame of the Marauders back home. Everyone was talking about them.

Elsewhere in K Force, there was a sense of foreboding at what lay ahead. Of the original 3,000 men who had volunteered for the Marauders a little over six months earlier, approximately 1,600 remained. The 1st and 3rd battalions were each operating at a strength of 550, and the 2nd Battalion was down to 500 men. Of these many were sick, but damned if they'd leave their buddies in the lurch. With the same bloody-minded determination that they had displayed at Nhpum Ga, the Marauders vowed to complete Stilwell's "end run" to Myitkyina. After all, recalled Capt. James Hopkins, one of K Force's doctors, "General Merrill's promise that the Marauders were to be flown out of Burma as soon as the airfield was captured was now common knowledge. This promise, from a general who had their confidence and trust, went a long way in boosting their resolve to accomplish the impossible."

CHAPTER 17

Blazing the Mountain Trail

The march to Myitkyina was one of the most awesome accomplishments of the war. One of the most awesome and most awful. It proved to be as bad as every Marauder secretly feared, what Bernard Martin described "as a trail of sadness."

Staff Sgt. James McGuire, like Martin a member of K Force, chronicled the agony in his diary.

4/28/44—Raining. 6:30am started hiking, went up 2600 ft, really a tough climb. We have 6000 ft mt to go over and it's really raining and muddy. Bivouacked at village, water scarce. The path is a 20% incline.

4/29/44—Really rained last nite. Went up 4000 more ft, going tough. Lost a lot of horses, they fell over cliffs, had to be shot. Lost about 12 horses and mules.

4/30/44 (5/2/44)—Raining . . . hills muddy you can't hardly climb them. Lost some more animals. Equipment has to be hand carried.

Cameraman Dave Quaid recalled that when a mule fell off the trail, "the men went down on ropes and picked up radios, picked up heavy weapons, picked up mortar rounds and ammunition, and got them back up on the trail." Some of the mules fell hundreds of feet to their death, taking their precious cargoes with them. Ammunition, mortars, and rations could be resupplied, but not the unit records, including recommendations for decorations earned at Nhpum Ga.

Halfway up the 6,100-foot pass, Quaid was "carrying an Eyemo camera that weighed about fifteen pounds, twenty-four rolls of film which weighed fifteen or twenty pounds, my rations, my carbine with four clips of ammo, first aid kit, machete, poncho, shelter half, two canteens, and my pack." On some of the short, steep sections of the trail, recalled Bernard Martin, the mules were unburdened of their hundred-pound packsaddles. "We would unload the mules to get them by and then, after they had been manhandled, the load had to be lugged up the mountain and the mule reloaded."

Men began reducing the weight they were carrying to the bare minimum. Some cut their blankets in half to save weight, others threw away letters from home, and one or two, like Quaid, cut the handle off their toothbrush. Anything to lighten the load.

With no man having passed up the trail for a decade or more, the jungle had long since reclaimed it, and its inhabitants were fearless of the sudden intruders. "You'd see pythons lying across the trail," recalled Martin. "They were so long, we didn't know which end was the tail and which end the head. You had a few hundred men carefully stepping over these huge pythons."

One time, some of the men in Logan Weston's I&R platoon were trying to push a recalcitrant 1,200-pound mule up the trail. "Get up, you son-of-a-bitch!" yelled one soldier. "You volunteered for this mission, too!" His buddies laughed, and two men got their shoulders behind the mule's rump and started to push, their feet braced against a fallen tree lying across the muddy trail. Suddenly, the tree "began to crawl" and the pair screamed and took to their heels. Weston estimated that the python was twenty-five feet in length.

The men slept on the trail, only a blanket for warmth against the bitterly cold nights, with their heads toward the summit. So steep was the incline that some Marauders had the sensation of standing up as they dozed.

On April 30, K Force approached the summit of the Naura Hkyat Pass, but the closer they got to the 6,100-foot pinnacle, the tougher the trail. Men dug steps in the mud with their entrenching tools and heaved themselves up, reaching back a hand in the rain for their buddy. Other times, they grabbed hold of a vine and pulled. It was exhausting, relentless, cruel work. "More than once I lay on my back, pushed my battle pack over my head, and with my heels digging into the slimy, spongy soil, I wormed my way up the steepest slopes," recalled Logan Weston.

Dave Quaid was struggling as they neared the top of the pass. On one of their hourly breaks, he slumped to the side of the trail, his camera bag at his feet and his head in his hands. "An infantry squad came up the trail," he recalled. "One of them reached down and picked up my musette bag. He was a bearded young man and he said, 'I'll see you at the top of the mountain, Sergeant.'"

Ashamed of himself, Quaid struggled to his feet and "started up the trail after the stranger." At the top of the pass, Pvt. Bill Toomey handed over the musette bag to Quaid and the pair then looked out over Burma. "While we were climbing the mountain to get to the crest, the officers who had maps were saying that once we reached the summit of the pass, it would be all downhill from there," said Quaid. "Now at the summit and looking south along the trail, all I could see was an endless series of razor-sharp ridges. Each looked as bad as the one we had just climbed."

From the summit of the pass, K Force descended through the jungle, eventually bivouacking in a small valley close to the deserted village of Salawng-Hkayang. By May 3, James McGuire was out of rations and subsisting on "banana hearts and bouillon." Captain James Hopkins went for a walk as they waited for a resupply and came across a raspberry patch heavy with ripe fruit. It was a welcome distraction for his troubled mind. Hopkins was concerned by the growing number of men falling ill with a mysterious disease. It began with a chilly sensation and then developed into a very high fever, blinding headache, and, in several cases, a rash. His fear was that it might be Tsutsugamushi fever, known also as scrub typhus, an often fatal disease transmitted by a bite from a mite, a human parasite about 0.01 inch in length that infested Burma's elephant grass.

★

H Force had started out for the Kumon Range on April 29 with Colonel Hunter full of good cheer, insisting that the Kumons were in fact hills and not mountains. He drove the men on at such a fearsome pace that soon the front of the three-mile column was closing in on the stragglers from K Force. Men riddled with disease lay by the trail too weak to go on, oblivious to the rain and uncaring of the plump leeches that sucked at their blood. Hunter, who roamed up and down his column of men, ordered them to their feet. "Sympathy is a luxury which I seldom passed out," he admitted, "and one which was embarrassing when offered to me by my subordinates." Nonetheless, inwardly Hunter felt for his men, aware that the hike was "slow, tedious and brutal." Onward he urged them, encouraging them to keep going because the end was in sight, and "with this mission under our belts even Stilwell would be incapable of dreaming up more misery with which to try our weary bodies and sear our already scarred souls."

Hunter allowed the column a ten-minute break every hour, counting down the time on his watch. To the weary Marauders, it felt like ten seconds. There was no shooting the breeze now. Talking required effort. Some men sat and stared off into the distance, their minds numb with the horror of it all. Others stepped into the jungle, lowered their drawers, and emptied their bowels. If there was blood in their diarrhea, they reported it; otherwise they pulled up their pants and carried on. As they neared the summit, the temperature dropped and the jungle thinned out, allowing the sun to lighten both the trail and the men's morale. "When I arrived at the top of the hill and felt the warm sunshine . . . my spirits perked up," remembered Hunter. "I headed for the drop zone to observe the drop already in progress."

By the time Hunter hiked the five miles to Salawng-Hkayang, the 3rd Battalion had moved to another bivouac area two miles beyond the drop zone to allow space for the Chinese 88th Regiment. It was raining but it was also stifling hot, and the men lay steaming under their ponchos, taking the weight off feet that in some cases were nothing more than lumps of rotting white flesh. Marauders who suffered from the severest case of what was termed "jungle foot rot" threw away their boots and marched with their swollen, bleeding feet swaddled in strips of blankets. Every man stank to high heaven, a terrible sour smell, the result of what happened when the rain drenched sweat-soaked uniforms and then the sun dried them out.

Lieutenant Logan Weston, a veteran of the South Pacific, had never encountered weather like it. "Hour after hour, day after day, week after week of being continually soaked to the skin," he recalled. "Accompanied by the ever-present cacophony of the rain beating on the jungle canopy overheard." Weston had his faith with which to sustain him; so did every Marauder, though it wasn't necessarily the same as Weston's. It was a more tangible faith, the belief in each other, the belief that only by sharing the misery and the hardships together would they accomplish their mission.

It was as if the monsoon had washed away each soldier's pretense, the façade that he had erected during his early adulthood, to reveal underneath the real man. For most Marauders, what lay beneath the exterior proved tough and durable, a steely inner core that earned the respect of their comrades. The Marauders may not have had the energy to go around slapping each other on the back and spouting trite words of encouragement, but a look was enough, a glance in another man's eyes to let him know they were going to see it through to the end.

K Force struck camp at 0800 hours and started southeast on the seven-mile march to Ritpong, a village that, according to Kachin scouts, contained a company of Japanese. Khaki Combat Team's I&R platoon led the way, and by sundown on May 5 they had reached a trail junction one mile north of Ritpong. Intelligence reports in the possession of Colonel Kinnison indicated there was a "trail which encircled Ritpong to the west and joined another trail south of the village." No such trail was found. "The situation screwed up, it's muddy and raining going tough," wrote Sgt. James McGuire in his diary that night. "Move on tomorrow."

Early on May 6, the men of the Khaki Combat Team began hacking their way through the jungle northwest of Ritpong with the intention of establishing a block on the trail south of the village. Once that was in place, two companies from the Chinese 88th Regiment would launch a frontal assault on the village.

Cameraman Dave Quaid accompanied Khaki as they waded into the jungle, their aching arms wielding machetes against the hard, unyielding bamboo. "The men cutting the trail could only last about five minutes," recalled Quaid. "Fresh men had to take over to move ahead . . . the bamboo was so thick and so heavy that two men in the lead were needed to chop with their machetes. The bamboo was like tree trunks, eight to ten inches in diameter; not the slim fishing rods we used as kids."

As the Khaki Combat Team soldiers neared the trail to the south of Ritpong, they spotted three Japanese soldiers approaching the village carrying bundles of food. Whatever it was, it smelled divine. As soon as the Marauders reached the trail, they established a block to prevent any further access to or from the village; then some were sent south to seek out the enemy kitchen. It was found a few hundreds yard down the trail, in a *basha* that was empty other than for "braised water buffalo, cans of Japanese fish packed in Japan, and many kinds of Japanese food." The booty was gathered up and shared among the ravenous Marauders.

Meanwhile, Quaid had crawled closer to Ritpong, taking refuge in a small trench dug around a clump of bamboo, one of many such trenches built by the Kachins to catch rainwater. This was then sucked by the bamboo, which provided the Kachins with an important source of water.

Quaid got to talking to the young Marauder already occupying the water-filled trench. He introduced himself as Charles Page from Samson, Alabama. Quaid asked him his age, and Page replied he would be turning eighteen in a few hours' time.

By nightfall, the Japanese were aware of the block to their south, and bored soldiers fired the occasional burst down the trail toward the Americans. Quaid was crawling through the bamboo when he suddenly "heard the sharp crack of a rifle, and simultaneously, I heard a strangled sound." Quaid hurried back to the trench to discover that Page had been shot in the chest by a fluke enemy bullet. He was carried back to the aid station, and Capt. Paul Armstrong, one of the battalion doctors, did the best he could with the scant resources at his disposal. But Page's wounds proved too serious, and he died a few days later.*

To the sound of bugles, the Chinese attacked Ritpong on May 7, launching their assault from the northwest as the Khaki Combat Team rained down mortar bombs on the village from the south. It was the first time in history that American and Chinese soldiers had fought together

---

*In some accounts, Page died a few hours after he had been shot, but according to the diary of James McGuire, he succumbed to his injuries on May 11.

against a common enemy, and by May 9 the alliance had overwhelmed the Japanese defenders of Ritpong.

The battle for Ritpong allowed H Force to close the gap on K Force, but it also presented a problem for Colonel Hunter: Their presence in the Hpungin Valley was now known by the Japanese. Hunter therefore ordered K Force to make a feint by heading for Tingkrukawng, twenty miles east, where the Japanese were holding out against a British-led Kachin and Gurkha force trying to capture a supply base at Nsopzup. This move would not only aid their allies, it might also fool the Japanese into diverting troops away from Myitkyina, allowing H Force to march unimpeded the thirty-five miles southeast to the airstrip.

While Hunter formulated this new plan, he ordered H Force to construct an airstrip at Arang, the headquarters of OSS in the area, so that casualties from the battle for Ritpong could be speedily evacuated and a resupply effected. However, it wasn't just battle casualties who needed airlifting to the hospital; the rate of soldiers succumbing to the mysterious illness had reached alarming proportions. Captain James Hopkins by now had the opportunity to discuss the situation with the medical team from H Force, and they disclosed that at Naubum several cases of scrub typhus had been confirmed among Marauders.

Waiting for Hunter at Arang was Frank Merrill, recently arrived in a liaison plane from Naubum and anxious to learn when H Force expected to reach its target. Hunter briefed the general on the situation, and the two men drew up a strategy for the seizure of the airstrip. Forty-eight hours before the estimated time of attack, Hunter would radio the code words "Cafeteria Lunch" to Merrill. Twenty-four hours prior to the attack, he would radio "Strawberry Sundae." The code words "In the Ring" would indicate that the assault was underway. Once the airstrip was secure and usable, Hunter would radio "Merchant of Venice."

Hunter then asked Merrill the role of H Force once the airstrip was secured. "You don't have to worry," replied Merrill. "I'll be the first man on the field." Hunter pressed Merrill for more information. Should he attack the town of Myitkyina, two miles east of the airstrip? "What is the big picture?" he asked. "Don't worry," said Merrill. "I'll be there and take over."

CHAPTER 18

A Force of Will

Early on May 11, K Force marched east from the Ritpong area toward Tingkrukawng. "The hottest [day] yet, some fell out from heat exhaustion," wrote James McGuire in his diary. They bivouacked near a river that evening, and the men bathed and washed their stinking clothes. McGuire lost his dog tags in the water as well as his lucky half coin that he'd carried for over two years.

The next day was even hotter, though the rain continued to fall in cords. There were still ten miles to Tingkrukawng, and the trail wound its way down through the jungle, a descent that lowered the altitude and increased the humidity—a paradise for all the worst forms of wildlife. "Swarms of insects thrived and leeches were continually attacking the men," recalled Capt. James Hopkins. One type of leech targeted its victims from above, dropping from trees on the Marauders as they passed underneath and burrowing its head into their warm flesh. There were also clouds of black buffalo flies and huge malaria-carrying mosquitoes.

There was now barely a fully fit man in K Force. Minds were dulled by disease and reactions blunted by fatigue, even in the I&R platoon of the Orange Combat Team. As they scouted the trail to Tingkrukawng, the lead scout saw forty or so soldiers a hundred yards ahead on a narrow ridge, one of whom shouted the Chinese greeting "*ding how.*" The scout waved back, and then the Japanese began firing. One Marauder was killed, and the rest went into their familiar wedge formation.

Further back down the trail, Lieutenant Colonel Beach began barking orders to the Orange Combat Team and issuing instructions to the mortar section. Then he strode toward the firefight. Dave Quaid went with him, his camera in his left hand and a carbine in the right. "I ran up a small jungle-covered slope, then down the other side in the direction of the

171

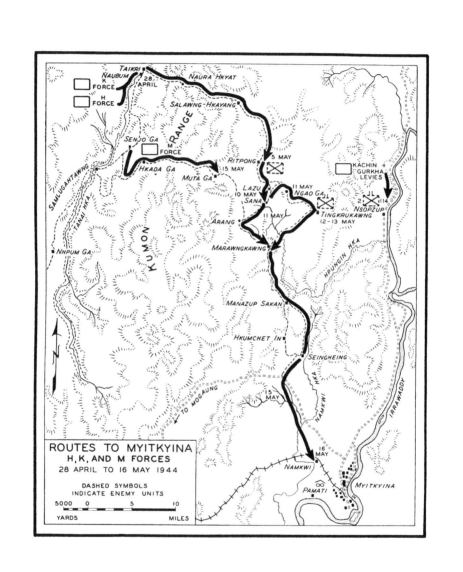

ROUTES TO MYITKYINA
H, K, AND M FORCES
28 APRIL TO 16 MAY 1944

DASHED SYMBOLS
INDICATE ENEMY UNITS

5000   0   5   10

YARDS   MILES

firing," he recalled. "Bullets were flying all around me, knocking pieces off the bamboo. Every time a shot went through a clump of bamboo, it exploded a number of sections. Every shot sounded like a machine gun."

Quaid crawled forward toward the skirmish line established by Beach, who appeared to be having the time of his life despite the fact that the Japanese were no more than twenty yards through the jungle. Quaid questioned what he was doing so close to the enemy. "My job," replied Beach. He invited Quaid to take some shots of his boys fighting the Japs. "I'm taking them right now," insisted Quaid. He captured Master Sgt. John Keslik on film firing a rifle grenade before turning the camera on the 3rd Battalion's commander. "At one point, Colonel Beach missed a shot and it irked him," remembered Quaid. "He jumped up and ran forward at the Japanese and threw a hand grenade right into their position."

Quaid moved back toward the trail to take some more footage, and then he sheltered behind a tree while he put a fresh hundred-foot roll of film in the camera. "I got it loaded and went trotting right up the middle of the trail, very excited, for I knew that I was getting good combat film," remembered Quaid. Suddenly from the jungle, he heard someone shout "Dave." It was Bill Toomey, the bearded Marauder who had carried his camera bag up the last section of the Naura Hkyat Pass. Toomey was setting up a fire position for his Browning heavy machine gun. "What the hell's the matter with you?" he asked Quaid. "What are you doing in the middle of the trail?"

Quaid stepped off the trail, and in the same instant a Japanese light machine gun began firing. "The Jap gunner was good," reflected Quaid. "He walked the bullets up the trail toward me. He fired low anticipating that I would hit the dirt, and he was just starting to raise the stream of bullets up." Quaid took a chance and dived right, and "as I flew through the air, I heard a smack like someone hitting a side of beef with a cleaver," he recalled. "The Jap traversed his gun after me as I rolled down the slope. When I got to the bottom, I found myself behind an eight-inch tree. I kept my head down, and heard tinkle, tinkle, tinkle on my helmet. I looked up very carefully with just my eyes, keeping my chin into the dirt, and all I could see were sharp, white splinters falling down on me. They were coming out of the back of the tree as the Japanese bullets went right through the trunk!"

For a moment, Quaid couldn't believe he was still in one piece. He checked himself out but, no, he hadn't been hit. Then the cry went up from somewhere above. "Medic!" Quaid scrambled up the slope and saw Father Barrett giving the Last Rites to a soldier. It was only when the Chinese stretcher-bearers arrived and lifted the dying man on to the litter that Quaid saw who it was. "The awful slap that I had heard was the bullet hitting and killing Bill Toomey," said Quaid. "Here was one of those tricks of fate when a man does another person a good deed and pays hard coin for it."*

The Marauders laid Toomey to rest later in the day after the Japanese had been driven back. Quaid got permission from Father Barrett to film the burial, and his camera began to roll as Toomey was lowered into the ground wrapped in his poncho. The dead man's buddies asked Quaid what the hell he thought he was doing. He was accused of being "sacrilegious." One or two were violently upset. Then Barrett spoke up on Quaid's behalf, calming them and saying Quaid needed to film the burial "to show people that war is not just exciting scenes, [that] there is a price to be paid in eighteen-year-old boys."

The fighting just west of Tingkrukawng continued for another twenty-four hours, until the late afternoon of May 13, by which time five more Marauders were dead and fourteen wounded. The Chinese had suffered comparable losses. With intelligence reports indicating that Japanese reinforcements were on their way, Colonel Kinnison decided that K Force had achieved its mission; it was time to withdraw and head toward Myitkyina to help H Force in securing the airstrip.

---

*Quaid was "always bothered" by the manner of Toomey's death and years later paid for a memorial bell in his name at his daughter's New York school.

CHAPTER 19

"Will This Burn Up
the Limeys!"

The suspense for General Stilwell as H Force closed on the airstrip at Myitkyina was excruciating. On May 1, three days after the Task Force had set out east across the Kumon Mountains, he had written in his diary: "Will they meet a reinforced garrison [at the airstrip]? Does it mean we'll fail on both sides, instead of only one? Can I get them out? . . . The die is cast, and it's sink or swim. But the nervous wear and tear is terrible."

Stilwell had taken his gamble without telling his Allies for fear of losing face in front of the British. Admiral Lord Louis Mountbatten, commander of SEAC, had always maintained that Myitkyina couldn't be taken in the monsoon season, but that, to Stilwell, was further evidence of British pusillanimity. It could be taken—by him.

On May 14, Colonel Hunter flashed the signal "Cafeteria Lunch" to Merrill at Task Force Headquarters, and Merrill in turn informed Stilwell. "I told Merrill to roll on in and swing on 'em," Stilwell wrote in his diary.

The following day, H Force suffered a setback when their Kachin guide stepped on a snake as they approached the upper Namkwi River. The snake vanished before it could be identified, but whatever it was, it was venomous. The guide rapidly deteriorated, and when medical officer John McLaughlin reached the scene, two officers were trying to suck out the poison. McLaughlin radioed Hunter further back down the column requesting permission to use a flashlight to treat the guide. "Affirmative," replied Hunter, who remained with his ear glued to the set waiting for news. A few minutes later, McLaughlin reported that the guide's leg was badly swollen and it was imperative that he rest up for the night. "Doc, he has got to go on until he collapses," replied Hunter. "Too much depends on this man."

A stand-off ensued over the airwaves, with McLaughlin insisting the man was too sick to be moved and Hunter appreciating the doctor's devotion to the "precepts of the Hippocratic Oath" but adamant as commander that he had to overrule the most humane course of action for the one "which shows promise of contributing to the success of the mission." Eventually, a compromise was reached with the sickening guide, a former forest ranger with an intimate knowledge of the best route to take toward the airstrip. The man would be strapped to a horse.

★

At dusk on May 16, the still feverish guide led H Force into the village of Namkwi, four miles northwest of the airstrip and close to the Mogaung-Myitkyina Railroad. Hunter had the inhabitants interned for the night, just in case any were in the pay of the Japanese. A telephone line was tapped and a Nisei interpreter eavesdropped on the enemy conversation: It was a quiet night in Myitkyina, no mention of a column marching down from the north. Hunter sent the code words "Strawberry Sundae" to Merrill. Twenty-four hours and counting.

That was the good news for Hunter; the bad news concerned the state of his men. There were now more sick than healthy, and the previous day thirty-two of the weakest men had been left in the village of Seingheing in the hands of a fit medic.*

Hunter's intelligence of the airstrip was minimal. He had a map and an aerial reconnaissance photograph, which showed the location of the enemy defenses but didn't tell him if they were occupied or not. The airstrip was in an unknown condition and surrounded by flat, open terrain. An advance on the airstrip without a proper reconnoiter could result in carnage.

Hunter called for Lt. Sam Wilson, but Wilson was sick with amoebic dysentery. Instead, he sent for Clarence Branscomb. Branscomb and Hunter had much in common; neither was sick, for a start, but they shared similar character traits: a dry wit, an intolerance of frippery, and a tough but compassionate inner core.

It was a little before 2100 hours when Branscomb presented himself to his commanding officer. Looking up from his map, Hunter—who was nursing a bottle of Canadian Club whiskey—instructed Branscomb "to investigate all the gun emplacements to see if they were manned, then walk

*Hunter asked for these sick men to be air evacuated, but low clouds prevented this and they were forced to stagger back to Arang, where they were eventually rescued.

the airstrip to see if all the bombs had been repaired." Hunter appreciated he was giving Branscomb "a hell of an assignment," so he sent him on his way with what remained of the whiskey.

Branscomb returned to the I&R platoon, briefed them on the mission, and asked for a couple of volunteers, dangling before their eyes the bottle of Canadian Club as if it were the juiciest carrot in Burma. Tom Frye and Walter Clark stepped forward, and the three of them "killed the Canadian Club." They then set off south using a luminous compass with Branscomb cradling his Thompson submachine gun. It was his weapon of choice, even though other soldiers found it heavy and prone to climb on automatic fire. Branscomb reckoned it was "effective when giving them little squirts."

For about two and a half hours, they saw and heard nothing. Suddenly, they stopped dead. "We heard talking and, as we crept closer, finally saw lights from work crews," recalled Branscomb. "We were fairly tense, and as we crept around in the grass trying to get a better view and find some pillboxes, the Japanese started packing and leaving."

Branscomb figured that the crews had knocked off for the night, now that it was 0000 hours. He watched as they climbed aboard their trucks and drove away toward billets on the east side of the strip near the southern end. Once the last light on the airfield had been extinguished, the three Marauders continued their reconnaissance. "We crawled around in the grass trying to work our way around the airport perimeter," recounted Branscomb. "After almost knifing each other a few times, at about 2.30 a.m. I picked up the radio and started walking down the middle of the runway, thinking if those emplacements were occupied we'd soon find out."

Branscomb walked the length of the runway without interference, noting that it was compacted gravel approximately 5,000 feet in length and 150 feet wide and "checkerboarded with fifty-five-gallon oil drums." Other than that, it was clear and in good condition. He communicated the fact to Hunter, who was stunned to learn that Branscomb had strolled brazenly down the middle of the airstrip as if it were a sidewalk in his native California. He praised the patrol for their "remarkable job," for furnishing him with a compass course that could be followed by H Force, and for a detailed layout of the defenses, including the important fact that there was no wire or occupied gun nests.

Working on the intelligence supplied to him by Branscomb, Hunter drew up a plan, then assembled his officers in the early hours and issued his attack order. "The 150th [Chinese] regiment was to deploy in front of the bivouac area on a broad front, move directly on, and overrun the airstrip stopping on the southeast side to dig in and hold against any counter-attack," Hunter recorded. Lieutenant Colonel Osborne's 1st Battalion was tasked with seizing the ferry terminal at Pamati, one mile southwest of the airstrip, thereby giving Hunter control of the nearest crossing of the Irrawaddy River.

★

The attack began at 1030 hours on May 17 with Hunter riding "up and down in front of the troops on my horse," exhorting them to drive the enemy away from the airstrip. They did just that in an almost flawless operation that by noon had secured H Force their objective. Most of the Japanese had chosen to flee and not fight, racing back to Myitkyina in a convoy of trucks.

Lieutenant Colonel Osborne left the Red Combat Team to hold the terminal, and with the White Combat Team he returned to the airstrip to find the 150th Chinese Regiment dug in on the east side and in possession of the runway. Having seized the airstrip, and the initiative, from the enemy, Colonel Hunter exploited his lightning success by ordering the White Combat Team to head two miles southeast to the village of Rampur from where, on May 18, they would go on to capture the ferry terminal at Zigyun, further down the Irrawaddy.

Hunter had flashed the code words "In the Ring" to Task Force HQ as the attack commenced, a signal that sent Stilwell into paroxysms of anxiety. The wait had been so unbearable that he ordered one of his staff officers, Maj. Gen. William Old, into a liaison plane to determine what he could see over the airstrip. *Nothing* was Old's answer when he returned. "We'll just have to sweat it out," wrote Stilwell in his pocket diary. Four hours later, at 1530 hours, Stilwell learned from Merrill that the code words "Merchant of Venice" had been received from Hunter. The Myitkyina airstrip was in American hands. Stilwell's narrow mind was delighted, not so much with H Force's magnificent achievement but with how the British would react. "WILL THIS BURN UP THE LIMEYS," he wrote gleefully in his diary.

Stilwell got his wish. The seizure of Myitkyina did "burn up" the British, Mountbatten especially, who was "outraged" that he hadn't been informed of the operation. The commander of SEAC also had to deal with a tart query from Prime Minister Churchill. He demanded to know how "the Americans by a brilliant feat of arms have landed us in Myitkyina."

Once he'd calmed down, Mountbatten was graceful enough to issue an Order of the Day addressed to General Joe Stilwell in which he declared:

> By the boldness of your leadership, backed by the courage and endurance of your American and Chinese troops, you have taken the enemy completely by surprise and achieved a most outstanding success by seizing Myitkyina airfield. The crossing of the 6,100-foot Naura Myket Pass is a feat which will live in military history. Please convey my personal congratulations and thanks to all ranks.

From Stilwell himself, the Marauders received nothing but silence.

CHAPTER 20

Broken Promises

Hunter established his headquarters in the southwest perimeter of the airstrip and sent signals to K Force and M Force, ordering them to join him as soon as possible. Then he waited for the promised reinforcements to arrive.

The first aircraft to touch on Myitkyina contained Col. Moe Asensio, an engineer officer who proudly pointed to an approaching flight of seven C-47s towing gliders. Inside the gliders, he informed Hunter, were his finest engineers. Hunter stared at Asensio in disbelief. He'd been expecting Merrill; instead he got a company of engineers flying in to repair a runway that didn't need repairing. Major General Old was the next to arrive. "I am sorry to say I lost my sense of humor [and] respect for rank," reflected Hunter, who demanded of Old that he "stop this fiasco."

"Where's Merrill?" Hunter asked of Old.

"I don't know," replied Old, who in attempt to placate Hunter announced that a large contingent of Chinese troops was on its way.

"But I don't want any more Chinese right now," said Hunter. "What I need is the ammunition and food Merrill promised to have."

Old grunted and walked away.

One of the few faces Hunter was pleased to see on the runway was that of Sgt. Clarence Branscomb, who had waved in the Marauders from a spot of high ground just north of the airstrip. He and Lt. Sam Wilson were eager to know when they would march on Myitkyina itself. Wilson asked the colonel and "got a negative." Hunter was powerless to press the attack because he had instructions to wait until Merrill arrived as he had promised.*

The rest of May 17 was a "nightmare" for Hunter as he stood in his

---

*Many histories of the Burma campaign state that Hunter ordered the Chinese 150th regiment to attack Myitkyina on the afternoon of May 17, an assault that ended in failure when the Chinese troops accidentally opened fire on one another. This is incorrect. His orders were to seize the airstrip and await further orders. Hunter did NOT launch an attack on Myitkyina. According to Robert Passanisi, one of the first Marauders on the airstrip, "no effort was made to take the town for at least a few days."

headquarters waiting for food, ammunition, and the commander of the Myitkyina Task Force to arrive. None did. But Stilwell arrived, early in the morning of May 18, accompanied by a dozen excited war correspondents and not long after by a detachment of antiaircraft troops.

By his own admission, Hunter no longer cut a very imposing figure. Never the tallest of men, he had lost two front teeth and more than 10 of 135 pounds during the march to Myitkyina and "had slept in the same decrepit jungle greens for some months." He was unshaven, red-eyed, and in one hell of a bad mood. Nonetheless, he was as "polite as possible" to Stilwell when he inquired as to Merrill's whereabouts. He received a vague reply, as he did when he pressed the general about food and ammunition.

Stilwell really didn't have time for Hunter and what he considered his petty cavils. He was here to glory in his triumph, one that was "nectar to a parched soul" after the humiliation of his retreat through Burma two years earlier. The war correspondents were putty in the general's hands as he described to them how he and his old friend, Frank Merrill, had dealt the Japanese their first body blow in Burma.

"Brilliant Stilwell Manoeuvre Seizes Myitkyina Air Field" was the front-page headline of the *Nevada State Journal* on May 19. Ohio's *Hamilton Journal* went with "Merrill's Jungle Troops Penetrate Myitkyina." Down in Mississippi, the *Daily Herald* carried a photo of Merrill on its front page with the caption "Merrill, commander of the famed 'Merrill's Marauders' studies his maps and brews more trouble for the Japs in Burma. Note his striking resemblance in this photo to Gen. Joseph Stilwell."

The *Washington Post* described how, "led personally by Merrill, the jungle-seasoned Marauders and American-trained Chinese troops seized the airdrome in a climax to a 700-mile winding trek afoot through jungles and mountains."

There was no mention of Col. Charles Hunter in the *Post*'s copy, or in any other newspaper. There was, however, an ominous quote from a "command spokesman" on Stilwell's staff. Asked what the capture of the airfield meant for future operations in northern Burma, he replied: "Monsoons won't necessarily put a pause to the fighting. The Japanese must fight on or be exterminated. It is of the greatest importance to keep the Japanese fighting in Burma."

Privately, out of earshot of the correspondents, Stilwell was "very upset" when he learned that the Chinese had not yet launched their attack on Myitkyina, two miles to the east, because their generals lacked food and ammunition. Stilwell urged action against an enemy garrison that he believed contained between 250 and 700 troops, a figure given to him by his son, Col. Joe W. Stilwell Jr., who was also his intelligence officer. Hunter told the general that the Marauders could take the town once K Force and M Force arrived at the airstrip, but Stilwell wanted the honor to go to the Chinese.

On the afternoon of May 18, Stilwell ordered a battalion of Chinese troops to probe the enemy defenses in the town. They got lost, but then an hour before sunset word reached Hunter that they had dug in on a road junction southeast of Myitkyina. Hunter set off in a jeep to consult with their commanding officer, but en route their vehicle was spotted by a Japanese patrol. Hunter's driver, Barlow Coon, was badly wounded, and Hunter had to reach over and reverse back down the road toward the airstrip. Hunter helped load Coon into an ambulance aircraft just as Capt. Williams Laffin climbed into an L-4 liaison plane to locate and deliver a message to K Force. Suddenly, a flight of Japanese Zeros came in low over the airstrip, shooting down the L-4 and strafing the ambulance aircraft. Both Coon and Laffin were killed, and Hunter was peppered with superficial shrapnel wounds to leave him looking "like I was in the last stages of syphilis . . . pock-marked all over my head, shoulders and forearms."

The Japanese, though now unable to reach Myitkyina from the south, west, and northwest, had, since the afternoon of May 17, begun drafting in reinforcements from the garrison at Tingkrukawng to the northeast. They flooded into the town in such numbers that within twenty-four hours, Colonel Maruyama had seven hundred able-bodied soldiers under the command, doubling his strength of the previous day.

When General Merrill finally showed up on May 19, he disclosed to Stilwell that aerial reconnaissance estimated that the Japanese now had "two and one-half battalions in Myitkyina," approximately three thousand soldiers, a figure that would rise by the end of the month to four thousand as more men poured into the town. That was about the extent of Merrill's usefulness at Myitkyina that day. The only communication Hunter had with the commander of the Myitkyina Task Force was a limp wave from the window of the aircraft as he prepared to take off for Stilwell's HQ at Shaduzup. That night, May 19, Stilwell wrote in his diary: "Merrill in— he has had another heart attack. Peterson [the NCAC surgeon] gave him morphine and put him to bed."

The following morning, three days after the airstrip had been seized, the first supplies of food and ammunition arrived. On the same day, Stilwell discussed the Marauders with his diary: "They are to finish the job [at Myitkyina]." Stilwell was confident the task wouldn't take long, not with the 150th Chinese Regiment poised to launch an offensive against Myitkyina. The attack began on the afternoon of May 20 and resulted in bloody failure. Initially, the operation had gone to plan, with the Chinese reaching the railroad station virtually unopposed. But then the lead battalion ran into a maelstrom of fire from Japanese defenders. The second wave of Chinese troops panicked and, according to Hunter, "stupidly opened fire on their own troops to the front. The entire regiment broke and ran, leaving close to three hundred of their comrades dead or dying in the city."

The Marauders watched the dazed survivors troop back to their positions around the airstrip. There was little sympathy. "The Chinese were not good soldiers," reflected Clarence Branscomb, a sentiment shared by Colonel Hunter, who believed the Chinese had two fatal flaws. First, "they were unable to tell their own troops from the enemy," and second, in combat "their motto seems to be 'every man for himself.'"

Not that these glaring weaknesses were any longer the concern of Hunter—or the Marauders. In the light of Merrill's incapacitation, Stilwell decided against the logical choice of appointing Hunter his successor and instead went for another "yes man," the amiable but inexperienced Col. John McCammon, who immediately got off on the wrong foot with Hunter by inquiring: "What are your plans for withdrawal if the stuff hits the fan?" Hunter could hardly believe his ears. The Marauders hold this airstrip, he replied. The Marauders will continue to hold this airstrip. The Marauders will not withdraw from this airstrip.

McCammon was promoted by Stilwell to brigadier general (the appointment was promulgated on May 22), declaring that McCammon was now commander of the Myitkyina area and all units therein. These were: the 88th and 89th Chinese infantry regiments, the 150th and 42nd Chinese infantry regiments, and the 5307th Composite Unit. Furthermore, two additional Chinese regiments—the 90th and 148th—plus the 41st Battalion—would arrive imminently.

With the Chinese now in the Myitkyina area in force, Hunter assumed that the 5307th would be relieved as promised and returned to India. But then a note he received from Merrill implied that it might not be so straightforward:

Dear Chuck,

   I feel like hell about what you have been up against and want you to know that I have greatly appreciated and recognize all that you have done. I'm sorry that our ending is bound to be rather unpleasant for most of us. I have talked with the boss [Stilwell] and have done all I could to get many things squared away but am afraid not much, except getting him to recognize that we weren't so far wrong in many things, resulted.

   Sincerely, Frank

It wasn't that unpleasant for Merrill, now on his way to Delhi and a comfortable job on the staff of Adm. Louis Mountbatten. But as far as Hunter and the battered, broken remnants of the Marauders were concerned, Merrill was right: Life was about to get rather unpleasant.

★

On May 17, K Force had received the message from Colonel Hunter instructing them to make haste to the airstrip that was now in their hands. The Marauders, already crippled by fatigue and sickness, summoned up their last vestiges of willpower and marched south as fast as they could. Then another message reached K Force, ordering them to seize Charpate, a village five miles to the northwest of Myitkyina that was on the Mogaung to Myitkyina road and two miles north of the railroad.

The Marauders emerged from the jungle trail on May 18 and began marching down the road toward Myitkyina. The road was flat, paved, and unobstructed, a glorious relief after weeks of tramping through dense jungle. Nonetheless, hundreds of men were now near the end of their tether. Both radioman Bernard Martin and his buddy Bill Smawley had been running dangerously high temperatures for days. Martin's head hurt so much that he thought it would split. "When we got down on to the road . . . the only way I was able to walk was to hang on to the ropes which were holding the radio equipment," he recalled. "I just could not put one foot in front of the other."

By the end of the day, the unconscious Martin was on a plane back to the 20th General Hospital, one of scores of men in the 3rd Battalion suffering from scrub typhus. The rest of K Force, those whose temperature didn't exceed 102 (the figure set by the medical staff as warranting immediate evacuation if it lasted a minimum of three days), advanced southeast along the road until they reached the village of Radahpur, three miles north of Myitkyina. There they ran into an increasing number of Japanese en route to reinforce Myitkyina, so K Force was ordered back toward Charpate.

The men were now so physically and mentally drained that lapses in concentration began to occur. On the night of May 22, one Marauder stood up in his foxhole to stretch his legs; a sentry five yards away fired at the sudden movement and killed the stiff man instantly. A day later, Sgt. John Dills mistook a Japanese soldier for a Chinese and was shot dead as he waved. The same evening, an enemy force on their way to Myitkyina walked right into a Marauders outpost. Lieutenant Warren Smith, the young officer who, with Logan Weston, had done such an effective job in slowing the Japanese advance toward Nhpum Ga two months earlier, was shot dead as he slept. In all, five Americans were killed because the foxholes had been dug too far apart from each other, allowing the Japanese to slip through the perimeter.

On May 24, Colonel Kinnison, himself fighting a fever, was ordered to withdraw K Force two miles south, to an area occupied by a Chinese regiment. Two days later, according to Capt. James Hopkins, "the roster of the 3rd Battalion now listed fewer than fifty sick and exhausted Marauders."

Sick but still on his feet was Staff Sgt. James McGuire, living in a flooded three-foot foxhole, his diary now his only companion. "Bullets was sure flying around our area last nite," he wrote on May 27. "The only way to get the men out of Burma is to evacuate them (I have 8 riflemen left out of the original 34 men). I feel sorta lonesome with most of plt. evacuated. It's like being away from home a long time, which I've been over 3 years. I hope Myitkyina falls soon."

Lieutenant Colonel Beach was evacuated a day or so later, as were Father Barrett and Colonel Kinnison, both of whom succumbed to scrub typhus a few days later. Captain James Hopkins went to see Colonel Hunter to ask what he should do—there was barely a fit man left in the 3rd Battalion. "He advised me to use my own judgment about giving evacuation tags to all who required them," recalled Hopkins. "Since the few remaining men all had good medical reasons for evacuation, they were sent to the airport for final evaluation by Major Melvin Schudmak, the regimental doctor. . . . None were turned down."

By the 31st of May, all but thirteen men and one officer of the 3rd Battalion had been evacuated. McGuire's turn had come on May 29 when he was one of twenty-five Marauders flown out of Burma. So, too, was Lt. Logan Weston, his I&R combat team down to twenty-three from its original strength of fifty-four. As the C-47 transport plane carried Weston north, he pressed his face to the window. "It was hard to believe that the beautiful, smooth, velvety jungle below us was the same steep, insect-infested, dark, blood-soaked cliff area we had been fighting for so long," he reflected. It was dispiriting too, thought Weston, that the plane accomplished in less than two hours what had taken them four months, an ordeal that would remain with them until their dying day.

That night, May 29, Staff Sgt. James McGuire made his final entry in his diary. "Went to 14th evac [hospital]. Took shower, burned all old clothes, put on pajamas, they really feel funny. I have sheets to sleep on. This is all new to me, the first time I've had it this easy in over three years. So this ends my going into Burma and coming out. I just hope I never have to go in again."

CHAPTER 21

The End of the Road

Lieutenant Colonel George McGee's M Force had set out for the Kumon Mountains on May 7. Eight days later they reached Arang, no longer a force but a column of pitiful, emaciated figures whose bodies were wasted even if their minds were still willing. "Most everyone was sick, weak, and exhausted," remembered Roy Matsumoto, who himself had violent dysentery. It was only the fact that his linguist skills could prove crucial that kept him going. "I knew I had to keep going, since everyone's life depended on me," he said.

Vincent Melillo, who had made it up to sergeant after Nhpum Ga, was so tormented by dysentery that he couldn't stand up. "They tried to put me on a mule, but I couldn't stay on it. So I held onto his tail as he pulled me up a mountain," he recalled. The animal broke wind in Melillo's face as it towed him up the Naura Hkyat Pass, a revenge that raised a smile despite his terrible condition.

Hell came in different forms and made no distinction between the Harvard eggheads, the tough kids from the east side of New York, and the country boys from the plains. Private Herb Clofine shed so much weight that he was down to ninety-eight pounds; Warner Katz's temperature reached 105.5 degrees. He would stumble along for a mile, lie down for ten minutes, stumble, then lie, stumble then lie. "If you ever would have seen our outfit going down into Myitkyina, you would have seen a bunch of dead people," he reflected.

One of the few men in the 2nd Battalion still strong enough to help others as well as himself was Pvt. 1st Class Gabriel Kinney. When one soldier collapsed on the trail and begged to be left to die in peace, Kinney and another Marauder fashioned a stretcher made from a parachute and two lengths of sturdy bamboo. "I think I was well past my limits, but there was no choice but to go on," recalled Kinney.

185

For Capt. Fred Lyons, every step toward the 6,100-foot summit of the pass "was like beating an open wound." He no longer cared about the Japanese; in fact, death from a bullet or a bayonet would have been a release. "All I wanted was unconsciousness."

But Lyons, like the rest of the 2nd Battalion, kept going, plodding forward, up and over the pass and down toward Arang. "Sometimes I'd look ahead at Doc Henry Stelling, who carried a pack twice as big as anybody else's, and I'd wonder how in the world he could make it," said Lyons. "Doc Stelling was a good man," said Gabriel Kinney. "The load he carried was tremendous, and a couple of occasions he slipped on the trail and without our help he couldn't get back to this feet."

The relationship between the 2nd Battalion and Doc Stelling was complex. The soldiers held him in high esteem even if, as Thomas Bogardus remembered, his naivety was often the butt of their jokes, as was his habit of writing love letters to his girlfriend each day. Stelling, a scholarly, sensitive, thirty-seven-year-old, admired the men's courage and resilience but recoiled at some of their more bawdy behavior. The ways of young soldiers were as alien to him as his eruditeness was to them. Nonetheless, Doc Stelling was now proving an inspiration, a man driven on by a burning sense of injustice toward Merrill and Stilwell for ordering them on such an endeavor. He blamed McGee, too, accusing him of being "so set on reaching Arang and being ready to push on to Myitkyina and so blind in his stubborn determination that he walked off with his usual very light pack and left most of his staff far behind."

But McGee was asking nothing of his men that he wasn't asking of himself. His weight had fallen from 180 to 120 pounds, and he "fainted several times during strenuous climbs."

Nonetheless, when the battalion reached Arang on May 15, Stelling's patience snapped. He was no longer prepared to tolerate this cruel mistreatment of sick men, fifty of whom "were completely incapable of marching" because of their illnesses. It was also his judgment that no soldier in the battalion "was in condition for combat at Arang and certainly the almost fifty miles which still lay ahead would not improve the condition of any of the men."

Stelling turned for support to Maj. Bernard Rogoff, the battalion surgeon, but it was his view that the majority of the 2nd Battalion was still fit for combat. Stelling was ordered to remain at Arang with the fifty sick men and oversee their evacuation by air.

The rest of M Force plowed on, marching south and receiving orders from Colonel Hunter to occupy Namkwi, a town four miles northwest of Myitkyina and one mile south of the railroad on the curve of the river after which the settlement was named. They arrived on May 19, and a pack train was organized to take twenty-five more sick Marauders onto the airstrip for immediate evacuation. By May 22, the 2nd Battalion boasted fewer than four hundred fit soldiers.

The next day, Lieutenant Colonel McGee went to the airstrip and learned of Merrill's heart attack and the appointment of Col. John McCammon as area commander. McCammon attached a company of the 209th Engineer Battalion to M Force, and Colonel Hunter instructed McGee to march his men toward the area occupied by what was left of the 3rd Battalion. En route toward Charpate, McGee's force ran into a unit of Japanese. One Marauder was killed, eleven were injured, and several more fell asleep as they fired their weapons at the enemy. One Texan Marauder kept himself awake by singing "When My Blue Moon Turns to Gold Again" over and over. Even McGee confessed to a "tendency to drop off." He knew his men had reached the end of the road.

On June 2, McGee requested that the 2nd Battalion be relieved and evacuated to India. Colonel Hunter agreed, as did Brig. Gen. Haydon Boatner, who had replaced the sacked McMammon on May 30. The 2nd Battalion began boarding transport aircraft for India on June 3, and the following day most of the men had left Burma behind. A few remained, however, including the fittest, such as Pvt. 1st Class Gabriel Kinney, who was tasked with instructing the engineers in a crash course of basic infantry skills.

Also detailed to remain on active service were Lt. Ted McLogan and his faithful sergeant, Paul Michael. Nearly a year earlier, Michael had goaded McLogan into volunteering for the "dangerous and hazardous" mission. Neither would quit before the other one did.

The pair remained with the 209th Engineer Battalion, most of whom had little experience firing a weapon, let alone fighting the Japanese. On June 5, McLogan was ordered to lead a patrol north from the airstrip in an attempt to identify the perimeter of the Japanese forces. "It was a scrubby area, slightly hilly," recalled McLogan. Approaching a large clump of brush, McLogan signaled for the eight engineers in the patrol to go to the right of the bush, while he and Sergeant Michael went left. "We were maybe three or four feet apart; we both saw this lone Japanese soldier rising from a foxhole," said McLogan. The soldier brought up his rifle. "He could have shot either one of us. I think he picked Michael because he had this huge red beard. He shot him right through the helmet."

For such a big, fine, brave man, Michael died with extraordinary gentleness. He sank to the ground, legs crossed. "He was just looking right at me," remembered McLogan, "air going out of him like a balloon." Paul Michael leaned forward as the last breath went out of him.

Two days after the death of Michael, Frank Merrill issued a valedictory memorandum to the 5307th Composite Unit (Provisional) from SEAC HQ in Delhi. "My farewell to the outfit will be as brief as my introduction was," began Merrill. He continued:

> I want everyone to know that I feel that I have been very fortunate and more so than any other commander in the war to have had the opportunity of commanding 5307. All of you know what you have accomplished and I will not waste your time on this. However I want you to know that I feel that no other outfit in the United States army could have accomplished the work which you have done.
>
> You now are undergoing the most difficult job of all. Waiting for something to happen is worse than either marching or fighting. I am sure that the gang who licked the Japs from Walawbum to Myitkyina can lick the war of waiting on the Ledo battlefront in the same way.
>
> I would have preferred to have remained with you but circumstances did not permit this, and it is with great regret that I am leaving. If at any time in the future I can ever be of assistance to any of you I hope you will not hesitate to write to me.

At first glance, the timing of the farewell letter might have struck one as odd. Merrill had flown to Delhi two weeks earlier, so why write now? He was probably asked by Stilwell, or perhaps Brig. Gen. Haydon Boatner, in the hope that his writing to the 5307th might quell a growing wave of discontent that was spreading among the men. Things had gotten so bad that Colonel Hunter could no longer guarantee the safety of General Stilwell in the presence of the Marauders, not since his visit to the airstrip when one soldier was overheard telling his buddy: "I had him in my rifle sights. No one would have known it wasn't a Jap that got the son-of-a-bitch."

But Merrill's letter did scant good. The Marauders felt betrayed, not so much by Merrill but by Stilwell. The deal back at Naubum had been clear: one final mission, the "end run" to Myitkyina, and then a flight back to India and some well-earned R&R.

The impression was gaining currency among the Marauders that they were Stilwell's "expendables," the Dead End Kids sent into Burma to kill and to be killed.

This was certainly the opinion of Col. Charles Hunter, though he pointed the finger of blame at Merrill as much as he did Stilwell. The 5307th was Merrill's unit, it was his responsibility, but he had run out on them using his weak heart as an excuse. If he was fit enough to fly to Delhi and take a job on Mountbatten's staff, then he was fit enough to remain in Burma and fight in the Marauders' corner. Hunter knew it wasn't just Merrill's heart that was weak; it was his character, his unwillingness to confront Stilwell. So Hunter did it instead.

On May 25, Stilwell flew in to the airstrip a week after his first visit. This time, there were no excited war correspondents in tow; they were already there, sheltering under the wreck of a C-47 transport plane and dodging Japanese sniper fire. So much for Stilwell's bold assertion that the enemy was on the run.

Hunter handed Stilwell a letter not long after his arrival on the airstrip, explaining to the general that he was delivering it personally instead of going through the official channels because he didn't wish the letter's contents to "be seen by every clerk in his headquarters."

Stilwell took the letter. Even before he began reading, he must have had an idea of its contents. He knew Hunter well enough, this fellow West Pointer who shared some of his traits: the same sharp temper; a man not afraid to voice his opinions, however unpopular. Stilwell probably had more respect for Hunter than he did for the rest of his staff combined. They were all "yes men," but Hunter, like Stilwell, was his own man.

But he was still shocked when he read the letter, a withering attack on his command and his treatment of the 5307th. Hunter began at the beginning, in India, and the housing of the unit in accommodations that were "a disgrace." There was the casual disregard for allocating the unit colors, insignia, and even a name that would have helped bond the men and boost their morale. Hunter reminded Stilwell that he had taken up this matter with his staff on several occasions "with no apparent results." There was the lack of interest shown by the CBI commanders (Stilwell wasn't mentioned by name) in the unit's training in India, something that hadn't gone unnoticed by the men. "American soldiers being of discerning nature and intelligent, naturally are sensitive to the treatment they receive from higher headquarters."

The 5307th was now "practically ineffective as a combat unit," said Hunter, because of its mistreatment, and its continued deployment in the Myitkyina area "is rapidly leading to a false sense of security, which is dangerous." And so it went on.

Hunter concluded by suggesting to Stilwell that in the future, "American infantry combat units assigned to this theater be treated in such a manner as to instill in the unit a pride of organization, a desire to fight, and a feeling of being a part of a united effort." This would be far better than the "don't-care attitude" meted out to the 5307th since the moment it stepped off the *Lurline* at Bombay.

Once Stilwell had finished reading, he looked up at Hunter over his steel-rimmed glasses and said: "This is a strong letter." Hunter replied:

"I intended it to be." Stilwell neatly folded the letter and slid into his shirt pocket.

Five days later, he wrote in his diary: "12 men left in 2 [Battalion] G[alahad]. Beach and Magee sick. Schudmak discouraged. [Galahad] is just shot."

For the first time, it seemed Stilwell understood, realized that the Marauders had been pushed to and then beyond the limits of human endurance. Military history coursed through Stilwell's veins; he had studied it at West Point, lived it on the Western Front a quarter of a century earlier. He had probably read what John Fortescue, the historian of the British Army, had written about the lessons learned from the horror of trench warfare, "that even the bravest man cannot endure to be under fire for more than a certain number of consecutive days, even if the fire be not very heavy."

In other words, every soldier, even a Marauder, needed a respite, the chance to rest and recuperate for a few days well away from the enemy, where they knew they weren't going to be shot by a sniper, strafed by a fighter, or blown up by a shell. Yet this basic requirement was ignored by Stilwell. For nearly four months, the Marauders had been operating in enemy territory, not always in close proximity to the Japanese but still within range of their aircraft or artillery. Nerves were shredded, a condition exacerbated by sickness, hunger, and exhaustion.

As Hunter pointed out to Stilwell, the 2nd Battalion had all but ceased to exist as a fighting force, the 3rd Battalion was being evacuated at a rate of 25 men a day, and by June 1 the strength of the 1st Battalion was down to 18 officers and 366 men. Lieutenant Sam Wilson had soldiered on as best as he could, but eventually one of the battalion doctors ordered his wasted body onto a plane, telling him: "You've had it, boy, out you go." Sergeant Clarence Branscomb went, too, suffering "from a bit of everything," his 180-pound frame whittled down to 135 pounds.

Wilson pulled through, but thirty Marauders died of sickness in the summer months, most from scrub typhus. Radioman Robert Passanisi was evacuated due to his 103-degree temperature. Nonetheless he felt fine, arriving at the 20th General Hospital with the "feeling I've got away with it." His clothes were peeled from his body and burned. Then a nurse took his temperature. It was 105. The next thing Passanisi remembered was waking up a fortnight later. Passanisi spent a further week in the hospital, taking pills and eating food in an attempt to regain some of the sixty pounds he had left behind in the jungle. Most of the Marauders' stomachs had shrunk so much in the jungle that they were advised to eat seven small meals a day rather than gorge on three large helpings.

Captain Fred Lyons was one of the men who had lain in a hospital bed hovering between life and death. He'd won the fight, but just barely. "I was in bed a week before I even wanted to look at my accumulated mail," he recalled. Mail meant America, meant sweethearts, family, the movie theater, steaks, and milkshakes. Such thoughts were still too painful—and too distant. The best tonic was talking to their buddies in the next-door bed. "In the hospital rooms, the men lived over again those weary hours of moving upward and downward, around and across, back and forth over the Burma hillsides," recalled Lyons. "They relived those days with the flies, the leeches, the ripping undergrowth, the rains, the mud, the moldy stench of ancient jungle and dead Japanese, the ever-present terror of ambush, the occasional grim quip. And this comprehending couldn't include return."

Passanisi and Lyons were sent to the convalescent center in the Staging Area at Dinjan, fifty miles south of Margherita, which turned out to be a "pasture surrounded by *bashas* in which cows would not have been stalled at home." There were no latrines, just filthy pits dug in the ground, nor were there any shower facilities. When the Marauders went to collect the personal belongings they had left in storage four months earlier on the eve of their march into Burma, they discovered "everything had been thoroughly ransacked, all valuables were missing, and the rest had been destroyed by rain and mildew." Morale, already low, sunk even further at the realization that while they had been fighting in Burma, rear-echelon troops had been helping themselves to their possessions.

Captains James Hopkins and Lewis Kolodny endeavored to make life as bearable as possible for the Marauders—no easy task, as there was no senior officer in the Staging Area and Northern Combat Area Command was reluctant to provide supplies and improve conditions. Another source of contention was the lack of decorations awarded Marauders, despite countless acts of gallantry in Burma that in any other theater would have been rewarded. It wasn't the medal itself that mattered to the Marauders, just the desire to have their effort recognized. But Stilwell wasn't a general who believed in dishing out decorations to American soldiers whose duty was to engage the enemy without "being patted on the back or [to] have their hands held." The medals he himself had been awarded, such as the Distinguished Service Cross and the Distinguished Service Medal, he had accepted reluctantly.

The final indignity came when Stilwell began ordering the return of Marauders to the frontline to help in the defense of the airstrip. "About two hundred men were literally shanghaied for the so-called emergency at Myitkyina," recalled Hopkins, himself just released from the hospital and still suffering chronic dysentery.

One of the men put on a plane to Myitkyina was Passanisi, just twenty-four hours after he'd been released from the hospital. "Without a chance to recuperate or convalesce, I got caught up in Stilwell's call for anybody who could walk to be sent back into Myitkyina," he reflected.

Also returned was Gabriel Kinney, one of the last of the 2nd Battalion to have left Myitkyina with a tag on the rags that passed as his uniform saying he was suffering from AOE—"Accumulation of Everything." "I didn't question the order to return; I just went," said Kinney.

Back at the Staging Area, Marauders' resentment at their treatment spread like the mildew inside their dilapidated center. Hopkins remembered that they were "disgusted by the failure of generals Merrill and Stilwell to meet them in small groups or as a unit to express some gratitude to them."

Finally, the resentment spilled over into something more serious the moment the men received their pay. There was the odd isolated outbreak of violence, but for the most part the Marauders just stocked up on alcohol and took to "living like bands of pirates . . . gambling and pitching empty beer cans out of the windows."

Lieutenant Charlton Ogburn, who had been assigned adjutant of the Staging Area, was ordered to write a report on the situation, and while he didn't condone the behavior of a minority of Marauders, he stated that their accommodation was a "pest-hole" and unacceptable for sick and battle-worn men. Ogburn tried to repair the threadbare morale of the men by helping to design an unofficial insignia for the unit. A blue shield with "Merrill's Marauders" embroidered in red at the top, the insignia features colors of four combat teams—red, white, blue, and green—with as its centerpiece "a bolt of red lightning cutting through a field of green between the Star of Burma and the Kuomintang of China."

★

Kinney, Passanisi, and the rest of the returned Marauders were told to dig in and defend the airstrip at all costs. It was now the height of the monsoon season, the airstrip dotted with flooded craters from the sporadic Japanese artillery fire. "Once or twice a day you would hear the whoosh whoosh of one of the Jap's 107mm guns, high overhead, followed by the report in the distance," recalled Passanisi. "No one ever paid any attention to it."

The Americans and Chinese now dug in around the airstrip were on the defensive as a result of Stilwell's monumental blunder. Myitkyina had been there for the taking on May 17 if only Stilwell, instead of gloating over the "Limeys," had executed a plan of attack that involved flying in additional troops and supplies within an hour or two of the airstrip's capture. If he'd done that, Hunter would have had the men and the means to wrest Myitkyina from the Japanese before they had the chance to bring up hundreds of reinforcements.

The moment had gone and Stilwell had blown it, though he couldn't bring himself to admit it. "Good God," he whined to his diary. "What goes on at Mitch?"

Stilwell could not now withdraw the Marauders. It would be a loss of face in front of the Chinese, and in front of the British, whose 36th Division would have been at his disposal had he not been so proud. Stilwell would not now relieve the Marauders, not until Myitkyina was his.

What was left of the 5307th amounted to no more than two hundred men, so additional American troops were flown in, green troops, some of whom were engineers unashamedly petrified at the prospect of combat. Others were like Francis Ponder, a twenty-year-old from Indiana, whose ship docked in Bombay on May 25, 1944. Four days later, he was on board a C-47 to Myitkyina. "We'd been issued rifles, machine guns, mortars, BAR, and hand grenades," recalled Ponder. "It was up to the infantrymen in the contingent to instruct the men who were not [infantrymen] how to load their weapons."

Ponder and the reinforcements were called "New Galahad" to distinguish them from "Old Galahad," the name given to the couple of hundred Marauders dug in around the airstrip. "We joined the Marauders in their defensive positions and tried to get an understanding of the situation," recalled Ponder. "They were glad to see us and eager for us to learn . . . and we listened to the Marauders and did what they told us to do."

The Japanese knew what was going on. Their frontline was now so close to the airstrip that snipers, as well as shells, were a constant menace to the Americans and Chinese. One night, they decided to put the reinforcements to the test with a nighttime attack on the airstrip. Dave Quaid, who along with several other reporters had set up camp under the fuselage of a damaged C-47, scrambled for protection as flares burst overhead and machine guns opened up. "I was lying behind one of the wheels of the plane and I had pretty good cover," recalled Quaid. "Swapp! A bullet went through the tire and the plane lurched down."

The reporters dashed across the runway toward the defensive positions established by Colonel Hunter. "We lay there in the torrential rain and became part of the perimeter guard taking care of our end of the perimeter," said Quaid. "There were voices below me from a dugout. I heard one of the voices say that he had left a whole basket of grenades in his tent." Quaid told the soldier to fetch them, that they might well need them before too long. The man, his voice quivering with fear, refused to leave his dugout. Quaid shouted at him, but still the soldier refused to fetch his grenades. Then Hunter appeared out of the darkness, slithering through the mud with Joe Doyer at his side. "Hunter yelled down to the dugout, 'Colonel Hunter here. Who's down there? Give me your names and rank!'" remembered Quaid. "One of the guys answered Major so-and-so, and another answered Captain so-and-so. All officers, but none of them Marauder officers, I'm glad to say. Hunter really chewed them out."

Despite the questionable quality of many men in New Galahad, Hunter remained bitterly opposed to the return of semi-fit Marauders to the airstrip. Nor was the irony lost on Hunter that Stilwell was displaying the same callous indifference to the Marauders that Wingate had toward the Chindits the previous year, one reason why General Marshall had agreed to the unit's transfer from British to American command the previous December.

Some Marauders arrived only to be sent straight back to the hospital by Hunter, who prescribed a medical procedure for every soldier ordered to return to the airstrip. It stated that three doctors had to agree that a man was too sick to stay. "The three-doctor bit sounded great, but to find three to examine a patient sometimes would take hours," recalled medic Richard Murch, back with the Marauders after having recovered from wounds sustained two months earlier.

Murch held a daily sick call at 7 a.m., an event that would often take hours. "Almost every member of our unit was suffering from either malaria, dysentery, exhaustion, or fever," he remembered. "Everyone looked like a skeleton—no flesh showing, just bones."

On June 19, Stilwell paid one of his infrequent visits to the airstrip, and Hunter made sure he witnessed the state of Old Galahad. "For the first time, he was witnessing good, rich American blood streaming from the agonized but silent bodies of American soldiers," reflected Hunter. "He saw no fear of death, no panic, no complaining."

On June 26, Mogaung fell, captured by the British and Chinese, leaving Myitkyina what Hunter called "the last rallying point for the Japanese in the area." On the same day, General Boatner was relieved of his command and replaced by Brig. Gen. Theodore Wessels, an officer regarded by Hunter as rugged and robust "with a good infantry military background." For once, Stilwell had made a judicious appointment. "Things could not help but improve and improve they did," reflected Hunter. "Now at Myitkyina for the first time was a commander with whom we could communicate."

One of the first requests communicated to Wessels was for increased aerial reconnaissance, the photographs of which were soon in Hunter's possession. On first examination, he couldn't understand why the photos, taken after a night of torrential rain, showed the roads leading from Myitkyina to the Japanese lines as dark in color for some distance and then lighter thereafter. "I studied it for hours trying to find the reason for this phenomenon, and then the solution hit me like an electric shock wave," recalled Hunter. "The roads changed color at the point where the nightly traffic ceased on each, and therefore a concealed Japanese position must lie near each of these points." Within days, the positions were destroyed from the air.

★

On August 1, Stilwell was promoted full general, the fourth star pinned on him by Frank Merrill. Two days later, Myitkyina finally fell to the Allies when the Task Force overran the sick, starving, and wounded Japanese defenders. "Over at last," wrote Stilwell in his diary. "Thank God. Not a worry in this world."

With Myitkyina taken, Stilwell no longer had need of Colonel Hunter, or what was left of his shattered 5307th Composite Unit (Provisional). Hunter was relieved of his command and ordered to return to the United States. Stilwell also issued explicit instructions that Hunter was to return by ship; that way, he would have time to bask in the glory of seizing Myitkyina without Hunter revealing the truth about the injustice perpetrated on his Marauders.

A week after the fall of Myitkyina, the 5307th was deactivated. Less than a year after the call went out for volunteers for a dangerous and hazardous mission, the Marauders were no more. Of the 2,600 men who marched into Burma six months earlier, 93 had been killed in combat, 30 had died from disease, and a further 301 were wounded or missing. An additional 1,970 Marauders had been hospitalized with sickness. Amoebic dysentery was the greatest scourge, accounting for 503 victims.

It was claimed that only two men from the original three thousand volunteers for the 5307th went through the whole Burmese campaign untouched by sickness. Master Sergeant Joe Doyer was one. The other was Hunter.

★

The 5307th was reconstituted as the 475th Infantry Regiment under the command of Colonel Osborne, erstwhile commander of the 1st Battalion. The 475th, together with the 124th Cavalry Regiment, formed "Mars Force," which in cooperation with the Chinese would march down the Old Burma Road in the spring of 1945.

By then, the majority of the Marauders who had survived Burma were back in the States, laid up in hospitals from Florida to California. Clarence Branscomb was in Santa Barbara, California, recovering from sickness in the Hoff General Hospital. Deploying the same initiative that he had in Burma, Branscomb began to "go out the window after lights out and head downtown." On one of these nocturnal escapades, he bumped into Charles Hunter and his wife on the sidewalk. "We threw our arms around each other and I said, 'I'm sure glad to see you,'" recalled Branscomb. "He asked me how I was finding it, being back home. I said it was hard, and he said, 'I know, people don't think we did anything out there.'"

"The Soldier's Soldier"

Stilwell's attempt to silence Hunter by shipping him back to the States didn't work out the way he'd planned. Hunter's letter of May 25 saw to that. To his credit, Vinegar Joe had ordered an investigation into the claims laid out by Hunter; he just hadn't expected the findings to be leaked to the press around the time that Hunter boarded his ship for the voyage back home.

"Marauders' Morale Broken by Hospital Faults, Promises" proclaimed the *Washington Post* on August 6. A similar headline appeared in the *New York Daily News*. In its article, the paper described how there had been "an almost complete breakdown of morale" within the Marauders, "one of the most famous American combat organizations." Quoting the Army investigation, the *News* stated that "ill-advised promises" to the men and faulty hospital procedure that sent convalescents back to the firing line were to blame.

The "promises" were those given to the Marauders the previous year, as detailed in a telegram from Gen. George Marshall to General Stilwell on September 30, 1943. Marshall said in the communication "that Galahad is provided for one major operation of approximately three months duration." Additionally, following the completion of this operation, the survivors were to be granted "three months hospitalization and rest with probably well-deserved furloughs in U.S." Although this information had never been officially transmitted to the Marauders, it was freely disclosed by officers during the months of training, and by Merrill in Naubum when he asked the men for their end run to Myitkyina.

Merrill was right to dangle the prospect of a furlough to the men; it renewed their spirits, gave them hope that the end was in sight—and hope is the best nourishment a combat soldier can have.

For the first time, Merrill had to contend with headlines that didn't portray him as the tough-as-hell combat commander. "Merrill has been relieved of his command and sent to India," commented the United Press, which added that since his departure, "hospitalization procedures has [sic] been changed in the Burma theater to prevent a recurrence of the incident."

Stilwell was forced to come to the defense of his friend, releasing a statement that was carried by numerous American papers on August 9:

> It [the statement] concerns the relief of brigadier Gen. Frank D Merrill from command of the 5307th Provisional Regiment and his subsequent assignment to head the CBI liaison group at SEAC headquarters.
>
> The only reason for his relief was his health. He was hospitalized from March 31 to April 16 and again from May 20 to June 13.
>
> I considered it unfair to a valuable officer to ask further effort on his part which might have a serious lasting effect upon his health, and I have therefore transferred him to less arduous but equally important duty in his present assignment.

At the same time, the Marauders were finally given some official recognition in the form of a Distinguished Unit Citation (in 1966, this award was redesignated the Presidential Unit Citation), which described how the "unit proved equal to its task and after a brilliant operation of 17 May 1944 seized the airfield at Myitkyina, an objective of great tactical importance in the campaign, and assisted in the capture of the town of Myitkyina on 3 August 1944."

★

With its forces engaged in two fierce conflicts in the summer of 1944, the American press was reluctant to probe too deeply into reports of mistreatment of its soldiers, so few newspapers raised questions about the allegations. The *Clovis News Journal* of New Mexico was an exception. Its editorial of Sunday, August 13, wouldn't have gone down well in Washington:

> One of the most disheartening news accounts to come out of the war is the reported breakdown of morale of that gallant band of men known as Merrill's Marauders. The report that the morale of the men

has broken probably will be pretty well hushed up until after the war but it is apparent even now that something is radically wrong.

For months and months these men fought a bitter battle with the Japanese under the most trying conditions. Their action behind enemy lines, against tremendous odds and under the most difficult conditions has been one of the bright pictures of the war. Now, according to latest reports, the men who had been promised that they would be given respite from their long fighting have understandably enough resented being returned to active duty.

Now Brig. Gen. Frank D. Merrill, their leader, has been assigned to liaison duty in the China-Burma-India theater. Gen. Joseph Stilwell is reported as saying that the transfer of General Merrill is in no way connected with the inquiry into the reported breakdown of the morale of the Marauders. But there obviously is more behind the story of the Marauders that some day will be made known.

One man who read the press reports with mounting concern was Robert Rice Reynolds, a Democratic U.S. senator representing North Carolina and a member of the Senate Military Affairs Committee. The day after the editorial in the *Clovis New Journal,* he wrote to Secretary of War Henry Stimson demanding that the committee should be "fully informed" on the following points:

1. The question of unauthorized promises of promotions, leaves of absence, and early relief for those who would volunteer for special duty in the jungles, and what action the army expects to take or has taken to prevent and discourage future use of such "bait" to induce men to volunteer for exceptionally dangerous assignment.

2. What has now been done with the volunteers of Merrill's Marauders who volunteered for a reported "three months" special duty?

3. What has been done to improve the reported breakdown in morale and the restoration of the confidence and faith these men should have in their leaders, but which they apparently lack?

4. What fatalities, casualties, etc., were suffered by the unit (the Marauders under command of Brigadier General Frank Merrill) as a result of the error in ordering sick men to the defense of the airport?

Alarmed by the furor, Stilwell ordered Merrill back to the States to smooth things over, although unlike Hunter he returned by air. Clearly the pair had concocted a plan prior to Merrill's return, one that pointed the finger at everyone but themselves. At a Pentagon press conference on August 26, Merrill dismissed the reports of shattered Marauders' morale as "a storm in a teapot." Then, with a series of snide insinuations, he delivered up the scapegoats to the assembled press corps; first, Charles Hunter. "This is what happened," Merrill explained when asked what had unfolded back at the end of May. "When we were attacking the town of Myitkyina, a local commander there thought the Japs were coming up in strength. He sent a message to me asking for reinforcements. I was in the hospital myself at the time. I asked General Stilwell to send back as many men as he could. In passing the general's message around, it finally got twisted to mean 'send back all the men fit to walk.'"

It was all lies. Hunter—the "local commander"—had done no such thing, and during the period in question Merrill had been released from the hospital and was on his way to Delhi to join Mountbatten's staff. Not satisfied with the response, the press corps persisted, demanding to know who was ultimately responsible for sending sick men to the frontline. "Our own doctors looked them over," said Merrill. "And if any of our men were in action who should have been in the hospital, it was due to an error by our own doctors."

It was extraordinary response, an unforgiveable slur on the character of the medical staff. Ever since the Marauders had marched into Burma, doctors such as James Hopkins, Henry Stelling, Paul Armstrong, John McLaughlin, and Lewis Kolodny had tended to the men with unceasing diligence and courage, frequently exposing themselves to enemy fire in order to treat the wounded. In one casual stroke, Merrill had betrayed them, portraying them as uncaring and impugning their integrity as officers and as doctors because he lacked the strength of character to admit that it was his idol, Stilwell, who was to blame.

Indeed, on June 22, 1944, Stelling and Hopkins had submitted highly critical reports of Stilwell's policy of returning convalescing Marauders to the frontline. Hopkins wrote that it "has resulted in the return of many sick men and soldiers who had not had adequate convalescence . . . we have found it necessary to readmit many men to these hospitals in order to prevent them from going back to combat, as casuals, before they are in reasonable condition."

The letter of Senator Robert Rice Reynolds to Secretary of War Henry Stimson resulted in a congressional investigation into claims that the Marauders had suffered a breakdown in morale following their treatment by Stilwell and his CBI staff. Beatrice Bouchard, the sweetheart of Lt. Ted McLogan, got time off from her job as a decoder for the Navy WAVES (Women Accepted for Volunteer Emergency Service) to attend the congressional hearing. She recalled that one of the findings of the investigation was a ruling that the "Marauders could never go into active duty again." Neither this nor any other outcome was seen fit for public consumption.

Merrill remained in the States for a month, doing what he did best: charming, schmoozing, and reworking history to fit the version he and Stilwell wanted written. He was stunningly successful. From September 14 to 21, the *Washington Post* ran a series of full-page articles describing the daring exploits of Merrill's Marauders. The serialization began under the heading: "Merrill's Marauders In the Burma Jungle." Naturally, there was a large photo of Merrill and several gung-ho quotes. Charles Hunter and George McGee were mentioned in passing, a line each, not enough to steal the old warrior's glory.

Reporters were invited to Merrill's home in North Woodstock, New Hampshire, where he regaled them with tales of derring-do. "A man of high intelligence and sensitivity," gushed the *Dixon Evening Telegraph*, "smoking a well-worn pipe, probably the relic of many a campaign in Burma."

The Marauders weren't fooled. When Maj. John Jones returned home in October 1944, he gave an interview to the Associated Press that was carried by several newspapers in which he talked of "Merrill's Marauders, directly under the command of Col. Charles N. Hunter."

When Hunter finally stepped onto American soil, there was no reporter waiting for him, and the War Department saw to it that he didn't open his mouth. Nor did it offer him any promotion. In contrast, Merrill was appointed deputy U.S. commander in the CBI Theater in December 1944. Fifteen months later, when he addressed the Commonwealth Club of San Francisco, Merrill omitted to mention Charles Hunter in his 6,500-word speech. "Hunter gave Merrill his total loyalty," reflected Sam Wilson. "Merrill did not quite do the same thing to Hunter. In fact Merrill, I know, badmouthed Hunter a bit to Stilwell, which was terribly unfair."

When World War II ended, the row had long been forgotten, as for the most part had the Allied effort in Burma. Returning GIs who had fought at Iwo Jima and Okinawa were feted, as were the brave men who had stormed the beaches of Normandy and repelled the German counter-offensive in the Ardennes in the bitter winter of 1944–45. The efforts of the Allied servicemen in the China Burma India Theater were largely overlooked. With the black humor associated with their race, Field Marshal William Slim's British 14th Army dubbed themselves the "Forgotten Army" when they returned home. The same moniker could have applied to the

Americans who had fought in Burma.

Then in 1959 came the publication of Charlton Ogburn's acclaimed war memoir, *The Marauders*, a book the *New York Times* described as "vivid, intimate, powerful." It was also unbending in its acclamation of Hunter. Toward the end of the book, Ogburn wrote:

> As for the feelings of the rest of us, we make no bones about them. Ask any of us what they are and the reply will be an expression of loyalty to Colonel Hunter and esteem for him such as few commanders arouse, and one also of distress that he has had so little of the recognition that was his due.

Merrill wouldn't have liked the book, but he had been dead three years, killed by that weak heart of his. At the time of his death, he was New Hampshire's public works and highway commissioner and on his way home from a Florida convention of state highway officials.

Ogburn's book inspired Hollywood to make a film of the daring jungle fighters, only they needed to make a few adjustments for the silver screen. The American public didn't know the name Charles Hunter, but the wartime generation was well aware of the dashing Frank Merrill, regardless of what Ogburn might have written. In September 1961, on the eve of the release of *Merrill's Marauders* (shot on location in the Philippines), there was a deep sense of unease among veterans that Hollywood was going to play with the truth. They had heard that Merrill, Stilwell, and Lewis Kolodny were the only "real" characters; everyone else was fictional.

The reservations were made known at the annual reunion—in South Carolina—but Warner Brothers "assured" the Marauders they would like what they saw. Hell, said a spokesman, the film is "so realistic there isn't even a woman in it."

When the film was released, with Jeff Chandler as Merrill, the *New York Times* described it as "a war drama of individuality and merit." Marauders left movie theaters appalled. "Just terrible," was Ted McLogan's verdict. "Shoot-it-up stuff; it didn't develop character. It was based on Merrill." Robert Passanisi derided it as "pure Hollywood" and as utterly unrealistic. Roy Matsumoto was deeply hurt by the fact that he was portrayed as a "a Filipino mercenary who just happened to speak Japanese." Hollywood in the early 1960s believed that cinemagoers weren't yet ready to accept that American Japanese had served their country loyally and with great courage during the war.

The film so angered Charles Hunter that he wrote his own book, *Galahad*, published to little attention in 1963. It was his attempt to set the record straight, but bitterness seeped through the pages, leaving some of his friends to wonder if he shouldn't have kept his counsel—and his dignity.

★

Fifty years on and only a handful of Marauders remain. Clarence Branscomb is one of them, now in his ninety-fifth year and, as he admits with a chuckle, not quite as nimble on his feet as he once was. For twelve years after the war, he worked on a farm, then he went into a tractor dealership before retiring to the West Coast.

By his own admission, Branscomb was for decades "pretty disgusted with the whole military establishment, including Merrill's Marauders." He reserves his fiercest criticism for Merrill. "He got the credit for the thing, got his name in it, but he never did anything," he said. "Hunter was doing the job at Mitch [Myitkyina] that Merrill should have been doing."

Branscomb never really got to know his fellow Marauders; casual friendships aren't in his nature. The two men he came to respect in Burma were Charles Hunter and Sam Wilson. "Hunter was a real soldier and a good man," remembered Branscomb. "And he was my friend."

In January 2013, Branscomb received a letter from Wilson, the first communication between the two men since the end of the war. Lieutenant General (Retired) Wilson, a former director of the Defense Intelligence Agency and regarded as one of the finest American soldiers of the Cold War era, had tracked down his old sergeant through Branscomb's son. His father, Wilson told him, was "one of the bravest and most capable soldiers I ever knew. We went through a lot together in North Burma and I have thought of him a lot over the years and wondered if he was still alive."

The words mean a great deal to Clarence.

Twenty-five years earlier, in 1988, Wilson had discussed his brilliant military career in an interview with Dr. J. W. Partin for the U.S. Special Operations Command. Asked to compare and contrast Merrill and Hunter, Wilson said of the former: "He thought more in politico-military terms, and [was] an outstanding conceptualizer when it came to dreaming up what the outfit might do. He tended to come apart a little bit on execution, where Hunter would take over and carry us through."

Wilson stressed that he liked Merrill, describing him as charming if a "little given to hyperbole." The problem in Burma, he added, was that Merrill should never have been put in charge of the Marauders in the first place. Smart as Stilwell was, said Wilson, "I think he was at times a poor judge of human character, a poor judge of people. I think he overrated Merrill. I think he underrated Hunter."

As for Hunter, Wilson had this to say: "Hunter was a dry-witted, laconic, tough, hard-bitten soldier's soldier. Tenacious to the point of stubbornness.

An excellent tactician, an absolutely super troop leader. . . . A better name for the outfit would probably have been Hunter's Harbingers or Hunter's Hawks, or something like that rather than Merrill's Marauders. But as you know, history doesn't always work like that."

WHAT BECAME OF THE MARAUDERS

Charles Beach: Beach joined a police force once hostilities were over, but the war in which he had served his country so gallantly was not finished for the commander of the 3rd Battalion. In July 1954, haunted by his wartime experiences, Beach shot himself.

Thomas Bogardus: After the war, Bogardus graduated from Northwestern University with a masters in journalism, married the girl he had played with in the sandbox, and worked for the *Palo Alto Times* in California as a business manager. Upon retiring in 1975, he and his wife settled on San Juan Island, where Bogardus was such an active volunteer for the Boy Scouts of America that their camp on the island was named in his honor. Bogardus began writing an account of his war service for his children, but regrettably he died in 1999 before he could finish.

Joseph Doyer: Fate was cruel to Master Sergeant Doyer, the First World War veteran who, along with Hunter, was the only Marauder to last the entire campaign without getting sick. After the 5307th was reconstituted the 475th Infantry Regiment, Doyer was promoted to chief warrant officer. In January 1945, he was wounded in an engagement with the Japanese and, while recovering in a hospital, contracted an illness and died.

James Hopkins: Now age ninety-nine, Hopkins was highly respected by the men of the 3rd Battalion, and he was similarly regarded by his patients during a long and distinguished career at his private thoracic surgery practice in Baltimore. He retired in 1989, and ten years he later coauthored *Spearhead*, the exhaustive 770-page account of the Marauders in Burma. In 2003 Charles Beck, erstwhile of the Orange Combat Team, 3rd Battalion, wrote to the Marauders newsletter: "I am not too well and thought before I left, this should go into our history. There wasn't a man in my platoon that didn't like Captain Hopkins . . . somewhere near Walawbum, Captain Hopkins was preparing to operate on a wounded soldier. Someone came by and said 'Hoppy' was told by another medic that this soldier doesn't have a chance of living. Hoppy was quoted as saying, 'Yes, I know but I am going to give him that chance.' Hoppy might have forgotten that incident but I didn't after sixty years. The soldier did die but from then on, Captain Hopkins gained our respect and admiration."

Charles Hunter: After the war, Hunter—who was married with three daughters (two of whom he outlived)—had an uninspiring military career. He served on the faculty of the Armed Forces Staff College for three years before being transferred to Europe in the mid-1950s as chief of the Military Assistance Division, U.S. European Command. He never rose above the rank of colonel. After leaving the military in 1959, Hunter retired to Wyoming, wrote his memoirs, and died in 1978 at age seventy-two. Not one American newspaper carried news of his passing.

Warren Katz: The German-born scout became a businessman after the war, marrying in 1950 and finally becoming an American citizen. He died in 2006.

Gabriel Kinney: Kinney was discharged from the Army in November 1945 and returned to his native Alabama, where he was employed by the Tennessee Coal and Iron Company (now U.S. Steel). Using his GI benefits, Kinney obtained his electrician's degree and for thirty-seven years worked as an electrician for U.S. Steel in Birmingham.

Married to Susan since 1945, Kinney has six children, fifteen grandchildren, and twenty-one great-grandchildren, and in July 2013 he cradled his first great-great grandchild. His experiences in Burma, and the camaraderie he found in the Marauders, are never far from his thoughts. Kinney said that "every minute of Nhpum Ga is still in my memory . . . thirteen days and fourteen nights that the English language cannot describe." Of his comrades, he said: "The Marauders were a well-trained group of soldiers who did what had to be done, when and where it had to be done."

Edward Kohler: One of the last of the 2nd Battalion to be evacuated from the airstrip, Kohler spent four weeks in the hospital recovering from malaria. During the rest of the war, he served in the States as an instructor of jungle warfare. Kohler returned to Ohio and got a job in Lima manufacturing boilers for locomotives. The decline of steam locomotives cost Kohler his job, and after a year painting bridges he bought a farm. Married in 1949,

Kohler and his wife raised four children and celebrated their sixty-fourth wedding anniversary in July 2013. "We have had a great life together and now we are on the road out," reflected Kohler, who considers himself blessed in his choice of wife and by his time in the Marauders. "All I can say is that I am proud to have been with such a wonderful group of men that took care of one another."

Fredrick Lyons: In 1945, Lyons gave an intensive interview to his local newspaper, the *Tampa Tribune*, about his time in the Marauders, anxious to correct the impression in some quarters that the unit had disintegrated toward the end. "We came home to hear it said of us that we cracked up but we didn't," said Lyons. "Yes, the men who had to go back did grumble and a lot of them didn't make it out there on the line, but that was not because our morale had cracked or we had fizzled. . . . No, the morale of Merrill's Marauders never ended. We never backed down. We just wore out!" Lyons died on October 31, 1986. Little is known about his postwar life.

Bernard Martin: Bernard Martin became an object of great medical interest upon his return to the USA. He was transferred from one hospital to another as doctors took samples of his blood in the hope of learning more about scrub typhus. He survived the disease, unlike his foxhole buddy, Bill Smawley, who died en route to Florida in June 1944. "I was lucky to survive. I don't know why I survived and Bill didn't," reflected Martin. He spent his working life in construction, building homes first in Florida and then in Las Vegas, before settling down to retirement with his wife in Nevada, where he still lives at age ninety-one. In Burma, Martin said, he grew a hard shell to protect him from the death of his buddies and the death of the enemy. "You had to be callous in your thinking," he said. "You're killing other men. You can't just kill another man and walk away with a smile on your face. It's not right. Even today I get bursts of guilt."

Roy Matsumoto: Despite suffering from dysentery, Matsumoto remained at the Myitkyna airstrip until the town was liberated. He was subsequently transferred to China and attached to Detachment 202, OSS, and then to the Nationalist Chinese Army guerrilla forces operating near the Indochina border. After the war, Matsumoto was reunited with three of his brothers, all of whom had served in the Japanese military. One was a veteran of the bitter fighting on Guadalcanal.

Matsumoto retired from the military in 1963 and, with his wife and two daughters, set up home on the West Coast. For decades, Matsumoto rarely spoke of his wartime service with the Marauders, opening up only in recent years. "I was really surprised," said his daughter Fumi. "He's really kind of this mild-mannered guy. Even now, I read about this stuff and I really have a hard time believing it." His other, daughter, Karen, is active in chronicling the sterling service of Japanese Americans during the war, and she recently made a documentary film about her father. Roy Matsumoto turned one hundred in May 2013 and is the sole survivor of the fourteen Nisei interpreters, all of whom are still held in awe by their fellow Marauders.

George McGee: McGee passed away in November 2007, the last of the Marauders' senior officers to die. In his obituary in the March 2008 edition of the Marauders' newsletter, Phil Piazza described McGee as "one of the finest officers I have ever known," sentiments echoed by Gabriel Kinney, who in 2013 reflected that "McGee's leadership was the main reason for our survival at Nhpum Ga." McGee fought in Korea and left the army in the late 1950s after twenty years of service. An honorable as well as courageous man, McGee felt compelled to answer some of Hunter's criticism of his command that had been detailed in the latter's war memoirs, *Galahad*. McGee's *The History of the 2nd Battalion*, which was privately published in 1987, was a rebuttal of many of Hunter's charges.

James McGuire: The avid diarist returned to his native Arizona, married, and raised a family. He died in January 1997 at age seventy-nine. His daughter, April, subsequently donated her father's diary to the Marauders Association.

Edward McLogan: Ted married his sweetheart, Beatrice, in October 1945 and spent the next sixty-eight years in a blissful marriage that ended only when Ted passed away in January 2013. His postwar career was spent in the retail business (he managed the family department store) and stockbroking, as well as raising seven children. McLogan was one of the few Marauders to have expressed any sympathy for Stilwell and his decision to order sick soldiers back to Myitkyina. "Looking back on it, I think he had no choice," said McLogan. "If we had been overwhelmed, we would have lost the airfield and Myitkyina, so I think he made the right decision." In late 1945, McLogan ran into Stilwell at the Pentagon and introduced himself as a former Marauder. According to Beatrice McLogan, "A few days later, Stilwell showed up at his office that was filled with many junior officers. In a loud voice, he asked, 'Where is McLogan?' Ted stood up and Stilwell said, 'Come with me, we're going to lunch.'"

Vincent Melillo: One of Melillo's most cherished possessions is his "short snorter," the name given to the dollar bill twenty-two of his buddies (including Roy Matsumoto) signed before he was flown to the States to receive treatment for malaria and dysentery. Not long after returning home, Melillo met Frankie, manager of the canteen at Camp Wheeler in Georgia. Shortly after the couple married in March 1945, Vincent was badly injured in a training exercise, resulting in his discharge from the military with a 50-percent disability. In 1949, he waived his disability, reenlisted, and was sent to Korea with the 7th Division, his first of three tours of duty in Korea. Offered a battlefield commission, Vincent turned it down because he didn't think he had the education for it. Vincent left the Army as a master sergeant in 1965 and subsequently worked as an inspector in small arms weapons repair. He retired from that position at Fort Benning in 1984. He continues to stay involved in military events, attending several Army reunions each year accompanied by his devoted daughter, Jonnie.

Richard Murch: Murch was one of the few Marauders who remained in Burma following the deactivation of the 5307th. He was promoted to 2nd lieutenant in December 1944 while serving with the 475th Infantry Regiment, and he returned to the States a year later. For over a half century, he did his best to forget Burma, finding it "all very upsetting. . . . It brings back too many things." In 2012, however, he decided to write an account of his service with the Marauders. "The one thing that stands out was the fellowship," he concluded. "The close relationship to your soldiers that seemed to increase as the danger increased."

Charlton Ogburn: Few Marauders had such an illustrious postwar life as Ogburn. His war memoirs, *The Marauders*, became a bestseller, and he wrote two novels, but it was his 1984 work, *The Mysterious William Shakespeare: The Myth and the Reality*, that brought him global attention, as he argued that Edward de Vere, the 17th Earl of Oxford, wrote the plays and poems attributed to William Shakespeare. Ogburn also worked in Army Intelligence and the State Department. Troubled by various ailments in old age, and with his eyesight failing, Ogburn took his own life in October 1998 at age eighty-seven.

William Osborne: Passanisi described Osborne as "a terrific leader; he seemed to know just what to do and how to do it." Osborne retired from the military in 1966 after serving as the assistant chief of staff for the 6th Army. He and his family settled near Monterey, California, and he died in 1985 at age seventy-one after a short illness.

Robert Passanisi: Shortly before leaving for the Far East, Passanisi married his sweetheart, Aileen, whom he'd met during a movie intermission at Brooklyn's Strand Theater. When he returned to Brooklyn in 1945, he finally got to hold their seventeen-month-old son. The couple went on to have three more children, and in December 2012 they celebrated their seventieth anniversary. Passanisi readily admits that his wife had to put up with much when he returned from the war. "Civilian life was difficult," he said. "Many things bothered me and my reaction was swift. My wife and others acknowledged that I had changed and not for the better. While in the service, we were respected and we were not to be fooled with, but in civilian life the feeling was more like, 'You did your job; so what?' You couldn't talk to anyone, except another Marauder, about your actions. They just couldn't understand."

But with the love of his family, Passanisi not only readjusted to civilian life, he thrived, launching his own TV service business before going to work for Fairchild Camera & Instruments in their Gyro test department. Passanisi then went back into higher education, graduating with an electrical engineering degree. He spent the rest of his working life employed on military radar projects, many of which were top-secret.

Passanisi retired in 1990, and for many years since he has been the tireless secretary of the Marauders Association. On the subject of the unit's chain of command, Passanisi had this to say: "Not to put Merrill down, but he was really Stilwell's representative. Hunter was a combat officer, and no question a lot of us owe our lives to Hunter's strategy. . . . General Stilwell felt that Hunter's concern for his men and the fact that he objected to the way they were treated by Stilwell might lead him to make life difficult for Stilwell upon his return to the States."

Asked to reflect on his time in the Marauders, Passanisi said: "Now that I know how unique we were, and the knowledge that no one ever before or since has accomplished what we did, I am very proud."

Philip Piazza: It took Piazza eighteen months to recover from the wounds he had sustained at the Battle of Inkangahtawng. Postwar he married, raised a family, and enjoyed a successful career in retail. He was also active in the American Legion/Disabled American Veterans and was also president of the Merrill's Marauders Association. A supporter of Merrill, Piazza said shortly before his death in 2011: "He was very close to his men. Some fellas say he wasn't, but from my personal experience I know he was."

David Quaid: After the war, Quaid became a cinematographer and university professor, winning a host of awards—including the Grand Prix at Cannes—and working on Hollywood movies such as *The Swimmer* (1966), starring Burt Lancaster. His documentary films included the 1961 Academy Award winner *Project Hope*, which detailed the maiden voyage of the hospital ship SS *Hope* to Indonesia. But Quaid never forgot his time with the Marauders; he was their official historian until his death in 2010.

David Richardson: At the time of his death in 2005, at age eighty-eight, Richardson had a reputation as one of America's most distinguished foreign correspondents. He had opened *Time*'s first postwar bureau in Germany and interviewed some of the postwar's most famous—and infamous— figures, including Gandhi, Ethiopia's Haile Selassie, and Colonel Gaddafi.

George Rose: Evacuated after the siege of Nhpum Ga while suffering from dysentery, Rose spent many months recovering in the USA, and it was while in the McGuire hospital in Richmond, Virginia, that he met the woman who would later become his wife. Upon his discharge from the Army in 1946, Rose spent thirty-six years and seven months working for a railroad company in Virginia. "I have many memories of Burma," he said, "but my fondest memories are the men I served and fought with in the godforsaken jungles of Burma. They were the bravest men I have ever known. To honor their memory and all who fought in Merrill's Marauders, my wife and I place flowers in our church each Easter Sunday." Rose died in 2003.

Henry Stelling: In his report of June 1944 (delayed by a month as he recovered from epidemic hepatitis), Henry Stelling accused CBI command of perpetrating one of "the greatest mass tragedies of gross injustice in the annals of the United States Army" upon the Marauders. The report wasn't well received by Theater Headquarters. Though Stelling was described as "an unquestionably fine surgeon and devoted to his work and to his men," General Boatner asserted that he had been "deeply affected by the destruction of human life caused by modern war [and] his report will illustrate the effect and should be read with the understanding that the report itself is the best evidence of the mental state of the reporting officer." Upon returning to civilian life, Stelling enjoyed a successful career as a family physician, and among his patients was Hollywood actress Patricia Neal. In an interview with the *Atlanta Journal and Constitution* in 1999, she said Stelling had helped her through her depression following the end of her love affair with Gary Cooper. "He was a fantastic man," she recalled. "He would just listen to me and listen to me and tell me stories. . . . It was a hard time, but he really saved my life." Dr. Henry Stelling died in 1990.

Joseph Stilwell: Ironically, Merrill ultimately outlasted both Hunter and Stilwell in Burma. A little over two months after Hunter was sent back to the States, Stilwell returned, recalled by Roosevelt after Chiang Kai-shek had informed the president that he was no longer able to work with him. General Albert C. Wedemeyer replaced Stilwell, whose reception upon reaching the States was as underwhelming as Hunter's had been. In June

1945, he was appointed commander of the 10th Army. Upon the surrender of the Japanese two months later, Stilwell returned to the States, where he was assigned to duty in Washington as president of the War Equipment Board. A year later in October 1946, Stilwell died of stomach cancer in a San Francisco hospital, five months before he was due to retire. "They'll have a hell of a time replacing him," said Frank Merrill, a view not shared by many other Marauders.

Stilwell continues to divide opinion, yet one of most measured assessments of the man comes from Sam Wilson, who met the general in Burma when he was a young lieutenant. In recognizing that Stilwell had "an impossible job" in CBI, attempting to defeat Japan while also maintaining an alliance with Britain and China, Wilson nonetheless believed that "Vinegar Joe" lacked the diplomatic and the strategic skills to fulfill the role. "He probably would have been the most magnificent corps commander in the United States Army, anywhere, in any theater during World War II," reflected Wilson. "He was definitely not our best theater commander." In Wilson's view, Stilwell was a master tactician who would have excelled had his sole responsibility been commanding general, Northern Combat Area Command.

Instead, Stilwell struggled to juggle his additional responsibilities as Mountbatten's deputy at South East Asia Command, commanding general of CBI, and chief of staff to Chiang Kai-shek. One consequence was his brutal disregard for the Marauders. But what did the fate of three thousand men matter when Stilwell had the fates of hundreds of thousands of men in his hands? Hunter never forgave Stilwell for his treatment of the Marauders, but Wilson is more compassionate. "I still have mixed feelings about him," he admitted in 1988. "The primary feeling, however, is one of kind of awed respect for his mind."

Logan Weston: In 1992, Weston published his memoirs under the title *The Fightin' Preacher*, chronicling his extraordinary military career in which he was awarded two Distinguished Service Crosses, five Silver Stars, and six Bronze Stars for gallantry in World War II and Korea. Upon retiring from the military with the rank of colonel in 1968, Weston was appointed secretary of the YMCA and coordinator of Campus Religious Life at Texas A&M University, a post he filled for thirteen happy years. Weston, who with his wife, Mary, raised four children, died in 2003 at age eighty-nine, and his service to God and his country was subsequently recognized by the South Carolina General Assembly. In a House resolution, they declared it is "appropriate for members of the House of Representatives to pause in their deliberations to note the passing of a distinguished South Carolinian and a gallant soldier."

ACKNOWLEDGMENTS

Such has been the overwhelming assistance and cooperation in the research and writing of this book that I really don't know where to start in lavishing thanks. Actually, no, that's not true, I do know where to begin—with Bob Passanisi, the secretary of the Merrill's Marauders Association. Put simply, this book probably would not have been possible without his help. To an Englishman such as myself, Bob is the personification of what I've come to believe of Brooklyn—straight-talking and no-nonsense. So Bob, from the bottom of my heart, I thank and salute you.

Jonnie Melillo Clasen, daughter of Vincent Melillo, has also been tireless in her support of the project, not only in interviewing her father on my behalf but also in offering advice and putting me in contact with several other Marauders' relatives. All this while she has had issues of her own to deal with. Jonnie, I admire your courage and tenacity. A chip off the block.

Sherry Cowling, daughter of Logan Weston, kindly allowed me to quote from her father's fascinating memoirs, *The Fightin' Preacher*, and supplied me with photographs. Thank you, Sherry, and I hope the book is a fitting tribute to your gallant father.

Members of the McLogan family were generous beyond the call of duty at a time when they were grieving for Mr. Ted McLogan. Matt and Jennifer supplied me with photographs, and Mrs. Beatrice McLogan was kind enough to provide some revealing insights into the life of a Marauder's sweetheart. I am very grateful, as I am to James Hopkins and his wife, Anne, who replied to my questions with patience and understanding and allowed me to quote from the magnificent *Spearhead: A Complete History of Merrill's Marauder Rangers*.

Thanks to the wonders of Skype, I was able to interview Roy Matsumoto and Gabriel Kinney "face to face," a privilege that wouldn't have been possible without the assistance and organization of Karen Matsumoto and Carol Crawford. In addition, both daughters also typed responses from their fathers to questions I had emailed, and I am humbled by their diligence and efficiency. Thank you.

Similarly, Jerrie Daly, daughter of Francis Ponder, went out of her way to aid my research and was unfailingly courteous despite my many questions. I am also indebted to Diane Quaid, who allowed me to read and quote from her father's absorbing autobiography, *Before I Forget*. David Quaid was a remarkable man. Jenny Kent, granddaughter of Ed Kohler, wrote up his memoirs, and it was a treat to include the memories of such a selfless soldier. Thank you, Ed and Jenny.

Pete Bogardus, son of Tom, is another relative to whom I owe so much, as is Mary Micele, niece of Dan Carrigan. Debi and Wes White have no blood relation to Clarence Branscomb, but they are friends, and because of their gentle persuasion, Clarence agreed to share his memories with me. I tip my hat to you both.

I also would like to thank the staffs of the Imperial War Museum and the Kew National Archives in London for their help during the research for the book. Additionally, the Library of Congress superb Veterans History Project was kind enough to grant me permission to quote from their archive. So, too, was Grand Valley State University, which archives interviews with Mr. and Mrs. McLogan from a few years ago.

My agent at Curtis Brown, Felicity Blunt, and her assistant, Rebecca Ritchie, have both been a great help in the planning and execution of this book, and knowing they are always a phone call away is reassuring. The editorial director at Zenith, Erik Gilg, has supported the book from the outset. His dedication has been inspiring, as was his patience in granting me an additional six weeks to complete the writing. What are deadlines for if not to be extended! Caitlin Fultz at Zenith has been a deft and lucid editor who has made the always onerous task of redrafting much more bearable.

Finally, the Marauders themselves: Gabriel Kinney, Roy Matsumoto, Robert Passanisi, Francis Ponder, Vincent Melillo, Ed Kohler, Bernard Martin, and Clarence Branscomb. My gratitude knows no bounds. It has been an honor to talk to you, to listen to you, and to record your bravery, fortitude, and fidelity from those faraway days of 1944. You will always remain "The Greatest Generation."

NOTES

Prologue

1. "swept through northern Burma": *Washington Post*, May 21, 1943
2. "the troops were supplied": *Waterloo Daily Courier*, July 6, 1943
3. "like the wrath of God and cursing like a fallen angel": Barbara W. Tuchman, *Stilwell and the American Experience in China, 1911–45* (Grove Press, 2001)
4. "We got run out of Burma": Ibid.
5. "indispensable to world victory": Ibid.
6. "greatly increase the flow of motor": George Marshall, *The Report of the Chief of Staff of the U.S. Army, 1943–1945* (War Department, 1945). This report was serialized in several newspapers, in this case *The Lima News*, December 12, 1945.
7. "When he began to talk": Trevor Royle, *Orde Wingate* (Weidenfeld and Nicolson, 1995)
8. "penetration affords greater opportunity": Ibid.
9. "expounded a large and very complex subject": Ibid.
10. "total of 2,830 officers and men": Charles Newton Hunter, *Galahad* (Naylor Publishing, 1963)
11. "Only 3,000": Tuchman, *Stilwell*
12. "We get a handful of U.S. troops": Tuchman, *Stilwell*

Chapter 1

13. "Newt has worn the gray": *Howitzer*, 1929
14. "Five feet seven": Charlton Ogburn Jr. *The Marauders* (Harper & Row, 1956)
15. "My only clue": Hunter, *Galahad*
16. "would suffer approximately 85% casualties": Ibid.
17. "discipline, self-control, and how to think logically": Interview with Samuel V. Wilson by Steven Pressfield in 2010, published online at http://www.stevenpressfield.com/2010/07/general-sam-v-wilson.

18. "We taught them out in": Wilson interview with Partin for the U.S. Special Operations Command, July 1988.
19. "He gave me all the responsibility": Ibid.
20. "rare among those who have": Ogburn, *The Marauders*
21. "ardent and idealistic": Ibid.
22. "An assemblage of less-tractable soldiers": Ibid.
23. "We've got the misfits": Ibid.
24. "He proceeded to read a": Robert Passanisi interview with Library of Congress Veterans History Project (LoC VH), AFC/2001/001/29947.
25. "There are many reasons that swirl": author interview, February 2013

Chapter 2

26. "I am not at liberty to say": From the unpublished memoirs of Capt. Thomas Bogardus, written in 1996 and kindly passed to the author by his son, Pete.
27. "Chow consisted of two meals a day": Written by Passanisi and published in the *Burman News*, the official publication of the Merrill's Marauders Association.
28. "bullnose pliers, wire cutters": Ibid.
29. "We thought we had learned something": In 1945 Lyons, upon his return to his native Florida, gave a lengthy interview with Paul Wilder of the *Tampa Tribune*.
30. "adventurers, musicians, drunkards": Ogburn, *The Marauders*
31. "mouth that was a straight line": Ibid.
32. "Then, lieutenant": Ibid.
33. "Jobs were hard to come by": author interview, December 2012
34. "At school in Japan": Ibid.
35. "I lost just about everything": Ibid.
36. "I did well at the language school": Ibid.

Chapter 3

37. "The main swimming pool": From the unpublished memoirs of Richard Murch, written by Richard in 2011–12.
38. "Would meet every morning": Ibid.
39. "and we were soaking wet": Bogardus memoirs
40. "The ship could stand a good": In early 2013, Ed Kohler relived his Marauders service in discussion with his granddaughter, Jenny Smith, who committed them to paper.
41. "I spent about two weeks on": author interview, December 2012
42. "picked up a long-handled broom": interview with Grand Valley State University Veterans Project

43. "So I got my guys out of their foxholes": Ibid.
44. "when the mission was complete": author interview, March 2013
45. "felt peace in my heart that": Logan Weston, *The Fightin' Preacher* (Vision Press, 1992)
46. "The houses as you enter": Bogardus memoirs
47. "To our knowledge": Ibid.
48. "the ship's safe": Ibid.
49. "The native Indians": Ibid.
50. "Bill and I became instant": author interview
51. "bring us hot tea and shake us": Bogardus memoirs
52. "The mouse must have fallen into the dough": Murch memoirs

Chapter 4
53. "Puzzled": Hunter, *Galahad*
54. "I don't want to see anyone": Ogburn, *The Marauders*
55. "This period of relative inactivity": James E. T. Hopkins and John M. Jones, *Spearhead: A Complete History of Merrill's Marauder Rangers* (Galahad Press, 2000)
56. "he only stood about five foot five inches": Grand Valley State interview
57. "told us every detail": *Tampa Tribune* interview
58. "He was rather Messianic": Partin interview
59. "dysentery can be controlled": LoC VH, AFC/2001/001/29895
60. "best defence in the jungle": Brig O. C. Wingate, "Report to Commander 4 Corps on Operations of 77th Indian Brigade in Burma," reference HS 1/47
61. "Rubberlegs": Tuchman, *Stilwell*
62. "across dry, rugged land": Bogardus memoirs
63. "They were double-layered": Ibid.
64. "My reaction to being transferred": author interview
65. "The answer I gave was the one": Ibid.
66. "Plebe year was safely passed": *Howitzer*, Class of 1937
67. "'Do you want to volunteer'": *Tampa Tribune* interview
68. "Our Trinidad unit boarded": George Rose's reminisces of his time with the Marauders were published in the March 2011 edition of the *Burman News* and were made available by the generosity of his daughter, Linda Burchett.
69. "Men who had volunteered": Ibid.
70. "Colonel Beach was a nice guy": author interview
71. "rarely if ever convened the battalion": George McGee, *The History of the Second Battalion* (privately published, 1987)
72. "squeeze the pin most of": LoC VH

73. "very inefficient compared": author interview, January 2013
74. "Physical disability, incompetence": Murch memoirs
75. "The Chindits were really tough guys": author interview
76. "They were much leaner, more conservative": Partin interview
77. "a fine officer and well respected": Author interview with Vincent Melillo in 2013. I emailed a series of questions to Vincent, and his daughter, Jonnie Melillo Clasen, was kind enough to transcribe her father's answers.
78. "a tall, lanky, soft-spoken man": *Burman News*, November 2006
79. "If you come under fire": Partin interview
80. "began to put pressure": Hunter, *Galahad*
81. "Louis [Mountbatten] is fed up on Peanut": Tuchman, *Stilwell*
82. "They have been driven absolutely mad": Ibid.
83. "If the bastards will": Ibid.
84. "so damn snotty": Ibid.
85. "For God's sake": Ibid.
86. "Wingate greeted us affably": Hunter, *Galahad*
87. "Long Range Penetration will prove": Wingate, "Report to Commander 4 Corps"

Chapter 5
88. "It sounds like a street address in Los Angeles": Ogburn, *The Marauders*
89. "He put the unit together, trained the unit": Partin interview
90. "Tasks have not always been easy": *Howitzer*, 1929
91. "Merrill was a neat guy, very softly spoken and easy to get along with": author interview
92. "Brilliant, innovative, and probably a better": Partin interview
93. "We decided if we are going to get killed in": author interview
94. "I was assigned a mule to carry": Murch memoir
95. "We found him to be friendly, unostentatious": Hunter, *Galahad*
96. "Little did I expect what I would luck into": David Richardson interview, LoC VHP, AFC/2001/001/4380
97. "the roughest, toughest bunch": *CBI Roundup*, March 9, 1944
98. "It was a greater mix than I'd ever run into in an outfit": LoC VHP, AFC/2001/001/4380
99. "He was right—we knew we were the castoffs": author interview
100. "hard as our green helmets": *Tampa Tribune* interview
101. "It was bliss": Ogburn, *The Marauders*

Chapter 6
102. "Ranges of hills form a barrier": Robert Talbot Kelly, *Burma*

(Adam & Charles Black 1908)

103. "The splotched camouflage": *Tampa Tribune* interview
104. "During training we occasionally": author interview
105. "Platoons were being disentangled": Ogburn, *The Marauders*
106. "I had dengue fever": author Interview, February 2013
107. "I hope this thing's over": *Tampa Tribune* interview
108. "And that his Royal Majesty's": Grand Valley State interview
109. "14 mi. tonite, saw some nurses": Sgt. James McGuire maintained a diary throughout his time in Burma. After his death, the diary was donated to the Marauders Association by his daughter, April.
110. "a hardworking, industrious, and trustworthy": Lt. Col. W. R. Peers, "Guerrilla Operations in Northern Burma," *Military Review*, July 1944.
111. "The pack was urging you": Hunter, *Galahad*
112. "It was quite evident that we were": Murch memoirs
113. "The life of a medical corps": Ibid.
114. "An Infantryman, after hours of brisk marching": *CBI Roundup*, March 23, 1944
115. "Each man passed back to the one": *Tampa Tribune* interview
116. "Old Doc Stelling seemed to be a gullible sort": Bogardus memoirs
117. "McGee was tireless": Grand Valley State interview
118. "The disgust generated by our battalion commander": James H. Stone (ed.) *Crisis Fleeting: Original Reports on Military Medicine in India and Burma in the Second World War* (Office of the Surgeon General, Department of the Army, 1969)
119. "He said 'Jesus Christ, dad, things'": Phil Piazza interview, LoC VHP, AFC/2001/001/29955
120. "easy and comfortable relationship": McGee, *The History of the Second Battalion*
121. "I noticed Merrill sort of gesturing": Partin interview
122. "to indicate the center": Hunter, *Galahad*

Chapter 7

123. "Took it easy got plenty of sleep": McGuire diary
124. "It is from four to eight inches": Peers, "Guerrilla Operations in Northern Burma"
125. "Aw, to hell with this": Donovan Webster, *The Burma Road: The Epic Story of the China-Burma-India Theater in World War II* (Harper Perennial, 2004)
126. "The boys all whooped and yelled": author interview
127. "Told what mission is": McGuire diary
128. "My pack is on my back": Hopkins and Jones, *Spearhead*

Chapter 8

129. "A soldier even under the best": Weston, *The Fightin' Preacher*
130. "If we ran into the enemy": Ibid.
131. "He was a loner who indulged": LoC VHP
132. "Some said this was a signal": Hopkins and Jones, *Spearhead*
133. "You're always scared like hell": Warner Katz, LoC VHP, AFC/2001/001/29918
134. "I don't know why but when": LoC VHP
135. "When the firing started, it seemed": author interview
136. "I never thought about dying": Ibid.
137. "When you see a guy get killed": LoC VHP
138. "Saw a lot of Burmese": McGuire diary
139. "Always the worst for me was": author interview
140. "I had doubts before we went": Ibid.
141. "Straight ahead and to the": Hopkins and Jones, *Spearhead*
142. "Crossed it Indian file": *Yank*, June 9, 1944
143. "We didn't have to wait very long": Weston, *The Fightin' Preacher*
144. "So I said to Weston": Gosho's interview was conducted with Dave Quaid, along with several other Marauder veterans, and is available to view through the LoC VHP, AFC/2001/001/29895.
145. "Saw a Japanese with a Nambu machine gun": Ibid.
146. "That last one he kinda crawled back": Ibid.
147. "as calmly as he were out for a walk": David Hurwitt quoted in Weston, *The Fightin' Preacher*
148. "They just kept coming across": Ibid.
149. "The knowledge that our sick": Hopkins and Jones, *Spearhead*
150. "I found myself on the ground": Murch memoirs
151. "When you are in imminent danger": author interview
152. "Ogburn was well educated and smart": Ibid.
153. "My mule was left behind": Ibid.
154. "one of the most valuable members of the platoon": Ogburn, *The Marauders*
155. "I didn't give any thought": author interview

Chapter 9

156. "I knew it was from a Jap operator": author interview
157. "Combat seems to seduce a guy": *Yank*, July 2, 1944
158. "The men ahead had pushed stalks": *Tampa Tribune* interview
159. "As I picked my way along": Ibid.
160. "We set to work digging the foxholes": Ibid.
161. "It was just like a regular handset": author interview

162. "I wanted to pee but didn't want": Ibid.
163. "I then heard a sergeant talking": Ibid.
164. "he was really upset and swore": *Burman News*
165. "We got our M1 rifles, had a fruit bar": author interview
166. "Pung had a walkie-talkie radio": *Yank*, July 2, 1944
167. "Minutes ticked by": Ibid.
168. "The noise was deafening": author interview
169. "The Dead End Kids were happy": *Yank*, July 2, 1944
170. "Those little bastards": Ibid.
171. "I know that I was scared as hell": *Burman News*, June 2007
172. "Beach shouted": author interview
173. "It was Lieutenant Colonel Beach who told us": Ibid.
174. "The spirit of the men was awe-inspiring": Hopkins and Jones, *Spearhead*
175. "They weren't afraid": author interview
176. "The hours dragged on": *Yank*, July 2, 1944
177. "Okay, gentleman": author interview with Bernard Martin, December 2013
178. "I believe we have killed": *CBI Roundup*, March 16, 1944
179. "We were underway": Murch memoirs
180. "bedded down in our midst": Hunter, *Galahad*
181. "Then we laid a bamboo across": author interview
182. "Between us and the Chinese": Hopkins and Jones, *Spearhead*
183. "Japs shelled us with artillery and mortars": McGuire diary
184. "She was pleasant to listen to": author interview
185. "You who fight on the Ledo Front": *CBI Roundup*, March 23, 1944
186. "So he ran away and joined the army": *The Portsmouth Herald*, March 7, 1944
187. "War at a theater commander's level": Hunter, *Galahad*

Chapter 10
188. "cloven-hoof marks": Ogburn, *The Marauders*
189. "The I&R led off with": author interview
190. "towering, tangled, resistant vegetation": Ogburn, *The Marauders*
191. "Sam was a good soldier": author interview
192. "Sam and I then withdrew": Ibid.
193. "I told Sam I wasn't going": Ibid.
194. "frantically pumping my fist": Ibid.
195. "As we crossed the river the water": Grant Hirabayashi, Loc VHP, AFC/2001/001
196. "We spread out": author interview
197. "pure 100-proof delight": Ogburn, *The Marauders*

Chapter 11

198. "Moved out 10:30am": McGuire diary
199. "the finest officers you could want": Jack Girsham, *Burma Jack* (Norton, 1971)
200. "open wounds about the circumference": Quaid, *Before I Forget*
201. "I began every morning": *Tampa Tribune* interview
202. "The Kachins were a very easy": author interview
203. "an exercise of no current or": McGee, *The History of the Second Battalion*
204. "regard for my feelings": Ibid.
205. "everyone was committed to doing": Girsham, *Burma Jack*

Chapter 12

206. "Walked 12 miles all day": McGuire diary
207. "was along the crest": Ibid.
208. "Our air photos had failed to arrive": Hunter, *Galahad*
209. "spent much of the day": Hopkins and Jones, *Spearhead*
210. "that we had crossed the Nampana": Ibid.
211. "I relied on sight, sound, and smell": author interview
212. "The Mogaung, from bank to bank": *Burman News*
213. "Lieutenant Grissom was a ballplayer": author interview
214. "Nearing the Jap road": *Tampa Tribune* interview
215. "They were very noisy soldiers": LoC VHP
216. "could see the trees": *Burman News*
217. "There was always a chance of being": author interview
218. "I should have had the battalion": LoC VHP, AFC/2001/001/29895
219. "I said 'And after that'": Ibid.
220. "First thing that came to my mind": Ibid.
221. "Suddenly someone yelled": Rose, *Burman News* reminisces
222. "A piece of shell had pierced his helmet": *Burman News*
223. "They were big Japanese marines": *Tampa Tribune* interview
224. "One thing about them": LoC VHP
225. "Divested of his arms": *Tampa Tribune* interview
226. "He was bleeding like a sieve": Hopkins and Jones, *Spearhead*
227. "I kept talking to him and": *Burman News*
228. "I plan to withdraw from this side": McGee, *The History of the Second Battalion*
229. "The water was a welcome relief": *Burman News*
230. "Urging the pilot to get down on the deck": Hunter, *Galahad*
231. "In my opinion this message should not have been sent": "Galahad: Intelligence Aspects," CIA Historical Review Program, September 22, 1993

232. "I told him bluntly that my orders were coming from General Merrill": McGee, *The History of the Second Battalion*
233. "since communication with Merrill": Hunter, *Galahad*
234. "an exceptionally fine action": LoC VHP
235. "The possibility of being surrounded": Hopkins and Jones, *Spearhead*
236. "I was disappointed when instead of getting permission": Hunter, *Galahad*

Chapter 13

237. "Every muscle in our": Weston, *The Fightin' Preacher*
238. "beat to a pulp, the physical": *Burman News*, November 2006
239. "A split second later": Weston, *The Fightin' Preacher*
240. "up and down for one": Hunter, *Galahad*
241. "Walked 428 mi": McGuire diary
242. "The Green Combat Team was moving": LoC VHP, AFC/2001/001/29895
243. "It seemed like a rather long time": Ibid.
244. "I figured this was": Ibid.
245. "We found another position": Ibid.
246. "When the word was": author interview
247. "'Let's go, Bill!'": Kohler memoirs
248. "They had been sent": LoC VHP
249. "'I'm not afraid, damn it'": Hopkins and Jones, *Spearhead*
250. "tree burst which wounded": McGee, *The History of the Second Battalion*
251. "possibility of holding at Auche": Ibid.
252. "Can Nhpum Ga be held": This conversation is recounted in McGee's memoirs.
253. "I had no warning of Merrill's": Hunter, *Galahad*
254. "We all agreed that he": Hopkins and Jones, *Spearhead*
255. "'He's having problems with his chest'": author interview
256. "perimeter had to have a figure-eight-shaped": Hunter, *Galahad*
257. "Our clothes are torn": McGuire diary

Chapter 14

258. "I always tried to fire short bursts": author interview
259. "We called him 'Pistol Pete'": author interview
260. "They were constantly shelling": LoC VHP, AFC/2001/001/29895
261. "There was absolutely nothing": Ibid.
262. "We have been hit on three sides": McGee, *The History of the Second Battalion*

263. "the hot spot on the hill": author interview

264. "I went forward with a litter": Hopkins and Jones, *Spearhead*

265. "Colonel Hunter had asked me": Acker's account of the howitzer guns is drawn from an interview with Dave Quaid (LoC VHP, AFC/2001/001/29895) and from an account published in the August 2005 issue of *Burman News*

266. "over the cliff to retrieve": author interview

267. "The thought of being overrun": Ibid.

268. "We cleared the bamboo": *Tampa Tribune* interview

269. "It was a patch of swampy ground": Grand Valley State interview

270. "You look wonderful this morning": Phil Piazza, LoC VHP

Chapter 15

271. "which of course": LoC VHP (AFC/2001/001/29895)

272. "Situation getting critical": McGee, *The History of the Second Battalion*

273. "Rather than do surgery": LoC VHP, AFC/2001/001/29895

274. "Some of the men became delirious": Stone, *Crisis Fleeting*

275. "Make Plans to fight your way out to the northwest": McGee, *The History of the Second Battalion*

276. "Gentlemen": Hunter, *Galahad*

277. "We've been attacking up": Ibid.

278. "I hope the mortar gang leaves some for us": Letter from Logan Weston to the parents of Dan Carrigan and reproduced with the kind permission of Mary Micele, Dan's niece.

279. "On New Georgia they got": Weston, *The Fightin' Preacher*

280. "We got hit": McGuire diary

281. "It was a light machine gun": Kermit Busher, LoC VHP, AFC/2001/001/29937

282. "The transmitter generator": This account was written by Bernard Martin in 2008 and passed to the author.

283. "One man lay to the southeast": Lt. Col. Henry L. Kinnison IV, "The Deeds of Valiant Men: A Study in Leadership," U.S. Army War College, 1993

284. "I wriggled and twisted": *Tampa Tribune* interview

285. "About all I could get out of Roy": Kohler memoirs

286. "They lined up in a line": Ibid.

287. "Able to say that we understood": Hopkins and Jones, *Spearhead*

288. "The Japanese were talking": author interview

289. "He was gone for twenty minutes": LoC VHP

290. "I want you to vacate your": Ibid.

291. "By the time I had fired five or six": LoC VHP

292. "I was happy": author interview
293. "I could literally see the bullets": LoC VHP
294. "I could recognize the clanging": *Burman News*
295. "When I saw those dangling": *Tampa Tribune* interview
296. "Just as the feast was being": Ibid.
297. "They began to look like skeletons": Stone, *Crisis Fleeting*
298. "Today was Good Friday": Kinnison, "The Deeds of Valiant Men"
299. "most of the men and officers": Henry Stelling, quoted in *Crisis Fleeting*
300. "After we pulled out of Shaduzup": author interview
301. "We all knew there": Ibid.
302. "I hope this is over quick": McGuire diary
303. "pointed hand-carved": Hunter, *Galahad*
304. "Extracting a slug from a cartridge": Ibid.
305. "We found a place about one thousand": *Burman News*, August 2005
306. "When I started to crawl up the hill": *Burman News*, August 2000
307. "Some infantry officer is": LoC VHP
308. "In the next 15 minutes": *Yank*, October 1, 1944
309. "There were Japanese dripping": LoC VHP
310. "The three scouts ahead of my": LoC VHP
311. "I had witnessed some horrible sights": Ibid.
312. "Being Easter Sunday and all": Ibid.
313. "The lower half of a bloated": Hunter, *Galahad*
314. "The first thing I saw when I got": LoC VHP
315. "the bodies more than anything": author interview
316. "Stunned to see that every inch": Hunter, *Galahad*
317. "Looked at us out of": Ogburn, *The Marauders*
318. "I was passing blood real": *Burman News*, July 2011
319. "Tears streamed down the faces": Weston, *The Fightin' Preacher*
320. "This is a hard letter to write": Weston letter to Carrigan family
321. "They had one of those grinding": author interview

Chapter 16
322. "Would be isolated in Burma": Tuchman, *Stilwell*
323. "Galahad is OK": Ogburn, *The Marauders*
324. "Then it dawned on us": Partin interview
325. "persisted like a mosquito": Ogburn, *The Marauders*
326. "Guy at the gaming tables": Partin interview
327. "a chance to put": Ibid.
328. "presented to General Stilwell": Hunter, *Galahad*
329. "drops as big": McGuire diary
330. "I guess it's another mission": Ibid.

331. "Would be relieved and flown to an already": Hunter, *Galahad*
332. "The first thing I did at Naubum": Quaid, *Before I Forget*
333. "General Merrill's promise": Hopkins and Jones, *Spearhead*

Chapter 17

334. "A trail of sadness": LoC VHP
335. "Raining": McGuire diary
336. "The men went down": Quaid, *Before I Forget*
337. "We would unload the mules": Ibid.
338. "You'd see pythons": author interview
339. "Get up, you son-of-a-bitch!": *Yank*, June 24, 1944
340. "More than once I lay on my back": Weston, *The Fightin' Preacher*
341. "An infantry squad came up the trail": Quaid, *Before I Forget*
342. "One of them reached": Ibid.
343. "While we were climbing": Ibid.
344. "Sympathy is a luxury": Hunter, *Galahad*
345. "With this mission under our belts": Ibid.
346. "When I arrived at the top": Ibid.
347. "Hour after hour": Weston, *The Fightin' Preacher*
348. "The situation screwed up": McGuire diary
349. "The men cutting the trail could": Quaid, *Before I Forget*
350. "braised water buffalo": Ibid.
351. "Heard the sharp crack of a rifle": Ibid.
352. "You don't have to worry": The conversation between Merrill and Hunter at Arang is related by Hunter in *Galahad*.

Chapter 18

353. "Swarms of insects thrived": Hopkins and Jones, *Spearhead*
354. "I ran up a small jungle-covered": Quaid, *Before I Forget*
355. "I'm taking them right now": Ibid.
356. "I got it loaded and went trotting": Ibid.
357. "What the hell's the matter": Ibid.
358. "The Jap gunner was good": Ibid.

Chapter 19

359. "Will they meet a reinforced": Ogburn, *The Marauders*
360. "I told Merrill to roll": Hopkins and Jones, *Spearhead*
361. "Doc, he has got to go on": Hunter, *Galahad*
362. "We heard talking and": author interview
363. "We crawled around in the grass": Ibid.
364. "The 150th [Chinese] regiment was to deploy": Hunter, Galahad
365. "WILL THIS BURN UP THE LIMEYS": Tuchman, *Stilwell*

366. "the Americans by a brilliant feat": Ibid.
367. "By the boldness of your leadership": *CBI Roundup*, May 25, 1944

Chapter 20

368. "Where's Merrill?" Hunter, *Galahad*
369. "Had slept in the same decrepit": Ibid.
370. "Nectar to a parched soul": Tuchman, *Stilwell<M*
371. "Merrill, commander of the famed": *Daily Herald*, May 19, 1944
372. "Led personally by Merrill": *Washington Post*, May 19, 1944
373. "Monsoons won't necessarily": Ibid.
374. "Like I was in the last stages": Hunter, *Galahad*
375. "stupidly opened fire on their": Ibid.
376. "The Chinese were not good soldiers": author interview
377. "Dear Chuck": Hunter, *Galahad*
378. "When we got down on to the road": LoC VHP
379. "The only way to get the men": McGuire diary
380. "He advised me to use my": Hopkins and Jones, *Spearhead*
381. "It was hard to believe": Weston, *The Fightin' Preacher*
382. "Went to 14th evac": McGuire diary

Chapter 21

383. "Most everyone was sick": author interview
384. "They tried to put me on a mule": Ibid.
385. "If you ever would have": LoC VHP
386. "I think I was well past my": author interview
387. "every step was like beating an open wound": *Tampa Tribune* interview
388. "Doc Stelling was a good man": author interview
389. "so set on reaching Arang and being ready to push": Stone, *Crisis Fleeting*
390. "fainted several times": Ibid.
391. "was in condition for combat": Ibid.
392. "It was a scrubby area": LoC VHP
393. "I want everyone to know": A copy of Merrill's statement was given to the author by Bernard Martin.
394. "I had him in my rifle sights": This quote has been repeated several times, including Tuchman's *Stilwell and the American Experience in China* and John Master's *The Road Past Mandalay*.
395. "This is a strong letter": Hunter related both the contents of the letter and Stilwell's reaction in *Galahad*.
396. "12 men left in": Ogburn, *The Marauders*
397. "That even the bravest man": Lord Moran, *The Anatomy of Courage*

(Constable, 1945)

398. "They relived those days": *Tampa Tribune* interview
399. "pasture surrounded by": Ogburn, *The Marauders*
400. "About two hundred men": Hopkins and Jones, *Spearhead*
401. "disgusted by the failure of generals": Ibid.
402. "living like bands of pirates": Ogburn, *The Marauders*
403. "a bolt of red lightning": Ibid.
404. "Once or twice a day you": Article written by Passanisi and published in *Burman News*.
405. "Good God": Tuchman, *Stilwell*
406. "We'd been issued rifles": author interview
407. "We joined the Marauders": family interview, 2005
408. "I was lying behind one of the wheels": Quaid, *Before I Forget*
409. "Hunter yelled down to": Ibid.
410. "Almost every member of": Murch memoirs
411. "Things could not help but improve": Hunter, *Galahad*
412. "I studied it for hours trying": Ibid.
413. "Over at last": Tuchman, *Stilwell*
414. "Go out the window": Branscomb wrote an account of this meeting in a 1989 letter to James Hopkins and repeated it to the author in 2013.

Epilogue

415. "An almost complete breakdown of morale": *Daily News*, August 5, 1944
416. "That Galahad is provided for": Hopkins and Jones, *Spearhead*
417. "Merrill has been relieved": *Daily Register*, August 7, 1944
418. "The only reason for his relief": *Kingsport Times*, August 9, 1944
419. "One of the most disheartening": *Clovis News Journal*, August 13, 1944
420. "fully informed": *Joplin News Herald*, August 14, 1944
421. "storm in a teapot": *Paris News*, August 27, 1944
422. "This is what happened": *Nevada State Journal*, August 27, 1944
423. "Our own doctors looked them": *San Antonio Light*, August 25, 1944
424. "Has resulted in the return of": Stone, *Crisis Fleeting*
425. "Merrill's Marauders In the Burma Jungle": The series was run in the *Washington Post* under the heading "The Inside Story of the Merrill's Marauders in the Burma Jungle."
426. "A man of high intelligence and sensitivity": *Dixon Evening Telegraph*, September 23, 1944
427. "Merrill's Marauders, directly under": Jefferson City News and

Tribune, October 8, 1944

428. "Hunter gave Merrill his total loyalty": Partin interview
429. "As for the feelings of the rest of": Ogburn, *The Marauders*
430. "so realistic there isn't": *Sumter Daily Item*, September 4, 1961
431. "a Filipino mercenary": Roy Matsumoto declined to reveal his reaction to the film, but his daughter, Karen, told me of his hurt.
432. "Pretty disgusted with the whole": Hopkins and Jones, *Spearhead*. (The letter from Branscomb was originally published in the *Burman News*.)
433. "He got the credit for the thing": author interview
434. "Hunter, *Galahad* was a real soldier": Ibid.
435. "One of the bravest and most capable": Branscomb disclosed the contents of the letter in a conversation with the author in February 2013.
436. "He thought more in politico": Partin interview
437. "I think he was at times": Ibid.
438. "Hunter, *Galahad* was a dry-witted, laconic": Ibid.

BIBLIOGRAPHY

Books

Calvert, Michael. *Fighting Mad*. Pen and Sword, 2004.

Fergusson, Bernard. *Beyond the Chindwin*. Fontana Books, 1955.

Girsham, Jack. *Burma Jack*. Norton, 1971.

Hanson, O. *The Kachins: Their Customs and Traditions*. American Baptist Mission Press, 1913.

Hopkins, James E. T., and John M. Jones. *Spearhead: A Complete History of Merrill's Marauder Rangers*. Galahad Press, 2000.

Hunter, Charles Newton. *Galahad*. Naylor Publishing, 1963.

Kelly, Robert Talbot. *Burma*. London: Adam & Charles Black, 1908.

Masters, John. *The Road Past Mandalay*. Bantam Books, 1979.

McGee, George. *The History of the Second Battalion*. Privately published, 1987.

McLynn, Frank. *The Burma Campaign*. Vintage, 2011.

Merrill's Marauders: February–May 1944. Historical Division, War Department for the American Forces, U.S. Government Printing Office, 1945.

Ogburn, Jr., Charlton. *The Marauders*. Harper & Row, 1956.

Rooney, David. *Mad Mike*. Pen and Sword, 1997.

Royle, Trevor. *Orde Wingate*. Weidenfeld and Nicolson, 1995.

Stone, James H. (ed.) *Crisis Fleeting: Original Reports on Military Medicine in India and Burma in the Second World War*. Office of the Surgeon General, Department of the Army, 1969.

Tuchman, Barbara W. *Stilwell and the American Experience in China, 1911–45*. Grove Press, 2001.

Webster, Donovan. *The Burma Road: The Epic Story of the China-Burma-India Theater in World War II*. Harper Perennial, 2004.

Weston, Logan. *The Fightin' Preacher*. Vision Press, 1992.

Newspapers/magazines

CBI Roundup
Clovis News Journal
Daily Herald
Daily News
Daily Register
Dixon Evening Telegraph
Ex-CBI Roundup
Hamilton Journal
Jefferson City News and Tribune
Joplin News Herald
Kingsport Times
Montana Standard

Nevada State Journal
New York Times
Ogden Standard-Examiner
Paris News
Portsmouth Herald
San Antonio Light
Sumter Daily Item
Tampa Tribune
Time
Washington Post
Waterloo Daily Courier

Journals

The Burman News. Official publication of the Merrill's Marauders
    Association, various issues from 1999 to 2013.
Howitzer. The West Point yearbook, 1929 to 1937.

Articles

"Galahad: Intelligence Aspects." CIA Historical Review Program,
    September 22, 1993.
Kinnison IV, Lt. Col. Henry L. "The Deeds of Valiant Men: A Study in
    Leadership." U.S. Army
War College, 1993.
McMichael, Scott R. "Common Man, Uncommon Leadership: Colonel
    Charles N. Hunter with Galahad in Burma." U.S. Army War
    College, 1986.
Peers, Lt. Col. W. R. "Guerrilla Operations in Northern Burma." *Military
    Review*, July 1944.

Unpublished memoirs/private papers

Bogardus, Thomas
Kohler, Ed
Murch, Richard
Ponder, Francis
Quaid, David, *Before I Forget*

Grand Valley State University
Veterans History Project interviews with:

McLogan, Beatrice
McLogan, Ted

Library of Congress, Washington, D.C.
Veterans History Project interviews with:

Busher, Kermit, AFC/2001/001/29937
Hirabayashi, Grant, AFC/2001/001
Katz, Warner, AFC/2001/001/29918
Passanisi, Robert, AFC/2001/001/29947
Piazza, Phil, AFC/2001/001/29955
Quaid, Dave, and various Marauders, AFC/2001/001/29895
Richardson, David, AFC/2001/001/4380

Imperial War Museum, London
The papers of Brig. James Michael Calvert

The National Archives, London
Wingate, Brig. O. C. "Report to Commander 4 Corps on Operations of 77th
    Indian Brigade in Burma." Reference HS 1/47.

Miscellaneous
Diary of Sgt. James McGuire (by kind permission of the Merrill's Marauders
    Association)
Interview with Lt. Samuel V. Wilson by Dr. J. W. Partin for the U.S. Special
    Operations Command, July 1988.
Interview with Samuel V. Wilson by Steven Pressfield, published online at
    http://www.stevenpressfield.com/2010/07/general-sam-v-wilson/

Author interviews
Branscomb, Clarence
Kinney, Gabriel
Kohler, Ed
Martin, Bernard
Matsumoto, Roy
McLogan, Beatrice
Melillo, Vincent
Passanisi, Robert
Ponder, Francis

Index